T0192002

Terrorism, Security, and Computation

Series Editor

V. S. Subrahmanian, Department of Computer Science
and Institute for Security, Technology and Society
Dartmouth College
Hanover, NH, USA

The purpose of the Computation and International Security book series is to establish the state of the art and set the course for future research in computational approaches to international security. The scope of this series is broad and aims to look at computational research that addresses topics in counter-terrorism, counter-drug, transnational crime, homeland security, cyber-crime, public policy, international conflict, and stability of nations. Computational research areas that interact with these topics include (but are not restricted to) research in databases, machine learning, data mining, planning, artificial intelligence, operations research, mathematics, network analysis, social networks, computer vision, computer security, biometrics, forecasting, and statistical modeling. The series serves as a central source of reference for information and communications technology that addresses topics related to international security. The series aims to publish thorough and cohesive studies on specific topics in international security that have a computational and/or mathematical theme, as well as works that are larger in scope than survey articles and that will contain more detailed background information. The series also provides a single point of coverage of advanced and timely topics and a forum for topics that may not have reached a level of maturity to warrant a comprehensive textbook.

M. D. Miller

Discovering Hidden Gems
in Foreign Languages

 Springer

M. D. Miller
University of California
Berkeley, CA, USA

ISSN 2197-8778 ISSN 2197-8786 (electronic)
Terrorism, Security, and Computation

ISBN 978-3-031-18481-9 ISBN 978-3-031-18479-6 (eBook)
https://doi.org/10.1007/978-3-031-18479-6

This Springer imprint is published by the registered company Springer Nature Switzerland AG
The registered company address is: Gewerbestrasse 11, 6330 Cham, Switzerland

Disclaimers and Copyright Notices

Other items are referenced in small amounts throughout this text in accordance with Section 107 of the Copyright Act (Fair Use).

Google, Google Docs, Google Drive, Google Keep, Google Translate, Google Trends, Google Chrome, and YouTube, along with their respective logos, are trademarks of Google LLC. This book is not endorsed by or affiliated with Google in any way. All images of Google owned items are published in accordance with Google's Brand Resource Center policies, which can be found at https://about.google/brand-resource-center/products-and-services/search-guidelines/. Google and the Google logo are trademarks of Google LLC.

Microsoft, Bing, Windows, Word, Excel, PowerPoint, and Edge, are trademarks of the Microsoft group of companies. Images of Microsoft products are used with permission from Microsoft. All images of Microsoft owned content are published in accordance with Microsoft's copyright policy, which can be found at https://www.microsoft.com/en-us/legal/copyright/permissions.

This book is an independent publication and has not been authorized, sponsored, or otherwise approved by Apple Inc. Apple and Apple Macintosh are trademarks of Apple Inc., registered in the U.S. and other countries and regions. Images of Apple owned software are published in accordance with Apple's copyright policy, which can be found at https://www.apple.com/legal/intellectual-property/guidelines-for3rdparties.html.

All images containing the Reddit brand are reproduced in accordance with Reddit brand policies, which can be found at https://www.redditinc.com/assets/images/site/reddit_brand_guidelines_version_2022_2022-04-01-160548_akmi.pdf. Special permission to reproduce one image was obtained from Reddit user u/octolink.

This book contains images from Wikipedia. Wikipedia® is a registered trademark of the Wikimedia Foundation, Inc., a non-profit organization. See: https://en.wikipedia.org/wiki/Wikipedia:Copyrights for more information on Wikipedia's copyright policies.

This book contains one image containing the Semrush logo and products. Semrush is a registered trademark of SEMrush Inc. The image included in this book is reproduced in accordance with the Semrush brand policy, which can be accessed here: https://www.semrush.com/company/legal/brand-policy/.

For all other images, the author requested and obtained written permission to reproduce images from the following organizations, listed in alphabetical order: Creative Commons (CCSearch), Dassault Systèmes (Exalead), Data.gov, Data Miner, DuckDuckGo, Gibiru, Glosbe, IPVanish, Internet Systems Consortium (ISC), Kapwing, Naver, OCR Space, SerpAPI, Seznam, Stack Exchange, Startpage, Swisscows, ThePashto, Thruuu, Veed.io, and Yandex.

Special thanks to all of the aforementioned organizations. Without your permissions, this book would be very boring.

Preface

I recognize that this book comes at a time when information is increasingly available online from regions of the world where information was previously unavailable or difficult to obtain. The need to narrow search results is not a new problem for today's researchers. The new problem is incorporating resources that capture an international perspective in our global society. What better way to do that than with resources from across the globe?

The modern researcher need not speak every language spoken on the planet—they only need the skill and prowess to discover and understand these resources. This is the purpose of this book. It provides tools to begin discovering the *hidden gems* that exist in other languages that provide a global perspective on a wide variety of topics. It is time for the modern researcher to step outside their comfort zone and seek perspectives which they might not normally understand. It is using these perspectives that the researcher may finally begin to challenge accepted norms and combat their own biases.

Indeed, foreign language research can be frustrating and uncomfortable; efforts to find certain resources may sometimes fail, too. This is ok—there will be times when the information sought does not exist in any language. However, if the information sought does exist, the researcher may now have a greater chance of finding it than ever before.

Generally, books that discuss online services do not age well. There is always the risk that websites, services, and links hosted online may cease to exist in the future. The year is 2023: the references contained therein existed at this time. Additionally, newer resources may come into existence in the future that would have been relevant to include here. The researcher will uncover new resources that support their research needs that are not in this book. This book does not aim to include every search engine, every database, or every link that the researcher may need in their research project. This would be an impossible task. Rather, it cites examples to demonstrate how research can be done and processes replicated. I encourage the reader to establish their own methods that work for their research needs. This book offers a starting place.

Finally, I would like to express my gratitude to those who helped and inspired me to write and complete this book. First, the editorial and administrative staff at Springer Nature, who gave me the opportunity to share my thoughts. It is a tremendous honor to share my work with this fine publisher, whose books I read all throughout college.

Thank you to the content creators who agreed to share their copyright materials with me, and allowed me to reproduce it here. Many of the images used throughout this book are not my own work; yet they offer an invaluable demonstration of how search techniques and tools serve our purposes. Without them, this book makes no sense.

I would also like to thank my colleagues at the various academic institutions I have studied, who showed me the need for such a book. Without them, I may have kept these thoughts to myself.

Finally, I would like to thank my husband and our tuxedo cats. You let me "suffer in silence," which was absolutely necessary for me to complete this book. It was not easy to sit at the computer and write when I knew you were sitting idly by. Thank you to the cats, for always keeping me company. These cats spent countless hours curled up on my lap as I typed.

Good luck, and enjoy!

Berkeley, CA, USA   M. D. Miller

Contents

About the Author

M. D. Miller has a passion for Internet research and studying foreign languages. She holds an academic degree in Slavic Languages and Literature from the University of California, Berkeley. She lives in the United States with her husband.

Chapter 1
Introduction to Foreign-Language Research

This chapter introduces the definition, concept, and overall need for foreign-language research. It describes the benefits of incorporating foreign-language resources in the context of a larger research question and scope of knowledge on a topic. This chapter also discusses the development and scope of research questions that have an inherent foreign-language nexus. That is, a research question that may otherwise only offer a perspective native to the author's geographic location and language can be expanded to include a foreign viewpoint. Another concern with foreign-language research is the veracity of foreign sources, which is also addressed here.

To get the researcher started, this chapter also introduces some fundamental language tools, including a step-by-step guide with instructions to set up foreign-language keyboards on a computer. The use of Virtual Private Networks, or VPNs, can also improve and resource discovery. Finally, this chapter includes examples of the key features of some common foreign alphabets to aid the researcher with the passive identification of languages as they may appear in the wild.

1.1 What Is Foreign-Language Research?

Foreign-language research describes the process of discovering and enumerating foreign-language resources into the context of the researcher's overall research goals. Incorporating resources from the researcher's native tongue, the foreign-language researcher offers an all-encompassing view of a subject by adding resources from different regions of the world. Foreign-language ability does not bound the modern researcher only to research in languages they speak—it provides an opportunity to add to the depth and breadth of the researcher's own original thoughts. It helps the researcher represent the thoughts of a globalized society, and captures how modern research does not exist in a vacuum.

© The Author(s), under exclusive license to Springer Nature Switzerland AG 2023
M. D. Miller, *Discovering Hidden Gems in Foreign Languages*, Terrorism, Security, and Computation, https://doi.org/10.1007/978-3-031-18479-6_1

To help capture the concept of foreign-language research, it is also helpful to describe what it is *not*: it is *not* simply using Google Translate to discover what something says. It is *not* just reading the auto-translated subtitles of a video: it is so much more than that. It requires the researcher to go out of their way to discover opposing thought, and interpret the content of the foreign-language resource in the context of the source itself.

1.2 Who Is this Book for

This book is for anyone looking to extend their research abilities beyond their current capabilities. Undoubtedly, anyone who might be interested in this book has already been conducting research for quite some time, and some may have even published works of their own. This book is for those looking to challenge themselves, and those looking to expand upon the aperture of their current research methods. In no particular order, this book will primarily be beneficial to:

- Academics, to include students and faculty at all levels.
- Authors, journalists, and members of the media.
- Open-Source (OSINT) researchers.
- Business Intelligence analysts.
- Investigators and Forensic Investigators.
- Monolinguals, or those interested in capturing the views of others who speak a foreign language.

The reader may have already picked up the OSINT research books by Don MacLeod, Michael Bazzell, Johnny Long, or other brave stewards of the OSINT research community—and these are excellent books. This book expands upon the existing books on Open-Source research by introducing how one might use these methods to discover foreign-language resources. Business intelligence professionals may be interested to know what their competition is doing; competing companies may have offices in foreign countries, and their resources may exist only in another language. A medical researcher may be interested to know how their counterparts in a foreign country are tackling today's most challenging research questions. Even the reader who speaks many languages cannot know every single language on the planet. The multilingual, too, will benefit from knowing the resources that exist in a language they do not speak.

1.3 Benefits of Foreign-Language Research

Simply put, foreign-language resources fall into the category of resources that the researcher would not otherwise know because they exist in a language that the researcher does not speak. Often times, when conducting a search online or even for print resources, these foreign-language results fall to the bottom of the list. A simple Google search for any common term will often yield *millions* of results, but rarely will the researcher see the millionth result, let alone the eleventh. The desired results, i.e., the results in question, exist somewhere in the middle of the pile. Why permit the search engine to decide which sources the researcher should see? Below are just some of the benefits of discovering and incorporating foreign-language resources into any project:

- Discover new resources.
- Take control of search output.
- Cut research time significantly.
- View the exact desired results without too much extra digging.
- Expand the aperture of research findings beyond the expected.
- Generate counterarguments.
- Capture the whole of opinion of a subject.
- Learn what those of a foreign culture believe about a topic.
- Discover new research goals entirely (i.e., ask research questions that would otherwise not be asked).

Once the researcher decides that there is value to their project in adding foreign-language resources, the researcher should establish the scope and goals of the research. To be successful in this endeavor, the researcher should acknowledge how the new sources available impact the goals of the research and the findings.

Another way to consider the benefits of foreign-language research is using the Matrix of Knowledge, shown in Fig. 1.1. This book aims to help the researcher identify the information in the fourth and most detrimental quadrant of information in the Matrix of Knowledge: the information they don't even know they're leaving out.

It assumes that the researcher has not considered sources in languages they do not speak, and therefore that information is unknown to the researcher. By applying the methods in this book and by incorporating foreign-language resources to existing research projects, the researcher will expand the aperture of their views to the most challenging quadrant in the Matrix of Knowledge.

I know what I know	I don't know what I know
I know what I don't know	*I don't know what I don't know*

Fig. 1.1 Matrix of knowledge

1.4   Establishing Research Goals and Asking a Research Question

Before making the decision to incorporate foreign-language resources into one's research, the researcher should determine the goals of the research. To determine the goals of the research is to ask a research question and hypothesize the answer. Then, the researcher can determine a methodology to answer the question and develop a data collection strategy. The acquisition of foreign-language materials should be part of the data collection strategy, but will also play a large role in the methodology: the methodology should consider the scope of the sources collected, because the incorporation of foreign-language resources itself changes the scope of the research and findings. If the researcher determines that foreign-language resources will support the answer to the research question within scope, the next question the researcher must ask is *how* and *to what extent* those sources will support the answer. The research question should capture the foreignness of the answer. They should also discuss the impact of these sources on the overall findings of the research.

Foreign-language research can either add to the answer of an already existing research question, or help the researcher generate new research questions that a researcher might not otherwise ask. The incorporation of these sources is sometimes more obvious than others. A research question such as "What does foreign country X believe about issue Y?" organically benefits from conducting research both in the researcher's native tongue, and the language spoken primarily in country X. It would be possible to answer the question only using resources from the researcher's country and in the researcher's native language, but the results will be heavily biased and one-sided.

On the other hand, consider a research question such as "How has biometrics technology altered the relationship between the government and their populations?" It would be all too easy for the researcher to answer this question using only sources from their government and only capturing the views and impact of their native population. It would also be possible for the researcher to answer this question using resources about foreign governments and foreign lands, but using resources from the researcher's country. The researcher's community will laud the researcher for a job well done, because they, too, largely see value in views from whence they came. The third option is to answer the question using resources from across the globe: these resources are often not in English, but the results will be profound and the impact much greater.

Some research questions are less obvious. Take for example the question "What are the implications of artificial intelligence technology for smart cities and individual privacy rights?" One could simply conduct research in the language they speak and find an example or two of how *their* government is implementing AI solutions *domestically*. To broaden the scope of the answer, the researcher could first identify countries other than their own who have implemented AI solutions in their cities. For example, an American researcher will find examples of this in the United States, but upon further examination they will also find examples in China, Brazil, and Canada, to name a few. With this list, the researcher can then begin to implement the methods in this book to discover how foreign countries are implementing AI technology. The overall answer to the research question will be vastly different.

The researcher, now knowing first-hand the value of foreign-language resources, may naturally begin to look at existing issues from a more worldly lens, and may find themselves asking questions they have never asked before. They will begin to ask questions such as "How do think tanks from country X portray issue Y in comparison with think tanks from country Z?" This question demands that the foreign-language researcher identifies foreign think tanks from the country in question, locates the resources from those think tanks, interprets and understands their contents, analyzes them in a specific context, and presents their unique findings in writing.

Foreign-language research is not appropriate for every research question. With practice, the researcher will develop the ability to see how foreign-language resources can supplement their existing research strategies and preferred resources, and how foreign-language resources may even change the way they ask their research questions altogether.

1.5   Veracity of Foreign Sources

In the research community, there is no question that the source of information is paramount to the veracity of the researcher's subsequent findings. For example, an American researcher citing solely foreign resources might not receive such positive feedback from Western critics, simply because the critics may not consider the underlying sources to be reliable or unbiased. The same can be said about the opposite: citing only sources from one perspective, and only in one language, is still limiting, even if they are sources from the author's own native land. So, it is the researcher's duty to capture the whole of thought on a topic, not just the thoughts and opinions of one's own people. If this is so, then the researcher has the duty to comment on the one-sidedness of their sources, even if they are from only sources which the researcher personally deems trustworthy.

Similarly, if the researcher anticipates criticism for the use of foreign-language materials, they should clarify their choice of sources in the text. Point to the one-sidedness of other texts that discuss a similar topic, and remind the reader why they should consider alternative views from foreign sources. This will perpetuate a global culture in the research community, as the international community begins to expand upon the quality and variety of sources they use in their research.

1.6 Language Keyboards in Microsoft Windows and Apple Macintosh

While conducting foreign-language research on a computer, the researcher may decide to add a foreign-language keyboard to their computer. Keyboards are not a requirement for conducting foreign-language research: there are other techniques to aid the researcher discussed later in this book. For the ambitious researcher, this short tutorial demonstrates how to add keyboards in Microsoft Windows and Apple Macintosh operating systems. Once this is set up, it is easy to toggle between foreign scripts. The researcher is encouraged to familiarize themselves with foreign scripts, especially for languages they plan to use frequently.

1.6.1 Microsoft Windows 10

To add a keyboard in Microsoft Windows 10, access the computer Settings. In the Settings dialog box, as shown in Fig. 1.2, select "Time & Language."

Figure 1.3 shows the "Time & Language" settings options. To add a language, select the plus symbol next to "Add a language."

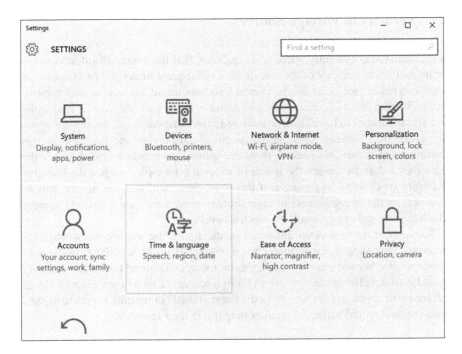

Fig. 1.2 Settings dialog box in Windows 10 © Microsoft 2021

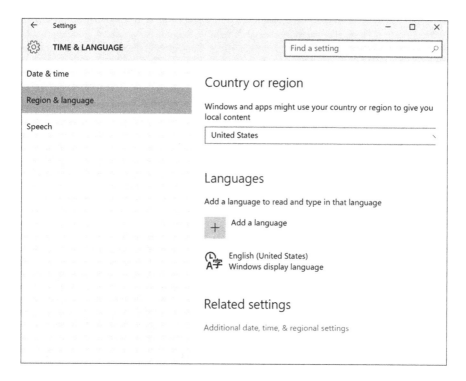

Fig. 1.3 Region and language settings in Windows 10 © Microsoft 2021

A list of languages will appear, as shown in Fig. 1.4. Select the language or languages to be added.

The list of all language keyboards added will appear in the "Time & Language" dialog box. Figure 1.5 shows the English and Armenian language keyboards added.

Upon adding multiple language keyboards in Windows 10, it is possible to view and toggle between the available keyboards directly from the Systray. In the bottom right corner of the Windows screen (where the date, internet connection, and other computer information settings options are located), a new icon should appear. Since the default language used in this example was English, the icon says "ENG." Click on the icon, and a list of all added keyboards will appear, as shown in Fig. 1.6.

Selecting a language in the language menu in Systray will change the character input on the computer. To change the language back, simply navigate back to this menu and toggle back to the desired language.

To view the keyboard layout of the added language, search the Windows main menu for "On-Screen Keyboard." This is demonstrated in Fig. 1.7.

Selecting the "On-Screen Keyboard" will display a new pop-up window containing the keyboard layout of the language currently selected.

Figure 1.8 shows the keyboard layout for the Armenian language. The user can type on their computer keyboard, or click on each button using the mouse. Using this method will allow the user to type any word in any language.

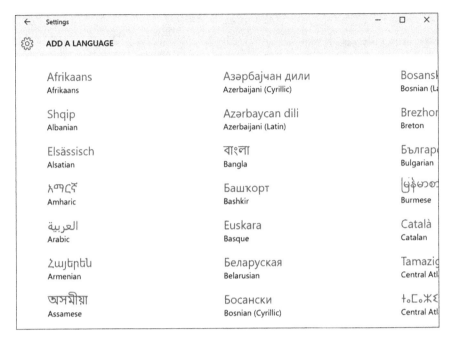

Fig. 1.4 "Add a Language" dialog box in Windows 10 © Microsoft 2021

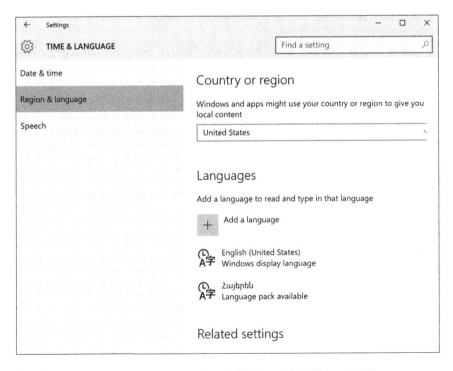

Fig. 1.5 Windows region and language settings in Windows 10 © Microsoft 2021

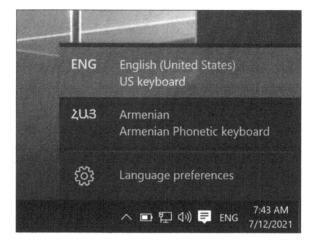

Fig. 1.6 Language preferences in Windows 10 © Microsoft 2021

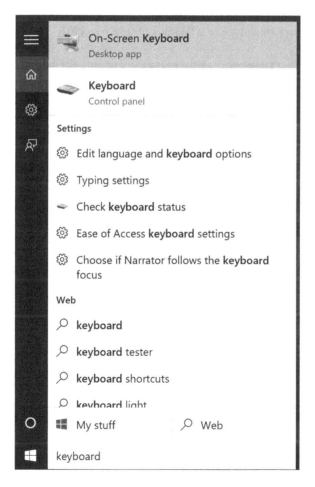

Fig. 1.7 Search for "On-Screen Keyboard" in Windows 10 © Microsoft 2021

Fig. 1.8 On-Screen Keyboard feature in Windows 10 © Microsoft 2021

Fig. 1.9 Accessing system preferences on Mac © 2021 Apple Inc.

1.6.2   Apple Macintosh

On an Apple Macintosh computer, it is possible to add a foreign-language keyboard in the System Preferences. On the top left of the screen, select the Apple symbol as shown in Fig. 1.9. From the drop-down menu, select System Preferences.

Fig. 1.10 The system preferences dialog box in Mac © 2021 Apple Inc.

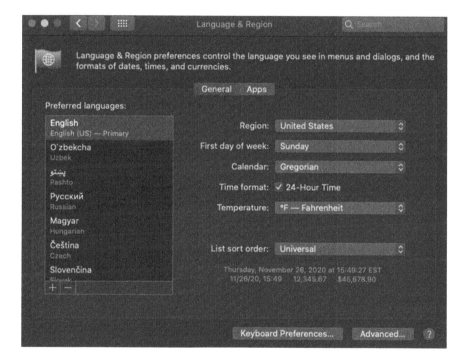

Fig. 1.11 The language and region dialog box in Mac © 2021 Apple Inc.

In the System Preferences dialog box, select "Language & Region." Figure 1.10 shows the "Language & Region" icon in System Preferences.

In the Language & Region window shown in Fig. 1.11, the language(s) already enabled will appear in the list of preferred languages. To add a new language, click the "plus" symbol beneath the list. To delete a language from the list, simple click on the minus symbol under the list of preferred languages. No further action is required.

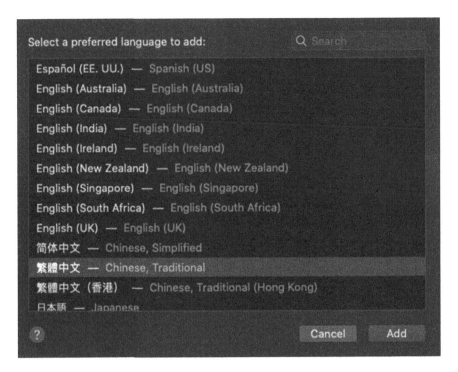

Fig. 1.12 The preferred language dialog box in Mac © 2021 Apple Inc.

After clicking the "plus" symbol at the bottom of the preferred language list, an additional drop-down menu will appear containing a list of languages to add. Figure 1.12 shows this menu. Select a language to add, or select multiple languages by holding down the "Shift" key.

After selecting the desired languages, click "Add." The drop-down menu will disappear. The language is now added. To view the keyboard for any language, select "Keyboard Preferences…" in the Language and Region dialog box. Click on any of the languages in the list to view which characters are associated with each of the keys on the keyboard. Figure 1.13 shows the list of languages added so far, including the keyboard layout for each.

Upon adding an additional language to the list of languages, a flag will appear among the icons in the top right corner of the desktop. As shown in Fig. 1.14, the flag of the country represents the language of the current keyboard. To change the language, click on the flag and change the language in the drop-down menu. The current language will have a check mark next to it in the list.

Another useful feature in this drop-down menu is the Keyboard Viewer (Fig. 1.15). First, select the desired keyboard language, and then select the Keyboard Viewer. This will open a dialog box containing the keyboard layout for the current language. For example, selecting Russian in the list and then selecting Keyboard Viewer will display a dialog box that can help when typing in that language.

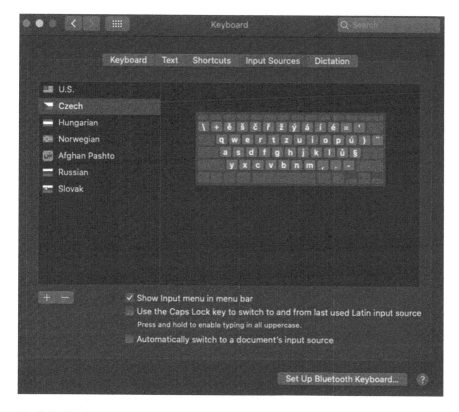

Fig. 1.13   The input sources dialog box in Mac © 2021 Apple Inc.

Fig. 1.14   The keyboard input drop-down menu in Mac © 2021 Apple Inc.

Fig. 1.15 Russian keyboard in keyboard viewer in Mac © 2021 Apple Inc.

It is also possible to type using the Keyboard Viewer by simply clicking the keyboard buttons with the cursor. This way, it is not required to type with the corresponding button on the keyboard, which can get confusing when trying to figure out which letter corresponds to which button on the English-language keyboard.

Another way to change the keyboard language is to hold down the "command" button and the space bar at the same time. Selecting this combination of keys will toggle the language back and forth between the current language and the most recently used language. If the user has multiple languages in the list, it will only toggle between these two. To use this shortcut to select a third language, hold down the "command" button and then hit the space bar multiple times. This will bring up a list of all the languages in the list in the center of the screen, as shown in Fig. 1.16.

Stop selecting the space bar when the desired language is highlighted.

1.7   Virtual Private Networks (VPNs) and Geographic Restrictions

One common concern when conducting foreign-language research online is the trustworthiness of foreign websites. Since this book is largely concerned with foreign-language research online, it is imperative for the researcher to know the risks associated with visiting websites they may not normally visit.

One recommendation is to use a VPN, or Virtual Private Network, to change the researcher's IP address. This obfuscates the apparent physical location of the researcher and makes it more challenging for the website administrator of the site the researcher is visiting to identify the researcher. *VPNs will not prevent malware*

Fig. 1.16 Changing the language input on Mac © 2021 Apple Inc.

or viruses! They only obfuscate the researcher's identity and make it more challenging for the website administrator or web browser to track the researcher's activity over time.

Besides privacy, another consideration for the foreign-language researcher is the location detection features within the web browser. Web browsers such as Google can detect the researcher's location, and will return particular results based on the location (or detected location). In other words, altering the IP address using a VPN may alter the results returned in search engine queries. This is of value to the foreign-language researcher, who may be interested to know the top ten search results for a particular topic based on region.

For example, setting the location to Atlanta, Georgia in IP Vanish will return results relative to Atlanta. Searching for "restaurants near me" will return restaurants near Atlanta, even if the researcher is not physically located in Georgia.

Figure 1.17 shows the VPN set to Atlanta, Georgia; Fig. 1.18 shows the corresponding results of the search in Google with the corresponding VPN settings. The results returned include websites that discuss popular restaurants in Atlanta, even though the search parameters did not include the words "Atlanta" or "Georgia."

The researcher will return different results if they conduct the same search for *restaurants near me* using a VPN located in Bratislava, Slovakia.

Figure 1.19 shows the VPN set to Bratislava, Slovakia; Fig. 1.20 shows the corresponding results of the search in Google with the VPN settings. The results returned include websites that discuss popular restaurants in Bratislava, even though the search parameters did not include the words "Bratislava" or "Slovakia."

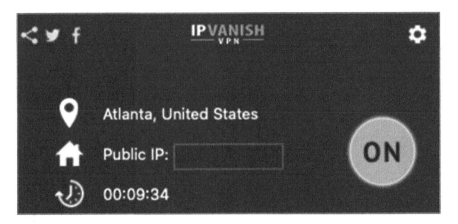

Fig. 1.17 IP Vanish VPN set to Atlanta, Georgia © 2021 Ziff Davis, Inc.

The difference in results will be an important consideration while conducting foreign-language research and will be discussed in detail throughout this book. Keep this in mind when interpreting the results shown throughout this book, or in one's own research projects.

To decide which VPN might be best for a particular project or goal, consider consulting the VPN Comparison Chart at: https://www.safetydetectives.com/best-vpns/ or https://www.bestvpn.co/vpn-comparison/.

1.8   Foreign Alphabets

To conduct foreign-language research often requires the researcher to identify foreign alphabets and associate them with a target language. As previously mentioned, this book assumes the audience for this book does not speak the language in which they are conducting research; it is not a prerequisite. Perhaps the researcher knows at least one foreign language, or at least has taken a beginner course in a language that uses a script other than their native language. This will certainly help the researcher—although, again, it is not possible to know all the languages in the world. It should always be possible to at least identify these languages.

Correctly identifying the language of the text is imperative for selecting the correct language for an automated translator, or correctly citing the work. It is not necessarily the case that conducting a targeted search for sources in a particular language or country will return results in that exact language. For example, a Chinese website may contain text in a language other than Chinese, and this is common. The researcher will develop a trained eye to identify differences and nuances between different but similar-looking alphabets.

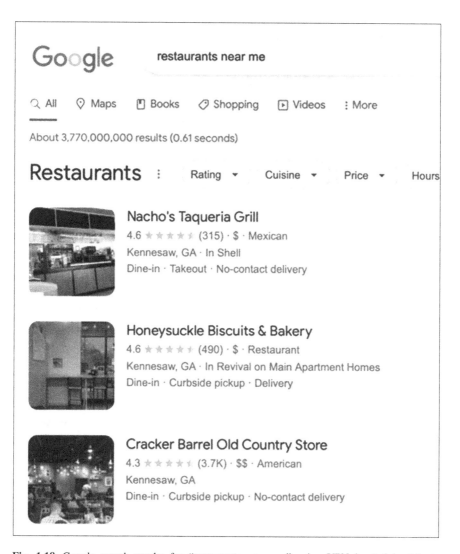

Fig. 1.18 Google search results for "restaurants near me" using VPN located in Atlanta, GA (Google and the Google logo are trademarks of Google LLC)

This book does not delve into all the different alphabets of *all* foreign languages—this could be its own book. This section only provides the researcher with a foundational awareness of the major differences between similar languages based on the script used or region. It also introduces nuances in orthography to which the researcher ought to pay attention when conducting research.

If the researcher is ever unsure of a language in question, they should identify the unique features of the alphabet, such as a unique-looking character in a word, and research that particular letter. Based on one or a few letters, the researcher may

Fig. 1.19 IP Vanish VPN set to Bratislava, Slovakia © 2021 Ziff Davis, Inc.

Fig. 1.20 Google search results for "restaurants near me" using VPN located in Bratislava, Slovakia (Google and the Google logo are trademarks of Google LLC)

identify a language or family of languages that may use these letters. For the beginner, this section briefly introduces the distinct features of prominent Latin, Cyrillic, Arabic, and Asian alphabets. This section also offers a few reasons the researcher should focus on this matter in the context of foreign-language research, and briefly instructs the researcher on how to use this knowledge to their advantage.

The primary reason patterns in orthography are so important for the foreign-language researcher is that the unique letters in foreign words can help researchers find the right subjects online with ease. Being able to use and identify these letters actively in a search or passively in the results will make research that much easier. For example, "kar" in Turkish means snow, but "kâr" means profit. Searching for the Hungarian word "időjárás," meaning "weather," versus "idojaras" without its appropriate diacritics will result in two different sets of results, even though the word without diacritics is not a word at all. The researcher's ability to visualize the minute differences and locate the correct characters on the keyboard will ensure the researcher will find the results they seek. This is especially important when the researcher does not speak the language in question.

Another consideration for language identification is the location where languages are spoken. For example, it is well known that Dutch is spoken in the Netherlands. However, there are several other countries where Dutch is also commonly spoken. The researcher must know this to conduct research effectively in this country. Knowing that Dutch is also a common language spoken in the Caribbean, Suriname, Indonesia, and other countries will change and improve the researcher's approach to discovering resources with a particular target in mind [1]. Afrikaans is actually the official language of South Africa and Namibia, but also has significant speaking populations in Zambia, Australia, the United States, the Netherlands, and elsewhere [2]. The researcher should consider this when planning their search and when interpreting the results. Later chapters in this book will demonstrate this concept. For now, let's discuss some common languages from around the world.

Latin alphabets are common among European languages, but not all languages that use a Latin writing system use the same characters as the English language. There are some characters that are only present in some languages. Knowing which letters are present in only one or a few languages can aid the researcher in identifying which language is in use.

Germanic languages, including English, German, and Dutch, are similar in their roots but are somewhat easy to distinguish, especially for native English speakers. Besides the letters found in the English alphabet, other letters in the German alphabet that stand out include ä, ö, ü, and ß. This makes German distinct from Dutch, which only has the 26 characters of the English alphabet; Dutch does not have any special characters.

Scandinavian languages, including Norwegian, Icelandic, Swedish, and Danish are written in a Latin script and have many similarities that make them difficult to distinguish. Letters commonly found in the Scandinavian languages include å, æ, ø, ä, ö, ð, þ, á, é, í, ó, ú, and ý. The letters å, æ, and ø are all found in Norwegian and Danish; the other letters in the list are not. The letter å is also found in Swedish, but the letters æ or ø are not. Instead, Swedish words will have ä and ö, whereas Norwegian and Danish will not. In Icelandic, the letters æ and ø can be found, in addition to ð and þ, and diacritics á, é, í, ó, ú, and ý.

Romance languages, including French, Spanish, Italian, Portuguese, and Romanian, are written in the Latin script and share letters with each other and other European languages. The French language is distinguishable from other romance languages by its use of the cedilla ç, even though this letter can also be found in other languages, including Turkish, Albanian, and Tajik, among others. The French language also uses several other diacritics, including the accented é; circumflex â, ê, î, ô, and û; the grave accent à, è, ì, ò, and ù; and the trema accent ë, ï, and ü. Many of these letters are not unique to French—but when seen amongst each other in a larger body of text, it may be easier to identify the language as French when many or most of these letters are present. The Spanish language is famous for the letter ñ, which can make it easy to identify Spanish. However, it is important to remember this letter can also be found in other alphabets, including Basque, Tatar, and Portuguese. The Italian language uses several diacritic vowels, including à, è, ì, ò, ù, é, í, ó, and ú. Since Italian only has 21 letters in its alphabet, perhaps what makes Italian easier to identify is that its words will never contain the letters j, k, w, x, or y, except loan words or proper names. At first glance, Portuguese can be difficult to distinguish from French based solely on the letters present in words because Portuguese uses the same diacritics on vowels as does French, except the letters ã and õ may also be present (also see comments on Estonian below). Romanian also uses diacritics on many of its vowels, as do French and Portuguese, but the Romanian alphabet also uses letters ş and ţ that make it easy to distinguish from the other Romance languages.

Slavic languages, including Russian, Bulgarian, Ukrainian, Polish, Lithuanian, Latvian, Croatian, Czech, and Slovak, are written in either Cyrillic or Latin script. The next two sections separate these languages based on the script used, with Russian, Bulgarian, and Ukrainian using a Cyrillic script, and the remainder using a Latin script.

The Russian script uses the Cyrillic script, identified by the use of the letters а, б, в, г, д, е, ё, ж, з, и, й, к, л, м, н, о, п, р, с, т, у, ф, х, ц, ч, ш, щ, ъ, ы, ь, э, ю, and я. The Bulgarian language uses the same alphabet, except it does not contain the letters ё, ы, or э. In many Russian texts, the letter ё is written without its stress, so this letter alone is not diagnostic of a Russian versus Bulgarian text. Ukrainian uses all the same letters as does the Russian language, but with a few exceptions: instead of the Russian и or й, Ukrainian uses the letters i or ї, respectively. Ukrainian also contains the letters г and є that the Russian alphabet does not use. Ukrainian does not use the Russian letters ё, ъ, ы, or э either. Figures 1.21 and 1.22 show sample text in Russian and Ukrainian. Note the major differences between the two.

Polish, Lithuanian, Latvian, Croatian, Czech, and Slovak are all Slavic languages that use a Latin script, and can be difficult to distinguish from each other. Polish contains acute accents ć, ń, ó, ś, and ź; the kropka ż; the ogonek ą and ę; and the stroke ł. The acute accents present on consonants rather than vowels help to distinguish Polish from Romance languages, in addition to the kropka and stroke. Lithuanian contains ogonek letters ą, ę, į, and ų; the caron letters č, š, and ž; the macron letter ū; and the diacritic letter ė. Caron letters can also be found in Czech, Slovak, Croatian, and Latvian, so the researcher should not base their diagnosis solely on the presence of caron letters. The macron letter ū is also found in Latvian, among other languages. Since Latvian contains many of the same special characters as Lithuanian, one way to distinguish these two languages is the presence of additional macron letters ā, ē, ī, and ū (whereas Lithuanian only contains ū), and the cedilla letters ģ, ķ, ļ, and ņ. As previously mentioned, Croatian contains the caron

Fig. 1.21 Sample Russian text [3] (CC BY 2.0)

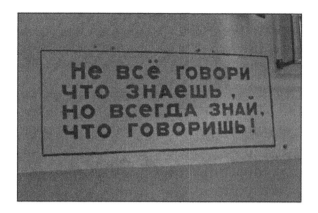

Fig. 1.22 Sample Ukrainian text [4] (CC BY-ND 2.0)

letters č, š, and ž; it also contains a diacritic ć, as does Polish. The Croatian language also contains three digraphs: dž, lj, and nj that make it distinguishable from other Latin-based Slavic languages. Perhaps most distinguishing from the other languages mentioned here is the presence of the letter đ, but this letter is present in Vietnamese and Sami, too. Croatian does not contain the letters q, w, x, and y, which may be another way to diagnose Croatian text. The Czech language contains many similar characters to the aforementioned Latin-based Slavic languages, but also contains a distinct ů (u with a ring diacritic) that can make Czech language text stand out. The Slovak language is very similar to Czech, making it difficult to distinguish the two. One way to distinguish them is that Czech words may contain the letters ě, ř, and ů, whereas Slovak does not. Similarly, Slovak words may contain the letters ä, ľ, ĺ, ŕ, ô, and dž, whereas Czech does not. Additionally, Slovak does not contain letters q, w, or x, except in loan words.

Figures 1.23, 1.24, and 1.25 show sample text in Polish, Lithuanian, and Latvian, respectively. Note the key characteristics in each as described above. For examples of text in the other languages, conduct online searches for "sample text in <language>."

Fig. 1.23 Sample Polish text [5] (CC BY-SA 2.0)

Fig. 1.24 Sample Lithuanian text [6] (CC BY 2.0)

Fig. 1.25 Sample Latvian
text [7] (CC BY 2.0)

Hungarian, Estonian, and Finnish are all Uralic languages written in a Latin
script, that can often be confused with each other and with other European languages. Hungarian uses the diacritics á, é, í, ó, and ú; the tremas ö and ü; and the
double acute accents ő and ű. The double acute letters are the easiest way to identify
and distinguish Hungarian from other Latin-based European languages. Estonian
contains the special letters š, ž, õ, ä, ö, and ü. Recall that the letters š and ž are also
common among other Slavic languages using a Latin script, and that ä, ö, and ü can
also be found in other Germanic languages (except the letter ü is not used in
Swedish). While õ is unique among the other Uralic languages listed here, this letter
can also be found in Portuguese, Vietnamese, and sometimes loan words in
Hungarian. Special characters found in Finnish include å, ä, and ö. Rarely are the
caron letters š and ž found in Finnish text: while they are not in the Finnish alphabet,
they can be found in foreign loan words. The Finnish language is possible to distinguish from Swedish because Finnish will have the letters ä and ö, but will not have
the letter å. Recall that å is often found in Scandinavian languages, including Danish,
Swedish, and Norwegian also.

Figures 1.26 and 1.27 contain sample text in Hungarian and Finnish, respectively.

Turkish, Kazakh, and Kyrgyz are all Turkish languages in origin, but use a variety of characters that Romance and Slavic languages also use. The Latin-based
Turkish alphabet contains the letters ç, ğ, ö, ş, and ü; some Turkish words may also
be spelled with the circumflex letters â, î, and û, even though they are not a part of
the alphabet. Perhaps the most distinctive aspect of the Turkish alphabet is that the

Fig. 1.26 Sample Hungarian text [8] (CC BY-SA 2.0)

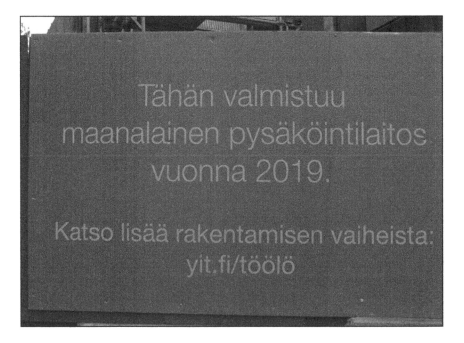

Fig. 1.27 Sample Finnish text [9] (CC BY 2.0)

letter I has both dotted and dotless letters in the lower-case and upper-case forms. These appear like so: the lower case dotless ı and the upper case dotless I, versus the lowercase dotted i and the upper case dotted İ. The dotted and dotless I can also be found in Azerbaijani and Kazakh. Currently, the Kazakh language is written in three different alphabets based on the country: Cyrillic, Latin, and Arabic. The Cyrillic alphabet is used in Kazakhstan, Mongolia, and former Soviet countries. Meanwhile, the Arabic alphabet is used in Iran, Afghanistan, and parts of China; the Latin alphabet is used among the Kazakh population in Turkey. However, the Government of Kazakhstan has a plan to adapt its language from a Cyrillic alphabet to a Latin alphabet between 2023 and 2031 [10]. Researchers should keep this in mind as they continue to conduct research in the Kazakh language (specific to resources from Kazakhstan). Letters found in the Cyrillic-based Kazakh alphabet are similar to Russian, but also contain ә, ғ, ң, қ, ө, ұ, ү, and ғ, which Russian does not use. Letters found in the new Latin-based Kazakh alphabet include ä, ğ, ñ, ö, ş, ū, ü, and the dotted and dotless I's. Letters found in the Arabic-based Kazakh alphabet are similar to the Modern Standard Arabic alphabet (discussed more in detail below), except the symbols ٵ, ٷ, ٸ, and ٻ. Some of these forms can also be found in Azerbaijani, Uyghur, and Kyrgyz. Kyrgyz is written in wither Cyrillic or Arabic, also depending on the country. The Cyrillic-based Kyrgyz alphabet uses all the same characters as does the Russian alphabet, along with the letters ң, ө, and ү (fewer additions than Kazakh). The Arabic-based Kyrgyz alphabet contains the four "wow" forms as does the Arabic-based Kazakh alphabet above, but it also contains the additional form ۉ that can make it possible for the untrained eye to distinguish Kazakh from Kyrgyz.

Armenian, Georgian, and Greek are grouped together here because, while not related, their alphabets tend to look similar to the untrained eye. Because they differ so greatly from many other languages, the easiest way to demonstrate their uniqueness is by simply listing them here as a reference for the reader. The Armenian alphabet is unlike any other alphabets listed so far:

ա, բ, գ, դ, ե, զ, է, ը, թ, ժ, ի, լ,
խ, ծ, կ, հ, ձ, ղ, ճ, մ, յ, ն, շ, ո, չ, պ, ջ, ռ, ս, վ, տ, ր, ց, ւ, փ, ք, o, ֆ, ու, and և.

As the reader can see, the Georgian alphabet looks similar, but, upon further inspection, does not contain any letters in common with Armenian:

ა, ბ, გ, დ, ე, ვ, ზ, თ, ი, კ,
ლ, მ, ნ, ო, პ, ჟ, რ, ს, ტ, უ, ფ, ქ, ღ, ყ, შ, ჩ, ც, ძ, წ, ჭ, ხ, ჯ, and ჰ

The Greek alphabet, too, is unlike any of the aforementioned alphabets, so it is worth listing here:

Α/α, Β/β, Γ/γ, Δ/δ, Ε/ε, Ζ/ζ, Η/η, Θ/θ, Ι/ι, Κ/κ, Λ/λ, Μ/μ, Ν/ν, Ξ/ξ, Ο/ο, Π/π, Ρ/ρ, Σ/σ/ς, Τ/τ, Υ/υ, Φ/φ, Χ/χ, Ψ/ψ, and Ω/ω

(upper- and lower-case letters are both listed here because many of them are different).

Languages using the Arabic script (not all necessarily Arab), include Arabic, Urdu, Persian, and Pashto. These languages are all written from right to left. The letters each have four forms, depending on their placement in the word: alone, initial, medial, and final. This can make it difficult, but not impossible, to distinguish nuances between languages that use the Arabic script. Figure 1.28 shows a table of the Modern Standard Arabic alphabet and all of its letter forms.

The letter forms in Fig. 1.28 are written in what is called the Naskh script, which is common in modern Arabic writing and official documents. This is important because other languages that use the Arabic alphabet or its derivatives are written in other scripts, which can make it easier for the non-Arabic speaker to identify (as opposed to identifying the presence or lack of unique characters). In particular, the

Fig. 1.28 Letter forms of the Arabic alphabet

Letter	Initial	Medial	Final
ا	ا	ا	ا
ب	بـ	ـبـ	ـب
ت	نـ	ـتـ	ـت
ث	نـ	ـثـ	ـث
ج	جـ	ـجـ	ـج
ح	حـ	ـحـ	ـح
خ	خـ	ـخـ	ـخ
د	د	ـد	ـد
ذ	ذ	ـذ	ـذ
ر	ر	ـر	ـر
ز	ز	ـز	ـز
س	سـ	ـسـ	ـس
ش	شـ	ـشـ	ـش
ص	صـ	ـصـ	ـص
ط	طـ	ـطـ	ـط
ظ	ظـ	ـظـ	ـظ
ع	عـ	ـعـ	ـع
غ	غـ	ـغـ	ـغ
ف	فـ	ـفـ	ـف
ق	قـ	ـقـ	ـق
ک	کـ	ـکـ	ـک
ل	لـ	ـلـ	ـل
م	مـ	ـمـ	ـم
ن	نـ	ـنـ	ـن
ه	هـ	ـهـ	ـه
و	و	ـو	ـو
ي	يـ	ـيـ	ـي

Urdu and Persian languages use the Nastaliq script. These writing styles have very different appearances that will help the researcher identify which language they are viewing at any given time.

One feature of Arabic that is also present in dialects of Arabic is the ة, or ta marbuta. While it is often written with two dots when it comes at the end of an Arabic word. This is uncommon in the other languages discussed here. The Urdu language uses a few letters that are not used in the Modern Standard Arabic alphabet, including ں, ژ, ڈ, ڈ, چ, ٹ, پ, and ڑ. The Persian and Pashto languages also use the letters ژ, چ, پ, so these letters alone cannot diagnose Urdu specifically. In addition, Persian also uses the letter گ, which is also seen in Dari. The Pashto language also contains extra letters that Arabic does not contain, including ک, ښ, ډ, ړ, ځ, څ, ، and ڼ. Pashto also uses five different forms of /yay/, which are: ی, ئ, ي, ی, and ۍ. A combination of the letters present and the script will help the researcher identify the language in question. There are examples of each of these scripts in Figs. 1.29, 1.30, 1.31, and 1.32 containing examples of Arabic, Urdu, Farsi, and Pashto, respectively.

Asian languages, including Chinese, Korean, and Japanese are grouped here because of the geographic proximity of the regions where these languages are primarily spoken. However, these languages are vastly different in many ways, and similar in others. Chinese does not have an alphabet; instead, it uses pictograms, or glyphs. This makes Chinese much more difficult for the nonspeaker to identify. These pictograms are most often square shaped, complex, and dense.

There are two primary dialects of Chinese: Cantonese and Mandarin. They use the same characters, which can make them difficult to distinguish from each other for the nonspeaker. However, it is important to consider because these languages are not mutually intelligible, and not all Chinese speakers speak the same way. Mandarin is the official language of China and is spoken in much of mainland China. Cantonese is spoken in Hong Kong, Macau, and some provinces in mainland China. The researcher should keep these dialectical differences in mind when conducting a targeted search in a specific region: making an extra effort to prepare searches in the correct dialect will ensure that the researcher gets the appropriate results and can interpret them correctly. There is more information about the Chinese dialects and regional differences at the reference in the footnotes [15].

Chinese also has two separate character forms that are more common based on the region. These are traditional and simplified. Traditional characters tend to be more complex than simplified characters in that they have more strokes. Chinese speakers in Hong Kong, Taiwan, Macau, and other countries tend to use traditional writing. Chinese speakers in mainland China, Malaysia, and Singapore tend to use simplified writing. The writing system used is dialect agnostic; that is, speakers of both Cantonese and Mandarin may use either writing style. Generally, there is an essence of elegance and professionalism in the use of the traditional writing style, which is often found in professional and government documents, contracts, or other formal situations [16]. The foreign language researcher may have to conduct searches in both traditional or simplified forms to discover the various Chinese language resources on a given topic. Figure 1.33 shows an example of Chinese writing.

Fig. 1.29 Sample Arabic text [11] (CC BY-SA 2.0)

There are online resources to help the researcher identify Chinese characters in simplified or traditional writing. One such resource is the Yellowbridge Chinese Character Search Tool, found at https://www.yellowbridge.com/chinese/adv-character-dictionary.php. Using this tool, the researcher can search by word, character, or component; it is even possible to draw a Chinese character using a computer's track pad to find it.

Different from Chinese, the Korean and Japanese languages use alphabets. The Korean alphabet is known as Hangul. Korean characters contain many more circles, ovals, and prominent vertical and horizontal lines compared to Chinese. They are less complex and dense than Chinese characters. The characters of the Korean

Fig. 1.30 Sample Urdu text [12] (CC BY 2.0)

alphabet are: ㄱ, ㄴ, ㄷ, ㄹ, ㅁ, ㅂ, ㅅ, ㅇ, ㅈ, ㅊ, ㅋ, ㅌ, ㅍ, ㅎ, ㅏ, ㅑ, ㅓ, ㅕ, ㅗ, ㅛ, ㅜ, ㅠ, ㅡ, ㅣ, ㄲ, ㄸ, ㅃ, ㅆ, ㅉ, ㄳ, ㄵ, ㄶ, ㄺ, ㄻ, ㄼ, ㄽ, ㄾ, ㄿ, ㅀ, ㅄ, ㅐ, ㅒ, ㅔ, ㅖ, ㅘ, ㅙ, ㅚ, ㅝ, ㅞ, ㅟ, ㅢ. These characters are used together to make syllabic characters. Sample Korean text is shown in Fig. 1.34. Notice the key differences between Korean and Chinese characters.

On the other hand, Japanese text is curvy and simple, and many characters can be written with one pen stroke. The primary alphabet of Japanese letters, known as Hiragana, is not bound by a "box," as in Chinese. Another distinguishing feature of Japanese is that it does not contain spaces between words! So, it is common to see strings of symbols in a row with no spaces. The Japanese alphabet is: あ, か, さ, た, な, は, ま, =, や, ら, わ, い, き, し, ち, に, ひ, み, り, う, く, す, つ, ぬ, ふ, む, る, を, え, け, せ, て, ね, へ, め, れ, お, こ, そ, と, の, ほ, も, よ, ろ,and ん. It is common for Korean and Japanese to use Chinese characters on occasion, too, so the researcher should not base their diagnosis solely on the identification of one or a few Chinese characters—they should look at the text from a glance. The Japanese name for borrowed Chinese characters is Kanji. Japanese also uses Katakana for spelling foreign loan words and names. Figure 1.35 shows an example of Japanese writing. See the reference in the footnotes for more information on Katakana and the Japanese writing system [19].

There are many other languages that are not mentioned here. The researcher who needs to conduct research in another language other than the ones listed here should research the orthography of that language before they begin. This is all part of the planning and preparation process and an integral starting point before proceeding to the more advanced methods and techniques discussed throughout this book.

جناب آقای محمدرضا بخشنده

با سلام و احترام،

بازگشت به نامه مورخهٔ ۸۷/۶/۹، اختراع شما با عنوان « تولید مستقیم پودر کاتد مس از سنگ معدن کم عیار و باطله های معدنی و صنعتی مس » در سطح ایران تازگی داشته و مورد تأیید می باشد. ضمناً هرگونه پیاده سازی یا تولید مورد اختراع نیازمند کسب مجوزهای لازم از مراجع ذیصلاح است.

با آرزوی توفیق الهی

دکتر محمدرضا بختیاری

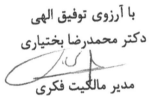

مدیر مالکیت فکری

Fig. 1.31 Sample Farsi text [13] (CC BY-SA 4.0)

Fig. 1.32 Sample Pashto text [14] (Pixabay License)

Fig. 1.33 Sample Chinese text [17] (CC BY 2.0)

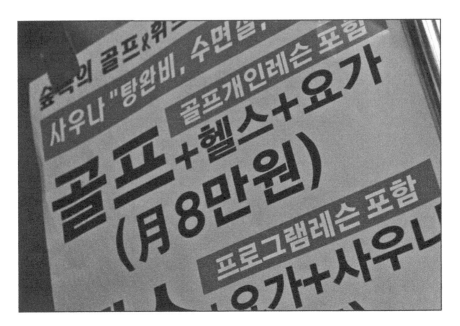

Fig. 1.34 Sample Korean text [18] (CC BY-SA 2.0)

Fig. 1.35 Sample Japanese text [20] (CC BY 2.0)

These languages are spoken around the world, not only in the country often associated with that language. It is easy to generalize that Chinese is spoken in China, Russian is spoken in Russia, etc. However, there are Chinese and Russian speakers across the globe. This is an important consideration for the foreign-language researcher that will be a common theme throughout this book as well.

1.9 Book Outline

The first chapter of this book introduces the justification for conducting foreign-language research and provides the researcher with fundamental tools to get started. Once the researcher has made the active decision to conduct research in a foreign language, Chap. 2 prepares the foreign-language researcher to conduct their research by introducing specialized search engines and foreign-language resources. Chap. 3 introduces the fundamentals of foreign-language resource discovery. Chap. 4 expands on the fundamentals from Chap. 2, focusing on country-specific domains. Once the researcher learns how to discover foreign-language resources, Chap. 5 offers methods and tools for translation and interpretation. Chap. 6 ties it all together, offering sample use cases. Chap. 7 proposes solutions for citing foreign-language resources so the researcher may legally use foreign-language materials in their formal work. Chap. 8 includes three valuable appendices, which contain list of useful websites for later reference.

Online Database References

1. "Dutch (Nederlands)," last modified September 26, 2021, https://omniglot.com/writing/dutch.htm
2. "Afrikaans," last modified September 26, 2021, https://omniglot.com/writing/afrikaans.htm
3. Dmitry Djouce, "Объект 825ГТС [Object 825GTS]," May 16, 2015, https://www.flickr.com/photos/nothingpersonal/17782466878, licensed under CC BY 2.0.
4. UNDP Ukraine, "Control Post "Dytiatky", entrance to the Chornobyl Exclusion Zone, Ukraine," July 7, 2008, https://www.flickr.com/photos/undpukraine/6035101199, licensed under CC BY-ND 2.0.
5. Krzysztof Belczyński, "Park Natoliński," June 17, 2012, https://www.flickr.com/photos/x-oph/7385804120, licensed under CC BY-SA 2.0.
6. jo.sau, "918," August 22, 2010, https://www.flickr.com/photos/johnas/4916247767, licensed under CC BY 2.0.
7. Anna Hanks, "untitled (443 of 1144).jpg," July 17, 2014, https://www.flickr.com/photos/annaustin/17431719798, licensed under CC BY 2.0.
8. Eli Duke, "Hungary: Walking around the Old Lake in Tata," January 13, 2015, https://www.flickr.com/photos/elisfanclub/15660812133, licensed under CC BY-SA 2.0.
9. TeaMeister, "Finnish - a simply extraordinary language," September 2017, https://www.flickr.com/photos/158710843@N02/37298704755, licensed under CC BY 2.0.
10. Assel Satubaldina, "Kazakhstan Presents New Latin Alphabet, Plans Gradual Transition Through 2031," February 1, 2021, https://astanatimes.com/2021/02/kazakhstan-presents-new-latin-alphabet-plans-gradual-transition-through-2031/

11. Pendolino, "old arab ads (5)," July 7, 2006, https://www.flickr.com/photos/pendolino/193835914, licensed under CC BY-SA 2.0.
12. Nevil Zaveri, "urdu, khuldabad," https://www.flickr.com/photos/43109416@N00/8225139925, November 23, 2012, licensed under CC BY 2.0.
13. Zarbarg, "IROST-MSRT.jpg," September 5, 2015, https://commons.wikimedia.org/wiki/Category:Documents_in_Persian#/media/File:IROST-MSRT.jpg, licensed under CC BY-SA 4.0. Altered from the original.
14. kaiser2b, accessed October 17, 2021, https://pixabay.com/illustrations/coronavirus-prevention-pashto-5030274/, available for use via Pixabay License.
15. Rory Boland, "What Is the Difference Between Mandarin and Cantonese?," April 14, 2020, https://www.tripsavvy.com/what-is-the-difference-between-mandarin-and-cantonese-1535880
16. Daniel Lal, "Traditional vs. Simplified Chinese: What They Are and Where to Use Them," accessed May 2, 2021, https://www.fluentu.com/blog/chinese/traditional-vs-simplified-chinese/
17. Phoebe Baker, "Chinese Receipt2," March 19, 2011, https://www.flickr.com/photos/23563006@N08/5541286498, licensed under CC BY 2.0.
18. Josh Hallett, "Seoul, South Korea," March 12, 2008, https://www.flickr.com/photos/hyku/2329396025, licensed under CC BY-SA 2.0.
19. "Japanese Alphabet: An Easy Guide For Beginners," August 31, 2020, https://www.lingua-junkie.com/japanese/japanese-alphabet
20. jam_232, "Bathroom sign in our hotel," November 13, 2012, https://www.flickr.com/photos/27549109@N06/8451685683/, licensed under CC BY 2.0.

Chapter 2
Preparing to Conduct Foreign-Language Research

This chapter prepares the researcher to conduct research in a foreign language they do or do not speak. Research always requires a plan or methodology to ensure rigor throughout the project. This chapter offers a method by which the researcher can begin their research, and assumes the researcher has already established a research topic or question.

To do this requires the help of online tools. This chapter introduces several resources, including the use of Wikipedia, country-specific search engines, and other search engines with unique features that demonstrate the unique results available in different medium. This chapter also offers a few examples of downloading search results, which can be used for further analysis.

2.1 Getting Started with Key Terms and Phrases

Once the researcher establishes the research question, one useful technique to discovering foreign-language resources is brainstorming key terms. Brainstorming key terms about the subject aids in initial topic discovery and helps the researcher uncover resources relating to, but not directly about the topic. The main idea is to narrow down search results to the exactly desired results. This can be counterintuitive: naturally, the researcher should want to have as many results as possible to increase the number of resources available to them. However, with the advent of the Internet and with so many resources available, more is not always better. Searching for the exactly right terms yields the exactly right results; searching the wrong terms yields the wrong results.

Consider the research topic of *demographics*. An online keyword search for just the term *demographics* in English, without any other keywords, returns 295 million results (see Fig. 2.1). Surely, the top ten results do not contain the desired

© The Author(s), under exclusive license to Springer Nature Switzerland AG 2023   35
M. D. Miller, *Discovering Hidden Gems in Foreign Languages*, Terrorism, Security, and Computation, https://doi.org/10.1007/978-3-031-18479-6_2

Google   demographics   ✕   🎤 🔍

🔍 All   🖾 Images   🖾 News   ▶ Videos   📖 Books   ⋮ More   Tools

About 295,000,000 results (0.46 seconds)

Fig. 2.1 The number of Google search results for the keyword *demographics* (Google and the Google logo are trademarks of Google LLC)

Table 2.1 List of terms relating to demographics in English

Birth rate/births	Ethnicity	Sex ratio
Death rate/deaths	Ethnic group	Children
Mortality rate	Emigration	Literacy
Infant mortality rate	Immigration	Education
Population	Statistics	Unemployment
Distribution	Age	Abortions
Life expectancy	Labor	Citizenship
Fertility	Languages	Census
Total fertility rate	Gender/sex	Urbanization
	Female/male	

information for an in-depth study of demographics issues. To sort through all of these results may take a lifetime. A more tailored search in this case will be better.

The first thing the researcher should do is take a moment to brainstorm the key terms associated with this topic in their native language. This will aid with key word searches later on. Words in this list may include synonyms or sub-areas of the topic. For assistance generating a list of key terms, one method is to simply start conducting simple search engine searches with the key terms the researcher already has. Another useful resource is Wikipedia. Generally, Wikipedia is not widely accepted as a citable academic source because anyone can edit pages. However, these pages are great for brainstorming key terms on a subject. To demonstrate this, a sample list of the terms relating to, but not directly about demographics is listed in Table 2.1.

Searching English terms for information about another country (that speaks a language other than English) will still yield English-language results. These results often offer an outside perspective, rather than an inward-looking perspective. In this example, English-language results on Russian demographics offer a Western view of Russia's demographics issues; Russian-language results are more likely to offer a Russian view of its own demographics issues. Each of these views can be equally valuable to the researcher, but they are likely to differ. So, it is to the researcher's advantage to seek out resources from both perspectives.

To do this, copy the words from the brainstorming list into an online translator, such as Google Translate. Keep a record of these key terms in a separate document for later use. Table 2.2 contains an example, where the Russian words for *Russia* and *demographics* have been added.

The researcher's next step is to conduct the previous searches using the Russian-language terms. Doing so yields primarily Russian-language results. Consider the example *демография*, the Russian word for *demographics*, as shown in Fig. 2.2.

Not only are there fewer results than the English-language search (only about 11.4 million), the top results are in Russian and from Russian sources. The search engine can detect that the search uses the Russian word for demographics instead of the English word, causing the results to differ drastically. This book delves into greater detail on methods for translation and use of foreign texts in Chap. 5. For now, it is up to the reader to simply notice the differences in the types of results returned.

Table 2.2   Terms relating to demographics in English with Russian translations

Russia	Россия
Demographics	Демография
Birth rate/births	Рождаемость
Death rate/deaths	Уровень смертности/смертность
Mortality/infant mortality rate	Коэффициент младенческой смертности
Population	Население
Population distribution	Распределение населения
Life expectancy	Продолжительность жизни
Fertility	Фертильность
Total fertility rate	Общий коэффициент фертильности
Ethnicity	Этническая принадлежность
Ethnic group	Этническая группа
Emigration/immigration	Эмиграция/иммиграция
Statistics	Статистика
Age	Возраст
Labor	Труд/работа
Languages	Языки
Gender/sex	Пол
Female/male	Женский пол/мужской пол
Sex ratio	Соотношение полов
Children	Дети
Literacy	Грамотность
Education	Образование
Unemployment	Безработица
Abortions	Аборты
Citizenship	Гражданство
Census	Перепись
Urbanization	Урбанизация

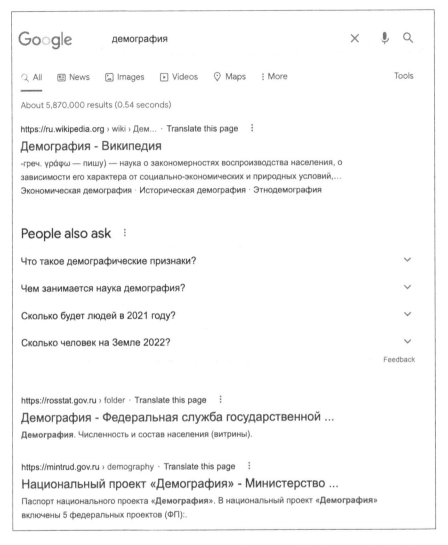

Fig. 2.2 Google search results for *демография*, the Russian word for *demographics* (Google and the Google logo are trademarks of Google LLC)

2.2 Foreign-Language Research Support Using Wikipedia

In the previous section, we used Wikipedia to brainstorm a list of key terms relating to the research topic of interest. Wikipedia is also useful for discovering other Wikipedia pages in other languages. While many communities often frown upon citing Wikipedia as a credible source (because anyone can edit pages anonymously), the resources listed on the foreign-language versions of these pages can be very helpful during research planning and initial resource discovery.

Another important consideration of the foreign-language pages on Wikipedia is that sometimes the content of foreign-language versions of web pages differs based on the language. That is, the content of the English-language page is not necessarily the same as the content on the Russian, Chinese, or Spanish page on the same topic. Not only that, pages in different languages on the same topic may cite different sources, which will point the researcher to different perspectives on the same topic.

Again, consider the example of Russia's demographics. The English-language Wikipedia page on this topic is titled "Demographics of Russia" as pictured in Fig. 2.3. On the left-hand side of many Wikipedia pages, there are links to similar pages in foreign languages. These pages are not always available on every topic, and each topic is only available in certain languages. A close-up image of the pages available in foreign languages is highlighted in Fig. 2.3.

To explore the foreign-language pages for the corresponding English-language page, select the language of interest. The thorough researcher should take some time to view the pages for each language available to see how much each page differs, based on the goals of the research. In this case, the researcher may first be interested in the Russian-language page. The researcher will quickly notice that the list of languages uses foreign characters itself. The researcher need not know 22+ languages to benefit from the knowledge on each of these pages. For the researcher who cannot read the foreign scripts in the list, begin by hovering over each link until the language of interest appears. A dialog box will appear that has the name of the page in the foreign language, followed by the language of the page. An example for the Russian page is seen in Fig. 2.4.

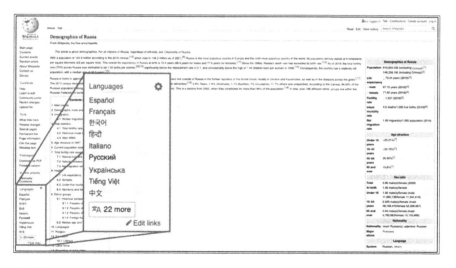

Fig. 2.3 Wikipedia page on the demographics of Russia, with the languages section highlighted in the bottom left (CC BY-SA 3.0)

Fig. 2.4 Hovering over
each language link in
Wikipedia (CC BY-SA 3.0)

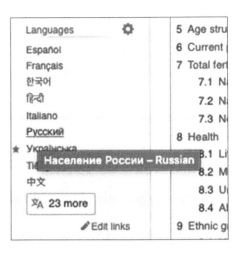

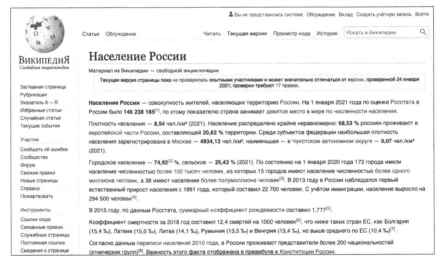

Fig. 2.5 The Wikipedia page titled *Население России*, meaning *Population of Russia* (CC BY-SA 3.0)

Selecting the Russian-language page reveals an entirely new page titled *Население России*, meaning *Population of Russia* in English (Fig. 2.5). Upon first glance, the page appears to have several images, maps, and charts that do not exist in the English-language version. Additionally, the resources listed at the bottom appear to differ greatly.

To see exactly how and to what extent the Russian-language page differs from the English, i.e., to translate and understand the full contents of the page, first copy the URL. Open a new tab in the web browser and paste the URL into the search bar as in Fig. 2.6.

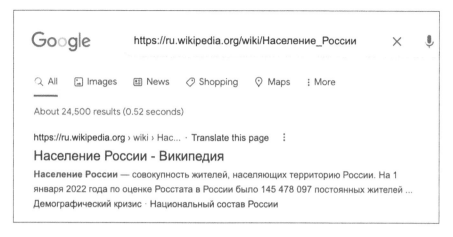

Fig. 2.6 Google search results for the URL of a Russian-language Wikipedia page (Google and the Google logo are trademarks of Google LLC)

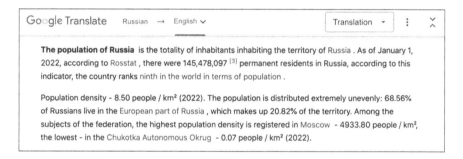

Fig. 2.7 English translation of a Russian-language Wikipedia page in Google Translate (Google and the Google logo are trademarks of Google LLC, content reproduced under CC BY-SA 3.0)

The Russian-language version of the Wikipedia page is the first result of the search. To translate the page, click on the "Translate this page" button to the right of the result. Figure 2.7 shows the resulting translation. This button appears in Google search results when the web browser can detect the language of the target website is uncommon to the geographic origin of the search (for example, conducting a search in Russian from America).

While not perfect, this English translation may offer the researcher different data, new perspectives, or counterarguments to the research that were only available in the researcher's native language. Differences in data and narratives may reveal significant inconsistencies in the context of the researcher's question. This book delves deeper into methods for translation in Chap. 5.

2.3   By-Country Website Popularity

It will be a common occurrence that the foreign-language researcher finds him or herself researching a country about which they know very little; or when other methods for discovering leads are ineffective. Another approach is to discover leads based on the websites that are most popular in that country. The researcher can then conduct a more targeted keyword search on the websites they know to be most popularly accessed in that given region. There are several online services that offer by-country lists of popularly accessed websites.

One such service is called Semrush, which can be accessed at https://www.semrush.com. Semrush lists the top 50 sites by country and category for free; a paid subscription includes greater detail. Figure 2.8 shows the top six news and media websites in Spain as an example.

Using this list, it is possible to conduct a more targeted search on a given topic by navigating to these websites and conducting keyword searches on each. These websites are more likely to contain up-to-date information from the target country and in the target language. The content of these websites will address all the common opinions and address all the likely biases of the people from the country.

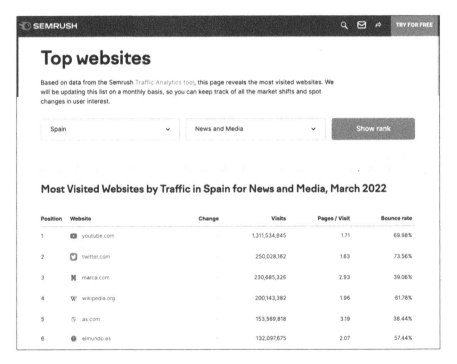

Fig. 2.8 List of most popular news and media sites in Spain as of March 2022 © 2008–2022 Semrush

From the researcher's perspective, Semrush is also a good justification to provide in the research methodology of a rigorous research paper, including theses and dissertations. When the researcher describes in the methodology how and why they collected information from a particular source, it is reasonable to say that the source is among the most popular websites accessed from within that country at this time.

Semrush is not the only service of its kind. This is important to know if, for some reason, the researcher wishes to see a list of popular websites in a country which Semrush does not offer its services. SimilarWeb is another online service that provides a list of the top websites by country. It has free and paid versions, and can be accessed at https://www.similarweb.com/top-websites/. For a specific country of interest, the researcher could also try searching the phrase "top websites in country X" in any search engine.

2.4   Country-Specific Search Engines

As the researcher can see from the previous section, the search engine in use dictates the results returned. Researchers may be more familiar with one search engine over another simply due to popularity of that search engine of their region. Unbeknownst to them, they may be missing valuable resources that will only appear in another search engine.

A web developer from a different region of the world may not be so concerned with their website's discoverability outside their own country. As a result, these websites are less likely to use the best practices of other search engines such as Google or Bing. For example, many Western search engines or websites may be inaccessible to people in China. These websites will not be maximized for discoverability in Google, Bing, or Yahoo. To maximize the relevance of results returned, the researcher should conduct searches in search engines that are native to the target region or language. First, the researcher must find out which search engines are most popular in the region where they are searching.

2.4.1   Seznam (Czechia)

To demonstrate the difference, recall the search in the previous section for Czech restaurants. Searches in Google and Bing each returned different results, and these results may or may not have contained the ideal websites. Another approach here is to conduct the same search in Seznam (https://search.seznam.cz), a search engine built just for Czech Internet users.

Consider the search shown in Fig. 2.9 for restaurants in Czech Republic using the Czech-language word for restaurants. When searching for Czech restaurants in Google and Bing, the researcher had to specify that they were interested in websites in Czech located in the Czech Republic. On the other hand, Seznam returned a list

Fig. 2.9 Seznam search results for *restaurace* using Czech VPN © 1996–2021 Seznam.cz, a.s

of restaurants in the Czech Republic by using only the one search term. This is much preferred. Not only is it easier for the researcher to craft their search parameters, it increases the relevance of the search results.

This raises the question: what is the most appropriate search engine to use for my current research problem? The answer is that there is no single correct search engine to use. Try a few and assess the varying results. Use Semrush to determine a strong starting point, but do not stop after just attempting the search in one search engine. It is also possible to conduct a search for search engines associated with a particular country. Ironically, this will require the use of a familiar search engine to discover another.

A quick Google search for *search engine popularity by country* returns several informal and incomplete lists. These are ok for getting started. It is also possible to search for *search engines in Malaysia* or the country of your choice. This book offers another short list, but be advised that websites are constantly changing—either they lose support or funding, are bought by another service and discontinued, or move to another URL. Not to mention, there are billions upon billions of websites on the Internet, making it impossible to provide one single comprehensive list of search engines. Undoubtedly, the researcher may know of other websites that are not on the lists provided here. The researcher is encouraged to use or augment the lists of websites in this book as they see fit.

Before moving forward with a discussion of search engines, keep in mind that web directories are not the same as search engines. Search engines return results based on automated computer algorithms; web directories are man-made structures that return only the results contained within its human-edited hierarchy. Generally, search engines should return more results than web directories because web directories are limited to the pages added manually to its hierarchy. Search engines are not necessarily better than web directories: sometimes, less is more. Searching the right web directory with the right perspective or scope may return fewer but more relevant and tailored results. On the other hand, the result the researcher seeks may not be indexed in the web directory they are searching, so it may not be found this way. This section focuses on search engines; however, Appendix 8.1 contains a list of some country-specific web directories that may be of use to the researcher.

When deciding to use one search engine over another, consider the intended target audience for that search engine. Compare the results in one search engine against the results of another. Also consider the language or regional features of the search engine, and whether or not that search engine possesses helpful functionality. Different search engines have different language-focused features beyond their affiliation with the target country.

2.4.2 Exalead (France)

For example, the French search engine Exalead lists the languages of all results of the search in a menu. This can be valuable when searching for words or symbols that may exist in multiple languages. Select the language of interest from the menu to filter the search, thus narrowing down the search results to the desired options. Figure 2.10 shows an example of a search in Exalead for the Mongolian word жор, meaning *recipe*. Exalead has detected that there are results in Russian, Mongolian, Ukrainian, Bulgarian, and English.

To narrow the search results by language, click on the desired language in the menu. In the example in Fig. 2.11, selecting the results only in Mongolian narrows down the six results in Mongolian. Notice that Exalead uses a *language:* operator that was automatically added upon selecting the language from the menu. The researcher can also add these to the search parameters of their initial search to eliminate a step.

One reason for conducting a search for Mongolian results in a French search engine may be to target the Mongolian population in France. Another reason simply

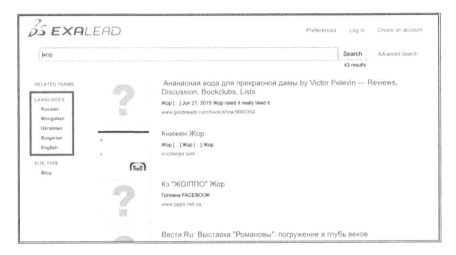

Fig. 2.10 Exalead search for *жор*, the Mongolian word for *recipe* © 2000–2022 Exalead - Dassault Systèmes

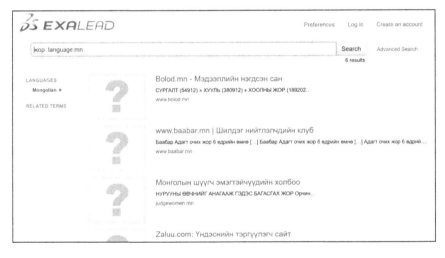

Fig. 2.11 Exalead search for *жор*, the Mongolian word for *recipe*, with the Mongolian language filter © 2000–2022 Exalead - Dassault Systèmes

could be to compare results between as many search engines as possible. Clearly, Exalead does not return results that are only in French or of interest to the French researcher. The key takeaway is not to limit the discovery of unique and relevant results returned solely by searching one engine.

2.4.3   Yandex (Russia)

The Russian search engine Yandex has a few country-specific domains, but only for Russia, Ukraine, Belarus, Kazakhstan, Uzbekistan, Turkey, and France. These are visible on the bottom of the Yandex.com site as shown in Fig. 2.12. The URLs for each are:

- https://yandex.com
- https://yandex.ru (Russia)
- https://yandex.ua (Ukraine)
- https://yandex.by (Belarus)
- https://yandex.kz (Kazakhstan)
- https://yandex.uz (Uzbekistan)
- https://yandex.com.tr (Turkey)
- https://yandex.fr (France)

This likely indicates that Yandex is most interested in Internet users from these countries. As a result, the researcher conducting research relevant to these countries or languages spoken in these countries should conduct their searches in the appropriate version of Yandex.

2.4.4   Baidu (China)

Baidu's search engine does not have other country-specific domains besides the .cn and .com, likely because the target audience of this search engine is Internet users in mainland China. However, it is possible to search specifically for simplified

Fig. 2.12   The Yandex.com homepage © 2015–2022 YANDEX LLC

versus traditional Chinese results, which are unique to Baidu. This may be one of the researcher's primary considerations when choosing to search Baidu for unique and relevant results in Chinese.

Like many other search engines, Baidu has an Advanced Search form located at https://www.baidu.com/gaoji/advanced.html. What makes this form stand out among other advanced search forms is the option to return results in simplified or traditional Chinese. This may be another feature that helps the researcher narrow down the results they wish to have returned in a search.

2.4.5   Yamli (Saudi Arabia)

The Yamli search engine from Saudi Arabia has a smart Arabic keyboard that recommends an Arabic transliteration of words based on Latin-character entries. It can be accessed at https://www.yamli.com. Yamli is not a translator, nor is it a standalone search engine: it will only offer the Arabic spelling of the word as it is pronounced letter-for-letter. For example, try typing "computer" in English into the search bar. The search engine will recommend Arabic-language search terms based on the English input. To search for the key term in Arabic, click on the appropriate option, and select search. Doing so will navigate the user to a new Google search page.

Yes, conducting a search in Yamli actually is the same as conducting a Google search, except with Arabic script. In this regard, Yamli is not really its own search engine—it simply adds its own unique Arabic script feature that may be helpful for the researcher who does not speak Arabic.

The websites discussed in this section only begin to scratch the surface of language and country-specific search engines. The examples presented here demonstrate the plethora of options and the benefits of careful consideration. They validate the old saying that "good stuff in, good stuff out," meaning that good quality searches will return meaningful results. Appendix 8.3 contains a list of country-based search engines discussed in this section. It also contains dozens of search engines not discussed here. The researcher is left to explore these resources on their own based on their research interests and goals.

2.4.6   Parsijoo (Iran)

Parsijoo is an Iran-based search engine that specializes in Persian language and culture, making it a top contender for Persian language and regionally focused searches. Accessible at https://parsijoo.ir, it hosts a robust suite of capabilities, including but not limited to image and video searches, music repository, news service, maps, and translation tool. It also has a mobile application with similar capabilities for smartphones. The Parsijoo home page has the appearance of any other robust search engine, with the search bar and other website features below it.

One noteworthy feature is the Persian translation tool built directly into Parsijoo. The translation tool is currently only available to and from Farsi and English; however, it is built with Farsi translation in mind, making it an important candidate for any Farsi-specific translations.

Another unique feature within Parsijoo is the website analysis tool called Shakhes. Shakhes offers website traffic information for many websites, enabling the researcher to assess the popularity and success of websites.

One application for the Shakhes analysis tool could be to aid in the data collection strategy discussion for a research project. The information contained within the analysis tool could provide real statistics from a uniformed source that the researcher can use to compare or rank pages in a given context. The researcher could also use these data points to compare websites or conduct some other web-based analytics project, to name a few additional examples. Again, this is largely focused for the researcher working on a project in Farsi; however, its use extends beyond the obvious.

2.4.7 MetaGer (Germany)

MetaGer is a privacy-focused meta-search engine made in Germany, meaning it and compiles results from several search engines simultaneously. By default, the web search includes results from Bing, Scopia, OneNewspage, and OneNewspage (Video) as of early 2022. Pictures, Shopping, and News searches use other combinations to conduct their searches. As MetaGer focuses on privacy, search results are available to "open anonymously": the Privacy tab explains how MetaGer uses user information, including IP addresses and user-agent strings. A sample search conducted in MetaGer is shown in Fig. 2.13 below.

In the search preferences, it is possible to toggle the search engines that are and are not used to conduct searches. It is also possible to select date and language filters, and blacklist websites.

Since MetaGer boasts privacy features, it is no surprise that it also hosts a TOR-hidden service, which is an equivalent search engine service for the TOR network. Navigate to the TOR-hidden service tab under the options from the main page to locate the TOR equivalent for the MetaGer search engine. MetaGer also has a mobile application for smartphone browsing.

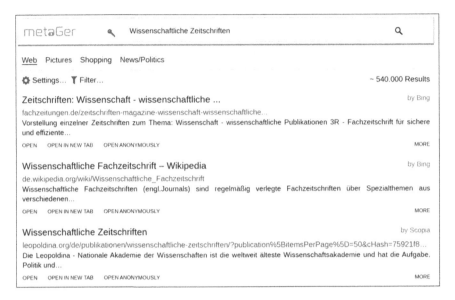

Fig. 2.13 MetaGer search for *Wissenschaftliche Zeitschriften*, meaning *Scientific Journals* in German (SUMA-EV)

2.4.8   Swisscows (Switzerland)

SwissCows is a privacy-focused search engine based in Switzerland. It uses Microsoft Bing to perform its searches, but offers a regional-focused search by country that enhances the relevancy of language and region-based searches, particularly for the Swiss-based searches. Figure 2.14 below shows an example of a German-language search for academic programs, with the filter for regional search set to Switzerland (de). The researcher is encouraged to try this search on their own—how to the search results compare with the same search parameters and various regions selected?

The Anonymous Preview option to the right of each result offers the opportunity to preview the website without establishing a full connection. This is an additional security feature that researchers who are conscious of their online security will surely appreciate.

2.5   Other Search Engines with Useful Features for Foreign-Language Research

Search engines need not boast foreign language or regional capabilities to be of use to the foreign-language researcher. The researcher may find certain search engines possess certain features that aid in foreign-language research besides their

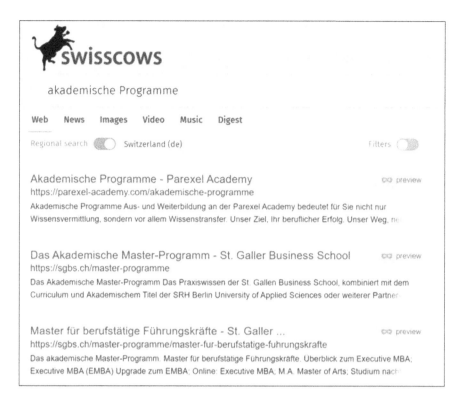

Fig. 2.14 Swisscows search for the German phrase *akademische programme*, meaning *academic programs* in the Swiss region © 2022, Swisscows AG

language-specific search features. For example, the researcher may need additional assistance discovering and searching translator resources online. A simple search for *translator resources* may not suffice. Other search engines return unique results in a specific context, such as open copyright resources or unfiltered results. This section introduces a few such search engines in a foreign-language context.

2.5.1   DuckDuckGo

DuckDuckGo has one unique feature (that includes special language capabilities) called Bangs. Bangs are a feature built directly into the DuckDuckGo search bar that allow the researcher to search directly on a website from the search engine. Typing the search using the Bang feature navigates the researcher directly to that website, not to DuckDuckGo search results. To invoke a Bang, simply type the exclamation mark and the known shortcut (with no space between), followed by the desired search parameter.

On the DuckDuckGo Bangs site, it is possible to search for a language or country. The results include a list of relevant Bangs using that search term. Figure 2.15 shows an example of Bangs relating to the search term *Norwegian*, many of which are relating to translation resources. Translation resources will be discussed more later in this book. For now, try searching the Bangs database for other topics, languages, or countries of interest.

From the list of search results, click on the Bang of interest to use it. This will add it to the DuckDuckGo search bar, and prompt the researcher to search for a key term afterwards. Fig. 2.15 shows the !sno Bang, which will redirect the search from DuckDuckGo to the StartPage.com search engine. Upon selecting the !sno Bang, the search bar appears above. The search in Fig. 2.16 will search the StartPage search engine for the Norwegian term *datavisualisering*, meaning *data visualization*.

Figure 2.17 shows the search results on StartPage.com for the term specified after the Bang.

2.5.2 Searx

Another search engine with unique features is the Searx metasearch engine. It is a crowd-sourced engine, meaning that the search engine community of interest (i.e., kind strangers on the Internet) have the freedom to download the publicly available source code for the site and customize its functionality to improve its performance for all to benefit. The Searx engine is designed to act as a proxy that searches multiple other search engines for the user all at once. As a result, Searx is a favorite for those who do not want search engine administrators to log or track their searches. Each result shows from which search engine Searx obtained each result.

The Searx search engine actually hosts 85 instances, each developed with different programming goals in mind (as of May 2021). Each instance is effectively a

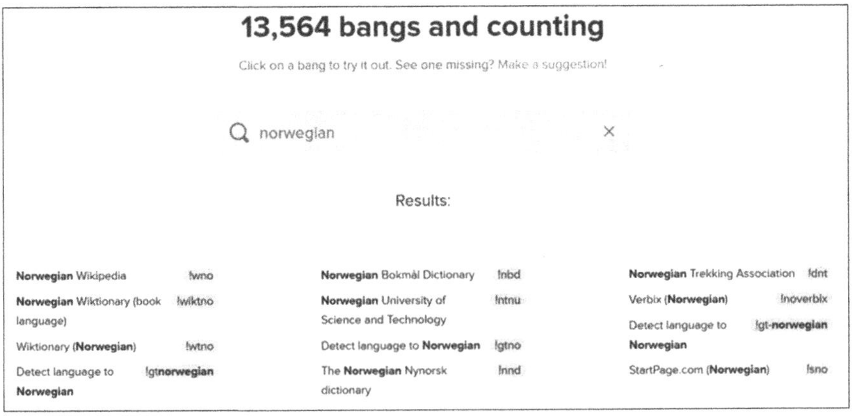

Fig. 2.15 DuckDuckGo Bang search for *Norwegian* [1] © DuckDuckGo

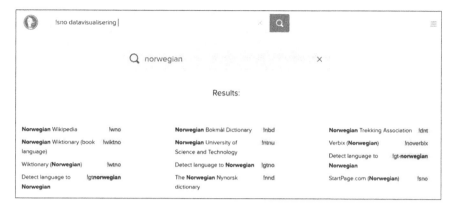

Fig. 2.16 DuckDuckGo Bang search using the !sno Bang with search parameter *datavisualisering*, the Norwegian word for *data visualization* © DuckDuckGo

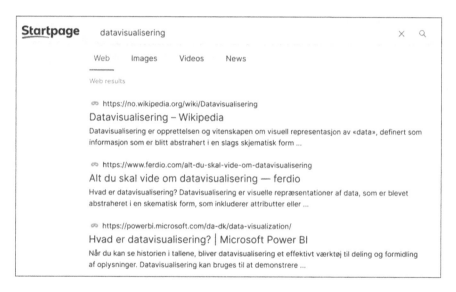

Fig. 2.17 Startpage search results for *datavisualisering*, the Norwegian word for *data visualization*, as redirected from the !sno Bang © 2022 Startpage

different search engine that may return different results, because each instance is designed to search certain search engines on the user's behalf. The list of instances, accessible at https://searx.space/#, clarifies which instances allow which search engines (see Fig. 2.18). When using one instance over another, it is important to consider which websites each instance includes in its search algorithms. If the researcher would like to know their Searx search will include both the Naver and Qwant simultaneously, the researcher should begin their search with the instance that purports to do so.

Fig. 2.18 List of working Searx instances as shown on https://searx.space/ and supported search engines for each (GNU AGPLv3)

Fig. 2.19 Searx search for *newspaper* in https://searx.tuxcloud.net with the Polish-language filter set (GNU AGPLv3)

Searx engine instances also have language functionality from a drop-down menu as shown in Fig. 2.19. In the https://searx.tuxcloud.net instance, a search for *newspaper* in English returns some Polish results from .pl domains. Notice also how each result shows the source of the Searx search: for example, the first and second results were cached from Wikidata, the third from DuckDuckGo, etc.

The language drop-down menu may filter only some foreign language results; however, because not all engines that Searx searches support foreign language searches. To see which engines do and do not support the selected foreign language, navigate to that instance's /preferences page. Usually there is a link in the top right corner of the search page; or, type "/preferences" after the URL. Figure 2.20 shows

Preferences

| General | Engines | Plugins | Answerers | Cookies |

| general | files | images | it | map | music | news | science | social media | videos |

Allow	Engine name	Shortcut	Selected language	SafeSearch	Time range	Avg. time	Max time
●	archive is	ai	not supported	not supported	not supported	N/A	7.0
●	wikipedia	wp	supported	not supported	not supported	0.189	2.0
●	bing	bi	supported	not supported	not supported	0.304	2.0
●	currency	cc	not supported	not supported	not supported	0.269	2.0
●	ddg definitions	ddd	supported	not supported	not supported	N/A	2.0
●	erowid	ew	not supported	not supported	not supported	N/A	2.0

Fig. 2.20 List of general-themed search engines turned on by default in the Searx instance https://searx.slash-dev.de (GNU AGPLv3)

the "general" tab under "engines" within the /preferences page for the https://searx.slash-dev.de/ instance.

Here, the researcher can decide if they would like to enable only sites that support the specified language, or simply consider these nuances when examining the results of their search. It is possible to manually allow that instance to search for a site that it does not inherently support; however, it will return no results. For example, the search in Fig. 2.21 below for *газета*, the Russian word for *newspaper*, in the https://searx.slash-dev.de instance shows that no results are returned when all sites are disallowed except for Yandex. This should be no surprise, as the matrix of supported search engines at https://searx.space/ clearly states that this instance does not support Yandex.

Instead, use the allow/disallow feature in /preferences to further limit the sites searched. For example, if the researcher is only interested in scientific results, navigate to the "science" tab under "Engines" and allow all engines in the list; navigate to the other tabs and disable all other engines (see Fig. 2.22). The https://searx.slash-dev.de/ instance has all scientific engines turned on by default, making this a good instance for a scientific search. Sadly, none of these purports to support foreign-language results. Still, let's attempt a search and see what types of results are returned.

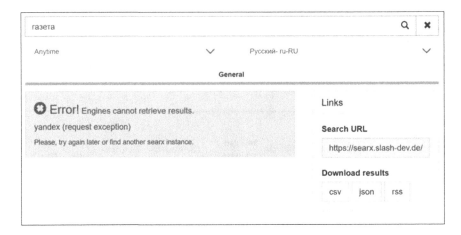

Fig. 2.21 Searx search results for *газета*, the Russian word for *newspaper*, in the https://searx.slash-dev.de/ instance with only Yandex enabled (all others disabled) (GNU AGPLv3)

Preferences

| General | Engines | Plugins | Answerers | Cookies |

| general | files | images | it | map | music | news | science | social media | videos |

Allow	Engine name	Shortcut	Selected language	SafeSearch	Time range	Avg. time	Max time
	arxiv	arx	not supported	not supported	not supported	0.748	4.0
	crossref	cr	not supported	not supported	not supported	0.864	2.0
	google scholar	gos	not supported	not supported	not supported	0.806	2.0
	microsoft academic	ma	not supported	not supported	not supported	1.956	2.0
	openairedatasets	oad	not supported	not supported	not supported	0.619	5.0
	openairepublications	oap	not supported	not supported	not supported	0.815	5.0

Fig. 2.22 List of science-themed search engines turned on in the Searx instance https://searx.slash-dev.de (Reproduced under GNU AGPLv3)

Figure 2.23 shows the results for the Polish-language search for *tłuszcze wielonienasycone*, the Polish phrase for *polyunsaturated fats*, in the https://searx.slash-dev.de instance. Note that the "Science" tab is selected instead of the "General" tab.

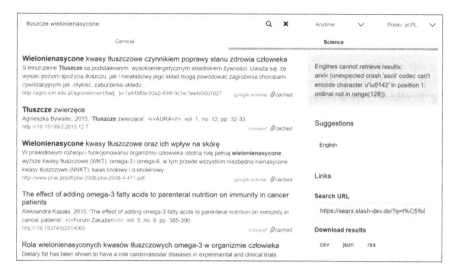

Fig. 2.23 Search for *tłuszcze wielonienasycone*, the Polish phrase for *polyunsaturated fats*, in the Searx instance https://searx.slash-dev.de with Polish-language enabled and all Scientific engines allowed (all others disallowed) (Reproduced under GNU AGPLv3)

Some, but not all results are actually in Polish. There also seems to be an error: Searx failed to search arxiv. If the researchers were interested in seeing the search results for this Polish term in arxiv, they should navigate to this search engine to see if there are any additional results of value missing from the Searx search.

Lastly, it is possible to download the search results into a file, which can be helpful for accessing these search results later. This functionality is built directly into the search results page, see right-hand side of Fig. 2.23. With this capability, it is possible to aggregate search results across multiple searches or import the results into a data visualization tool for analysis. The possibilities are endless.

2.5.3   CCSearch (Creative Commons Search)

CCSearch, short for Creative Commons Search (available at https://search.creative-commons.org), hosts content that is free of copyright restrictions for reproduction. Even though CCSearch does not overtly boast foreign-language search capabilities, it does search databases across the globe (it lists which ones on its site)—so, it is possible to search CCSearch in foreign languages. One useful feature within CCSearch is the ability to search for multiple spellings of a word. The researcher can specify the number of letters variance that the results may contain, based on the spelling.

This is helpful because nouns in foreign languages often decline, meaning that the ending of the word changes based on their part of speech, gender, plurality, or articulation. For example, the Russian word *город*, meaning *city*, is its dictionary form. When the Russian word for city is a direct or indirect object in a sentence, its ending changes to *город*. And there are other forms, too, such as the plural *города* or prepositional *городе*. This word will appear in all its forms online, but not all databases will return results that contain a form that does not match the exact spelling. In other databases, to cover their bases, the researcher may have to include the word in all its forms to guarantee that the search engine will find as many relevant results as possible. In other words, the researcher would have to search *город OR город OR города OR городе* to get results containing this word in some of its many forms.

In CCSearch, it is possible to search for all three spellings without using the Boolean OR operators and listing each of the relevant spellings. This is important for the foreign-language researcher who is not an expert in the target language. In CCSearch, the tilde symbol followed by a number denotes the number of letters variance in the spelling returned form the search. Consider the results of the search for the Russian word for *city* as shown in Fig. 2.24, which does not afford any variance in the spelling of the search term.

Now, compare these results with those of the search *город ~ 2* as shown in Fig. 2.25. This search will return all results containing the key word within two letters' difference. This will make the search broader in scope, effectively broadening the search results to include results with other spellings, type-o's, and results that may be in Ukrainian, too.

Note that the number of results in the first search is 287, and the number of results in the second search is 3,264. This is because the number of results with a slight spelling variance is greater than the number of results spelled exactly one way.

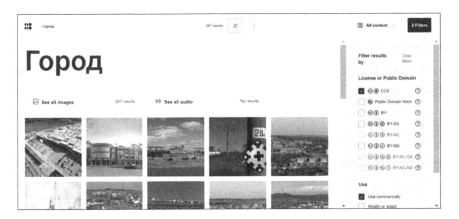

Fig. 2.24 CCSearch for *город*, meaning *city* in Russian (Images licensed under CC0)

Fig. 2.25 CCSearch for *город ~ 2*, meaning *city* in Russian with two-letter spelling variance (Images licensed under CC0)

2.5.4   Gibiru

Another search engine worth mentioning here is Gibiru, which is accessible at https://gibiru.com/. Gibiru purports to be an uncensored anonymous search engine, with a primary focus on user privacy. It uses a modified Google search algorithm to return its results: Google's algorithm displays results at the top that it believes will be most relevant to the searcher. It bases this assessment on the key terms searched, geolocation, and website popularity rankings.

Consider the search for *deutsche politik*, meaning *German politics* in German using Gibiru as shown in Fig. 2.26 above. The results contain some well-known resources, including the Encyclopedia Britannica and the University of Chicago's academic journal, among others.

One of Gibiru's most unique features is its uncensored search, which is accessible in the menu just above the search results. Gibiru uncensored search ignores geolocation and website popularity rankings, which makes for interesting results. These results are often entirely different than a search conducted in Google or another search engine, because most search engines focus their top results on websites it expects are most relevant to the searcher (based on location and website popularity, among other variables). Compare the top results for the German-language search *deutsche politik* across "all results" (Fig. 2.26) and "censored content" (Fig. 2.27) and note the key differences.

Fig. 2.26 Gibiru general search results for *deutsche politik*, meaning *German politics* in German
© 2022 Gibiru

2.5.5   Million Short

Like Gibiru, Million Short is a search engine that modifies Google's search algorithm to examine results in a different way. Million Short, which is accessible at https://millionshort.com/, allows the researcher to conduct a search in a foreign language, but then skip ahead to the 100th, 1000th, 10000th, 100000th, or millionth result. It also has a geolocation functionality, and displays which websites were removed by skipping ahead in the results. This affords the researcher the opportunity to easily see which results were simply not optimized for discovery in the most popular search engines, but are still of interest to the researcher. Just because a website is not optimized does not mean it is not valuable.

To experience how this works, conduct a search for the Lithuanian phrase *regioniniai rinkimai*, meaning *regional election*. The filter for the nth degree results is on the top left, and the country filter is below. A list of sites skipped appears to the right of the results. A brief glance at the results in this example demonstrates the

Fig. 2.27 Gibiru censored content results for *deutsche politik*, meaning *German politics* in German © 2022 Gibiru

obscurity of the results that often sit thousands of results down the list. The researcher will rarely see these, but again, this does not mean they are invaluable resources.

The purpose of this section was to demonstrate that different search engines with unique features may have an indirect applicability to the foreign-language researcher's problem set. Researchers are encouraged to challenge the prescribed limitations of available tools and discover new ways to find information online. The search engines discussed here are only a small set of those available for the researcher to start their search. The researcher is encouraged to try the search engines in this section, and find others, too.

2.6   Downloading Online Search Results and Specialized Website Content

The researcher may also be interested in exporting the list of results from their search into a document, which they can then analyze and use to enhance or substantiate their claims. With a list of sites returned from a search, the researcher can gain insight to craft better searches in the future, gain insight into which search engines are more useful for their research, or discover gaps in their own resources. Some search engines enable downloading the search results to a file directly from the search page. Others may require external tools to do so.

2.6.1 Searx

The "download results" feature in Searx has this capability, as shown earlier in Fig. 2.24. Simply click on the file type (either .csv, .json, or .rss) to initiate the download. This data can be very valuable for the researcher interested in analyzing the results returned in the context of their research. For example, an academic researcher may include a discussion of the searches they conducted to obtain the resources they used in their project. An analysis of this data may demonstrate biases and gaps in the research, which will add rigor and credibility to their analysis and findings. The researcher could use these results to identify trends in website popularity based on country, or demonstrate the value of incorporating foreign-language resources into their research methodology, among other goals. Consider correlating data from multiple searches to discover correlations. This type of analysis makes for unique and impactful research on topics ranging from market analysis to business analytics.

2.6.2 Thruuu

There are a plethora of third-party tools available that also allow the researcher to scrape and download search results. One tool by Samuel Schmitt called Thruuu scrapes search results and gives the researcher the option to export the results into an Excel file. Accessible at https://app.thruuu.com/, Thruuu can search by country or location, country-specific Google domain, and language for any keyword. It also allows the researcher to select the number of results to scrape, up to 100. Consider the business owner of a construction company who wants to see a list of other construction companies that appear in a keyword search. The business owner can see who their competition is by conducting keyword searches and comparing the results in a data analysis tool. Figure 2.28 shows the main search interface on Thruuu.

The results will be returned below the search box. To download the results, click "download" as shown in Fig. 2.29. This will initiate the user to save the file to their computer for further analysis.

The downloaded file (Fig. 2.30) contains the list of websites returned from the Google search, including their ranking, type, title, and URL. The researcher is now free to use this data to support their research.

Thruuu also contains several analytic features that add wonderful context to search results and specific web pages. Within the "Topics" tab, it is possible to view key search terms in context. For example, it shows other search terms that other Internet users searched to reach the same website. Under the "Outline" tab, it is possible to see the breakdown of a website's structure based on the way the website was written in HTML. The "Sources & Links" tab shows which pages are the most cited within the search results. Consider another example, this time using a foreign-language search term.

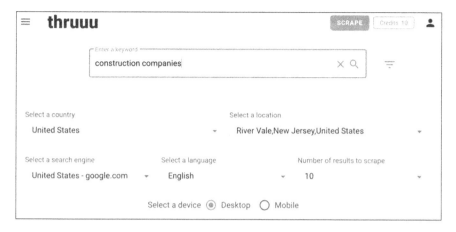

Fig. 2.28 Thruuu search parameters for *construction companies* in the United States on Google. com (Printed with permission from Samuel Schmitt)

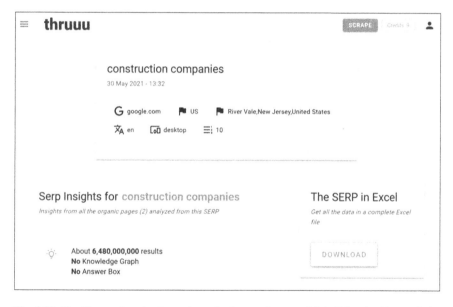

Fig. 2.29 The Thruuu download search results feature (bottom right) (Printed with permission from Samuel Schmitt)

Consider the search for *ngắm chim*, which is the Vietnamese phrase meaning *bird watching*, using the Vietnam country setting and Google.com.vn search engine. The Vietnamese language is also set to guarantee results will be in the Vietnamese language.

Figure 2.31 shows a screenshot from the "Topics" tab in Thruuu after conducting the search in Vietnamese. Thruuu is able to recommend dozens of related topics, all

Fig. 2.30 Thruuu search results for "construction companies" in the United States via Google. com (Printed with permission from Samuel Schmitt)

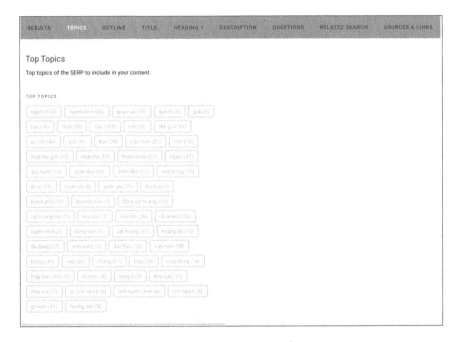

Fig. 2.31 Top topics from the Thruuu search results for *ngắm chim*, meaning *bird watching* in Vietnamese (Printed with permission from Samuel Schmitt)

of which are in Vietnamese. This list can be very helpful for the researcher who does not speak Vietnamese or know much about bird watching; hopefully, it can inspire further web searches to discover more resources, too.

Also in the "Topics" tab is a list of the most frequent topics used by the top ten results from the search. Scroll past this list of top topics to view top topics by result. Figure 2.32 shows a list of the top ten Vietnamese-language keywords found in the top search results of the same search for *bird watching* in Vietnamese. This can be used to conduct a word frequency analysis of all results returned in the SERP, which would make for a unique analytic paper on any search topic.

Thruuu requires free account registration to use. Additionally, each account user is allotted ten free scrapes per month—to conduct more than ten searches within a

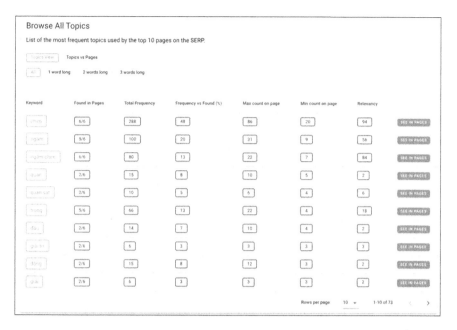

Fig. 2.32 List of most frequent topics found within the top ten results of the search *ngắm chim*, meaning *bird watching* in Vietnamese (Printed with permission from Samuel Schmitt)

month or to return more than 100 results using the bulk scrape feature, a paid subscription is required.

2.6.3 Data Miner

Another way to scrape search results or specialized content from any web page is with web browser extensions. Google Chrome hosts one extension called "Data Scraper" by Data Miner, available at https://dataminer.io/. This is available for free in the Google Chrome Web Store and requires the user to log in with a Gmail account [2]. Once installed into the Google Chrome browser, navigate to the extension menu, which is shaped like a puzzle piece, in the upper left corner of Chrome. Access the Data Miner extension by selecting it in the drop-down. Figure 2.33 shows what Data Miner looks like when it is pinned to the main menu in the Chrome web browser.

Data Miner introduces a list of recipes, or algorithms it uses to scrape certain types of information from the current site. Hovering over the list of recipes will inform the researcher if that recipe will be successful on that current page. If it is not, it will not scrape any results. In this case, the researcher is interested in scraping Google search results. To use this, the researcher must first conduct a Google search to scrape.

Fig. 2.33 The Data Miner extension menu in Google Chrome © 2021 Data Miner (Google and the Google logo are trademarks of Google LLC)

Consider the example in Fig. 2.33, which is a search for the phrase *vabatahtlike andmebaasid*, meaning *volunteer databases* in Estonian. Access the extension in the upper right of the browser, and hover over "Google Search Results – Get All Links 2021." Select the double arrow to scrape. Click the double arrow until the desired number of rows scraped appear in blue.

To view the scrape results, click on the blue link specifying the number of rows. In this example, there are 98 rows available to scrape, which is the same number of results as our search. This will open a Data Miner page displaying the results in a grid, as shown in Fig. 2.34.

Click the blue "Download" button on the right to download the results to an Excel file. The Excel file in Fig. 2.35 shows the first 36 rows of results, which includes the URLs and website titles of all 98 results.

Tools such as this must exist because Google does not inherently support scraping of its search results. Keep in mind that this extension may exist today, but these tools are forever evolving. Developers are creating newer and more advanced tools every day. The researcher is encouraged to seek alternatives based on their needs and the tools available at any given time. Certain scraping and downloading options may work only in certain cases—it really depends on the source of the information.

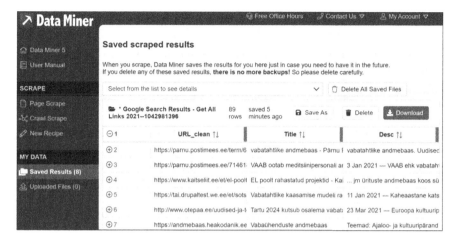

Fig. 2.34 Data Miner scrape results for the Google search *vabatahtlike andmebaasid site:ee*, containing the Estonian phrase for *volunteer databases* © 2021 Data Miner

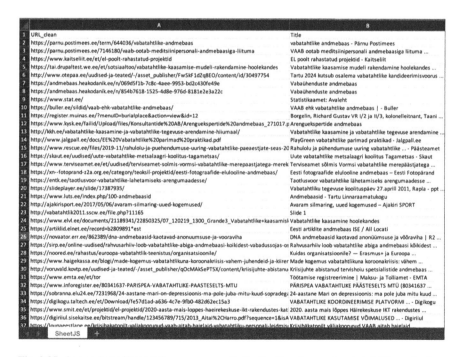

Fig. 2.35 Screenshot of Data Miner scrape results for the Google search *vabatahtlike andmebaasid site:ee*, containing the Estonian phrase for *volunteer databases* (Printed with permission from Data Miner)

2.6.4 Google Trends

Some services, even some Google services, offer the option to download data directly from the site that may be of significance to the foreign-language researcher. For example, it is possible to download search-related data directly from Google Trends. This is not scraping per-say, but it may be data of significance relating to search frequency of terms in relation to geographic region and time. Google Trends, which is accessible at https://trends.google.com/trends, shows the search frequency of terms based on how frequently that term is searched in Google. Google Trends will not include data for other search engines besides Google—however, since Google is a very popular search engine across the globe, this data may still be of value to the foreign-language researcher.

Figure 2.36 shows an example search in Google Trends for the Spanish word *fútbol* with the geolocation set to Argentina. From here, it is possible to download the data displayed in the chart by selecting the download button in the top right corner of the table. Scroll down to view and export data by subregion, related topics, and related queries [3]. This information may be valuable to the researcher interested in reporting on current or popular topics in a particular region of the world over time, or comparing research topics between two or a few geographic regions. In this case, a scraping tool is not needed—the download feature is built right into the service.

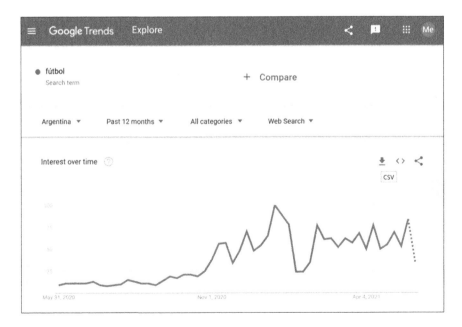

Fig. 2.36 Google Trends download to .csv feature as demonstrated using the Spanish search term *fútbol* in Argentina (Google and the Google logo are trademarks of Google LLC)

For information on other websites, this may not be so easy. Some more advanced researchers may prefer to write their own custom Python scripts that can perform the exact tasks specific to their desired goals. This is outside the scope of this book; however, the researcher should know that this may also be an option if all else fail.

2.6.5 SerpAPI

APIs, or Application Programming Interfaces, also require a little more technical expertize to implement from scratch. APIs are sets of rules, specific to a service, that allow a user to customize its communication between that service and another. There are some tools, such as SerpAPI, that will do this within a tool—no programming required. SerpAPI's interactive playground is available for free at https://serpapi.com/playground. SerpAPI also offers paid internet scraping services, available at https://serpapi.com/search-api. This service offers search and scraping solutions for Google, Yahoo, Bing, Baidu, Yandex, and others, and in foreign languages, too.

Figure 2.37 shows an example from the SerpAPI Playground for the word *coffee* in Baidu. The interface is split into three panes: the top pane contains the search parameters available for Baidu, the bottom left pane shows the Baidu search engine GUI, and the bottom right pane shows the output in JSON format (copy-pasteable). The language settings available are all languages, Simplified Chinese, or Traditional

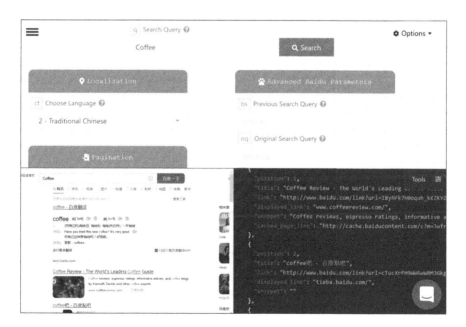

Fig. 2.37 SerpAPI Playground search for "coffee" in Baidu set to Traditional Chinese © 2022 SerpApi, LLC

Chinese; the language selected in this example was Traditional Chinese, with the search parameters in English. The Playground is only a sample of what API is capable of accomplishing for the researcher.

The key takeaway here is that there is more than one way to download search results. It depends on the source of the data the researcher is trying to extrapolate, the desired format, and the technical prowess of the researcher.

Online Database References

1. Results for this query found at https://duckduckgo.com/bang?q=norwegian
2. According to the Data Miner website, the service can only see the user's email and name. Get 500 scrapes per month for free, otherwise pay for a monthly subscription plan to scrape more than 500 times.
3. Read more about how to interpret Google Trends data and understand how Google normalizes the data at "FAQ about Google Trends data," accessed May 30, 2021, https://support.google.com/trends/answer/4365533?hl=en

Chapter 3
Discovering Foreign Language Resources Online

Dorking, also known as "hacking," refers to the use of tailored operators that can perform specific tasks directly in the search bar. Search engines that support dorks, or hacks, recognize these special operators and treat them not as search parameters themselves, but as functions that it will perform upon the other keywords in the search. These operators add an extra layer of complexity and detail to the results returned in search engines. This chapter introduces dorks in the context of foreign-language research. In this section, the term dork, hack, and operator are used interchangeably.

Not all search engines support dorks; not all search engines that do support dorks support the same dorks. Many resources often call this "Google Dorking" or "Google Hacking." These features not only work in Google—they also work in other search engines. One thing is certain: dorks are compatible with foreign-language keywords, which is the main focus of this section. Some dorks even allow the researcher to specify a region of the world or language, which can further tailor searches to return much more meaningful results.

Recall the example from Chap. 2 on Russia's demographics. This section uses this example throughout to demonstrate how tailored searches using dorks alter (and improve) the quality (and quantity) of results.

3.1 Discovering Exact Phrases with Quotation Marks

Quotation marks around search terms or phrases return exact results contained within the quotation marks. As a result, quotation marks limit searches drastically by omitting similar phrases or alternate spellings. Quotation marks work in almost every search engine and database, not only Google. A Google search for *"Russia demographics"* within quotes should return similar results to the same search without quotes because the key terms are the same. However, adding quotation marks

© The Author(s), under exclusive license to Springer Nature Switzerland AG 2023   71
M. D. Miller, *Discovering Hidden Gems in Foreign Languages*, Terrorism, Security, and Computation, https://doi.org/10.1007/978-3-031-18479-6_3

returns only results that contain the exact wording *"Russia demographics"* some-where on the page. This means that this search will not include results that contain the words *"Russia's demographics"* or *"Russian demographics,"* unless one of these phrases coexists with the search parameters. In other words, web pages con-taining both *Russia* and *Russian*, for example, will be returned in either search.

Consider the results for the search *"Russia demographics"* as shown in Fig. 3.1. First, the researcher will notice that there are only 415,000 results returned, com-pared to the millions of results for the same search without quotation marks. This is because the results must contain the spelling *Russia* at least once on the page. The page may also return results that contain other spellings of Russia, such as *Russian* or *Russians*, but the spelling *Russia* must be contained somewhere in the page. For the researcher, this can either be helpful or limiting, depending on the research goals. When conducting research using quotation marks, it is important to be aware that spelling matters.

Now consider the results for the Google search *Russia's demographics* as in Fig. 3.2. First, notice how there are even fewer results returned, compared to the 415,000 results from the previous search. The first result is also different than in the previous search because the search only returned results that have the exact spelling of *Russia's* instead of *Russia*. In this case, it is easy to see that spelling really does matter. This phenomenon will also be an important consideration when conducting searches in foreign languages using foreign characters.

But first, what about a search for the phrase *Russian demographics* as in Fig. 3.3? There are nearly twice as many results returned compared with the results of the search *Russia demographics*. Again, the top result is different. This search did not include the pages returned in the first two searches because these pages did not include the wording in this search.

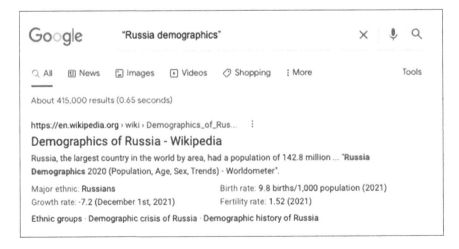

Fig. 3.1 Google search results for *"Russia demographics"* within quotation marks (Google and the Google logo are trademarks of Google LLC)

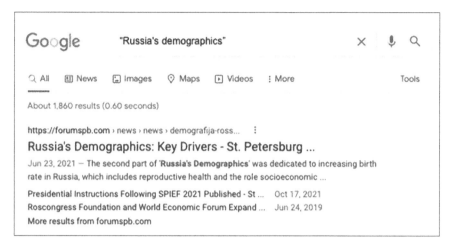

Fig. 3.2 Google search results for *"Russia's demographics"* within quotation marks (Google and the Google logo are trademarks of Google LLC)

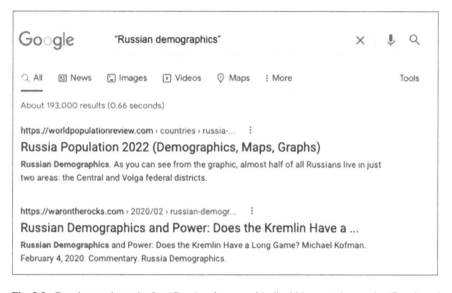

Fig. 3.3 Google search results for *"Russian demographics"* within quotation marks (Google and the Google logo are trademarks of Google LLC)

Another important lesson learned from comparing these three searches is in the wording frequently used within the demography community of interest. Based on the number of results returned, it is possible to say that most experts on demography tend to use the phrasing *Russian* when talking about Russian demographics, as opposed to *Russia* or *Russia's demographics*. The researcher might want to consider this phrasing in their own writing and when crafting subsequent searches.

Quotation marks also work with foreign alphabets. Using Google Translate, it was easy to obtain the Russian phrase *демография россии*, meaning *Russia's demographics*. First, conduct the search without quotation marks, as shown in Fig. 3.4. This search returned about 4.32 million results in Google. The researcher will notice that the top results are all in Russian. This is because the search engine is attempting to return results it believes are most relevant to the researcher. The researcher has conducted the search in Russian, so it believes the researcher would like to see results in Russian.

Fig. 3.4 Google search results for *демография россии*, the Russian phrase for *Russia's demographics*, without quotation marks (Google and the Google logo are trademarks of Google LLC)

Wikipedia is still among the top results, except this time it returned the Russian version of the page. The second result is registered with a .ru domain, and is also an official government website. Google search engine also suggests similar questions, asked in Russian, the answers to which may provide some useful context.

These results were not at the top when conducting the search in English. The researcher who does not speak Russian will have to take extra steps to understand the content of these sites. See the section that covers online translation services later in this book for assistance on translation. For now, the researcher should be concerned only with identifying the differences in results returned and their foreign affiliation.

Also, it is important to notice here that since this search did not use quotation marks, the results returned did not necessarily contain the exact phrase *демография россии*. Although, the fourth result at ruxpert.ru did contain the exact wording in the title. As for the other results, as long as the page contained either word anywhere on the page, it met the search criteria and was included in the list of results.

Now conduct the same search, but with quotation marks around the phrase as shown in Fig. 3.5 below. The results are drastically different – first, note that there are only 34,400 results returned, which is significantly lower than the search without quotation marks. That is because quotation marks dictate that all results must contain the exact phrase, with the exact word order and spelling, as the text within the quotation marks.

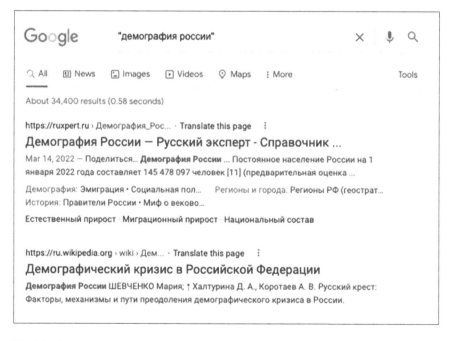

Fig. 3.5 Google search results for *"демография россии,"* the Russian phrase for *Russia's demographics*, with quotation marks (Google and the Google logo are trademarks of Google LLC)

Also, the top result in the search with quotation marks (ruxpert.ru) was the fourth result from the search without quotation marks (not shown). This is because this was the first result that met the new criteria; the previous top three results were filtered out because they did not meet the new criteria. Explore the other results to see how these searches differ.

Again, quotation marks will search for the exact spelling of a word; a misspelled word within quotation marks will drastically alter the results. Figure 3.6 shows the search results for *демография россии*, or *Russia's demographics*, but the word for demographics is misspelled. Many search engines, such as Google, will offer to display the results for the search as if the words were all spelled correctly. However, Fig. 3.6 shows what will occur when a word is misspelled: in this case, there is one result where the site owner has spelled the Russian word for demographics with the same spelling error in the search parameters.

Another reason the spelling of a word is important is because, as mentioned previously, words in foreign languages also have different spellings that are not errors. Just as in English, there is a difference between Russia, Russia's, and Russian, so too is there a difference between possessive, plural, and other forms of nouns in other languages. Using Wiktionary, it is possible to look up some of these forms. For example, the plural of демография is демографии [1]. This is also the form of the word in other declinations. Searching for the word in this form will return results where the phrase for *Russia's demographics* is in the middle of the sentence rather than as a standalone header or title. This is where a little understanding of the target language's grammar and spelling rules helps the researcher greatly.

Figure 3.7 shows the third, fourth, fifth, and sixth results from the search for *"демографии россии,"* where the Russian word for demographics is declined in other cases. Looking at the content of the top few results, it is possible to see that the

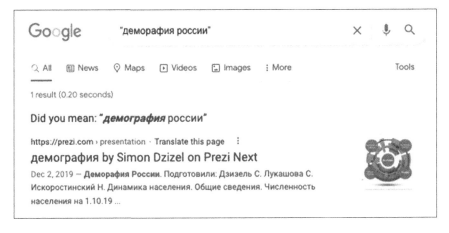

Fig. 3.6 Google search results for *"деморафия россии,"* misspelled, within quotation marks (Google and the Google logo are trademarks of Google LLC)

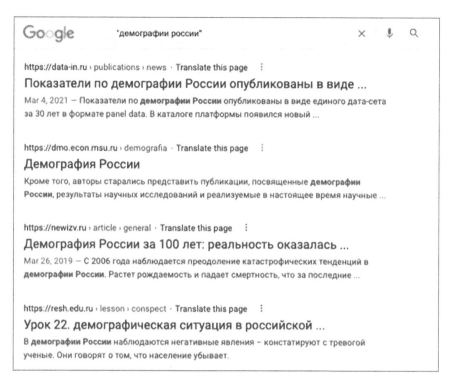

Fig. 3.7 Google search results for *"демографии россии,"* the Russian phrase for *"demographics of Russia"* with quotation marks (Google and the Google logo are trademarks of Google LLC)

references against which Google pulled these results match according to content from the middle of text and not just major headers or titles.

This is not to say that one search is better than another – knowing this, the researcher should be aware that every symbol and letter counts when searching in English or a foreign language.

Quotation marks work in most other search engines and databases besides Google, too, including (but not limited to) Bing, Yahoo, DuckDuckGo, Gibiru, Baidu, Yandex, etc. Since different search engines return different results, the researcher should attempt the variations of their search in different search engines, too.

Figure 3.8 shows the same search for *деморафия россии*, the Russian phrase for *Russia's demographics*, in Yandex (without quotations). A few of the top results come from similar sources, but as the list goes on, the results begin to differ. For example, this is the first time Yandex Zen has appeared in search results on this topic.

Conducting the same search with quotation marks limits the results slightly from the search without quotations: there were 9000 results without quotations (see Fig. 3.8) and only 8000 with quotations (see Fig. 3.9). Again, the search without quotations will return all pages with either word anywhere on the page, in any order.

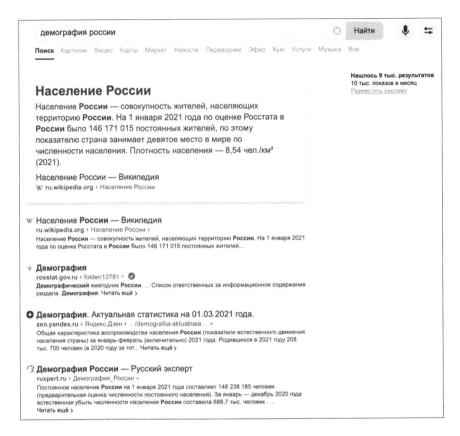

Fig. 3.8 Yandex search for *демография россии*, meaning *Russia's demographics*, without quotation marks © 2015–2022 YANDEX LLC

The search with quotations will return all pages with the exact phrase existing in the exact order as they are in quotations, and with the exact spelling. Both searches are very similar, which is why many of the results will be similar. However, the search with quotation marks is narrower in scope, so it returns slightly fewer results.

Also, the way the search engine displays the results is different. When quotations are used, the search engine highlights the entire phrase as it appears in each result. This makes it possible to view the exact context of the phrase as it exists on the site before viewing the full result. Figure 3.9 below highlights these instances as they stand out more distinctly in comparison with the search without quotations.

One final thought on this search topic is the use of the appropriate search engine. Since Yandex is primarily a Russian search engine made for Russian researchers, it is optimized to return results that are most relevant to the Russian researcher. So, instead of searching for *"Russian demographics"* in Russian, why not just search for *демография*, or demographics, in Russian using Yandex? Figure 3.10 below shows the top results for this search.

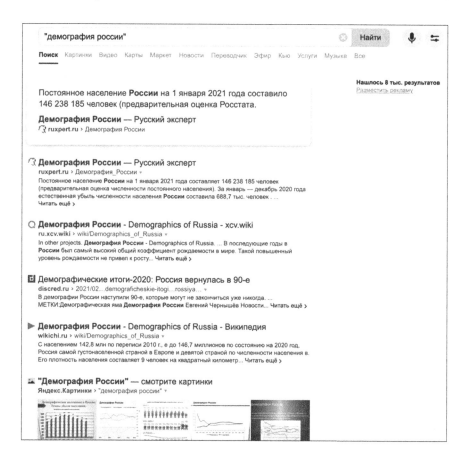

Fig. 3.9 Yandex search for *"демография россии,"* meaning *"Russia's demographics,"* with quotation marks © 2015–2022 YANDEX LLC

Upon further inspection, this search returned results on the broad topic of demographics. The results are all in Russian, but not necessarily about Russia. The key takeaway is that <u>different searches return different results</u>. It simply depends on what the researcher is trying to find. No single search is better or more correct than another; they are simply different. The researcher should now have a heightened awareness of how spelling, word order, and quotation marks alter results in search engines.

3.2 Discovering Combinations of Words with AND and OR

The AND and OR operators are Boolean terms that search for combinations of words. Generally, the AND operator restricts results and the OR operator expands results: AND will require all terms specified to be present in the results, but OR will

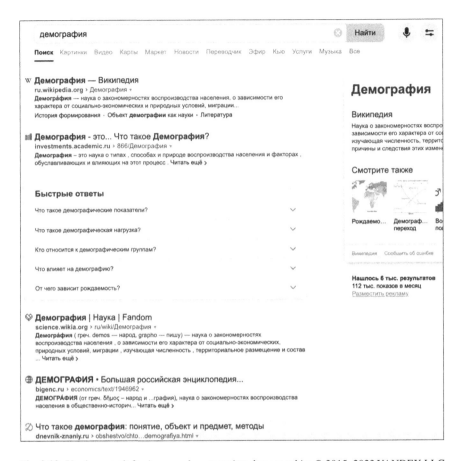

Fig. 3.10 Yandex search for *демография*, meaning *demographics* © 2015–2022 YANDEX LLC

return all results where at least one of the terms specified is present. These can be particularly useful in cases where the researcher needs to return results for multiple spellings or multiple aspects within one search.

Consider the search *(Russia AND Russian AND Russia's) demographics* as shown in Fig. 3.11. The results of this search include pages with combinations of all three spellings. The second result is a perfect example of how the AND operator behaves: it is easily apparent that the page contains the spelling *Russia* in the title, and *Russia's* and *Russian* in the body of the page. All other 5.55 million results should be of the same pattern.

Now consider the search *(Russia OR Russian OR Russia's) demographics* as shown in Fig. 3.12. The results returned should have either one, both, or all three spellings somewhere on the page. As a result, there are millions more results compared to the AND search: when using AND, there were 5.55 million results. When

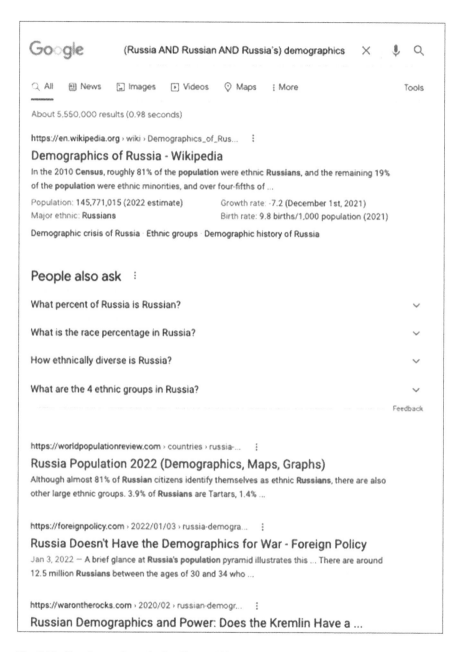

Fig. 3.11 Google search results for *(Russia AND Russian AND Russia's) demographics* (Google and the Google logo are trademarks of Google LLC)

using OR, there were 139 million results. All of the results that appear from the search using AND are a subset of the results returned from the search using OR. The search the researcher chooses in this case depends on the scope of the results in which they are interested.

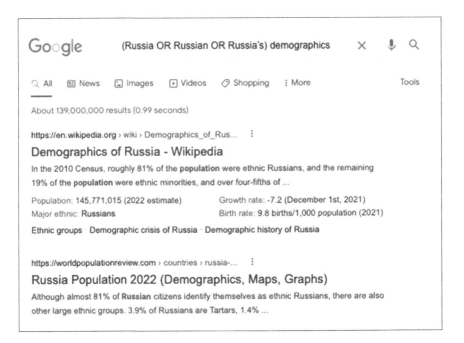

Fig. 3.12 Google search results for *(Russia OR Russian OR Russia's) demographics* (Google and the Google logo are trademarks of Google LLC)

It is also possible to use the AND and OR operators on alternate spellings of foreign words. This is helpful in languages where words have endings that change, which is common among nouns (which decline) and verbs (which conjugate), or to explore adjectival forms of the word. With the help of Wiktionary, it is possible to see one derived word that is similar to the Russian word for demographics is демографический, the Russian word for *demographic* [2]. This word is the adjectival form of the noun we have been exploring thus far. The adjectival form has the same root as the noun, but it is an entirely different word. To be sure that results on Russian demographics are included in search results, it may be wise to include the noun and adjective forms of the word in the same search. Figure 3.13 shows an example of the search containing both words, along with the Russian word for *Russia*.

While this top result has appeared several times already in the examples shown earlier, the researcher can know with 100% certainty that this word is now included in the search results shown. A further exploration of results beyond the first page will show results that differ from previous searches. Another added benefit to conducting the search including an alternate part of speech of the word is to explore other common use cases for the word. With these, the researcher can expand their searches even further.

First of all, демографический is an adjective, which means that a noun will often follow it. Since the search results highlight the search parameters, it is easy for

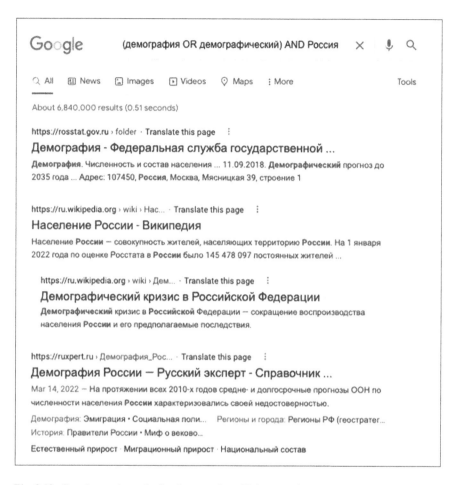

Fig. 3.13 Google search results for *(демография OR демографический) AND Россия*, containing the Russian noun and adjective for demographics and demographic, respectively (Google and the Google logo are trademarks of Google LLC)

the untrained eye to identify the terms in the result on which the search engine pinged, because they are in bold. The word following the bolded adjective is likely a noun, and in the context of demographic issues, this is likely a useful phrase. Copying and pasting the word that follows, *кризис*, into an online dictionary, the researcher will discover the meaning of this word is *crisis*, and the entire phrase means *demographic crisis*. This phrase was not likely to appear using the noun form of the Russian word for demographics, because this is not how Russian speakers discuss this topic.

In the search results shown in Fig. 3.14, the exact phrase *демографический кризис*, the Russian phrase for *demographic crisis*, appears in all 272,000 results. Some of these results have not appeared in some of the similar searches previously conducted. These results add an extra dimension of context to the search: rather than

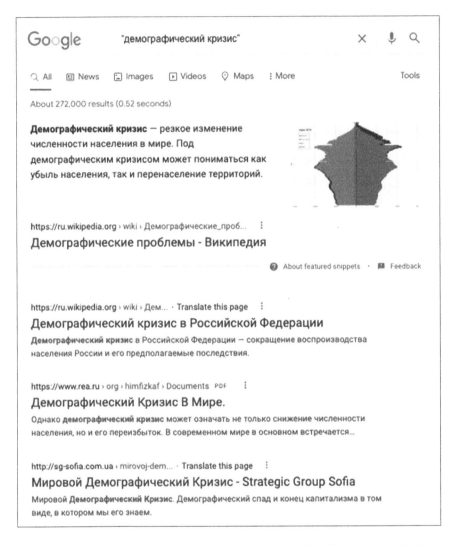

Fig. 3.14 Google search results for *"демографический кризис,"* the Russian phrase for *demographic crisis*, in quotation marks (Google and the Google logo are trademarks of Google LLC)

searching for the broad concept of "demographics," the search now focuses on a deeper context within the overall topic.

There are other contexts in which authors use the adjectival form of the Russian word for demographics. Consider the tenth result of the search *(демография OR демографический) AND Россия*, as shown in Fig. 3.15. On rbc.ru, the word demographic is used with the noun *прогноз*, meaning *prognosis* or *forecast*.

Now knowing these are two acceptable uses of the Russian adjective for demographic, it is possible to conduct a follow-up search for sources that contain results

https://www.rbc.ru › economics · Translate this page   ⋮

Власти ухудшили прогноз по убыли населения России ...

Apr 24, 2021 — Соответственно, скорректированный **демографический** прогноз следует ждать в конце 2021 — начале 2022 года, после того как будут ...

Fig. 3.15 The tenth result in the Google search for *(демография OR демографический) AND Россия* (Google and the Google logo are trademarks of Google LLC)

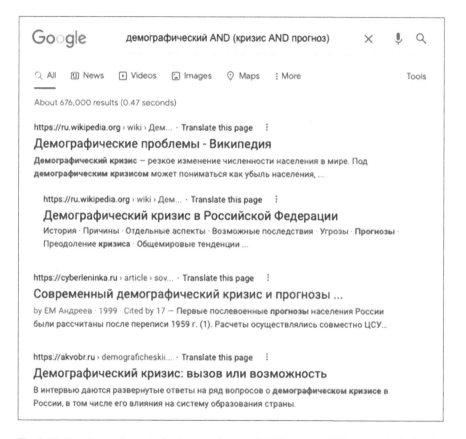

Fig. 3.16 Google search results for *демографический AND (кризис AND прогноз)*, the Russian words for *demographic AND (crisis AND prognosis)* (Google and the Google logo are trademarks of Google LLC)

covering Russian demographic crisis and forecasts. Since this phrasing appears at least in the top 10 searches for these terms, it is fair to say that this wording is common enough to appear in other searches. Figure 3.16 shows the results of the search for pages that contain the words *demographic*, *crisis*, and *forecast* in Russian. The

Fig. 3.17 Gibiru web search results for *демографический AND (кризис AND прогноз)*, the Russian words for *demographic AND (crisis AND prognosis)* © 2022 Gibiru

results offer a unique context to Russia's demographics that are more likely to be relevant to the researcher looking to discover information about this very specific problem set.

The results shown in Fig. 3.16 demonstrate how the results contain various combinations of the search terms, effectively offering an organized method for searching for common use phrases. The AND and OR operators also work with other search engines besides Google. Consider the same search as above, this time using the Gibiru search engine. Figure 3.17 shows the web results for this search, and Fig. 3.18 shows the censored results.

The results in Gibiru differ greatly from the Google search results, especially the uncensored search results. Not only that, the AND and OR operators clearly worked in this search engine, too. The researcher is left to try the AND and OR operators in other search engines using key terms of their choice.

Fig. 3.18 Gibiru censored web search results for *демографический AND (кризис AND прогноз)*, the Russian words for *demographic AND (crisis AND prognosis)* © 2022 Gibiru

3.3 Discovering Key Terms in Website Titles with intitle: and allintitle:

The *intitle:* and *allintitle:* operators search for key terms that are explicitly in the title of a website. Search engines have this capability because of the underlying tags in websites written in HTML, the common language for writing web pages. Each web page in HTML contains a <title> tag. Specifying the terms using the intitle: and allintitle: operators will specifically search for words within the <title> tag. While both of these operators will search for terms in the title of an HTML webpage, the major difference between the two is that the intitle: operator will only look for one key term. The allintitle: operator will look for all key terms listed after it.

Consider the search *intitle:Russian demographics* as in Fig. 3.19. The intitle: operator will return websites that contain the word *Russian* in the title and the word *demographics* anywhere on the page. This means that the word *Russian* must be in the title, but the word *demographics* may be in the title, body, links, or anywhere else. Sometimes, Google search will provide results containing synonyms: in this example, Google search considers "population" to be a synonym of demographics.

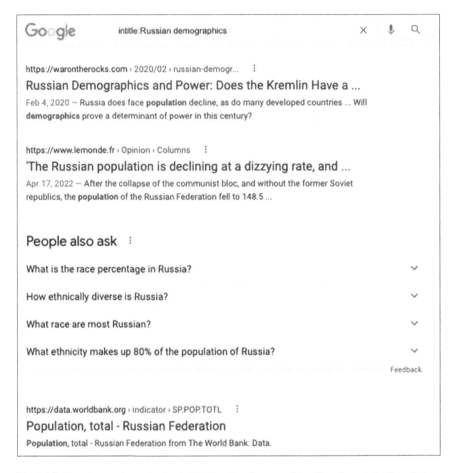

Fig. 3.19 Google search results for *intitle:Russian demographics* (Google and the Google logo are trademarks of Google LLC)

Note how there is no space between the colon after the operator and the first search term. Spaces will make the search misbehave.

Using the intitle: operator with quotation marks will search for web pages containing an exact phrase in the title. This will narrow down the search results significantly. Consider the three searches in Figs. 3.20, 3.21, and 3.22. The first search returns only results containing *Russia demographics* in the title, the second search returns only results containing *Russia's demographics* in the title, and the third search returns only results containing *Russian demographics* in the title. Notice how there are only 278 results in the first search, 81 in the second, and 802 in the third. This is consistent with our earlier assessment that most experts in this field use this language when discussing *Russian* demographics issues.

The allintitle: operator returns pages containing all words listed in the title. Unlike the intitle: operator with quotation marks, the order of the words listed after

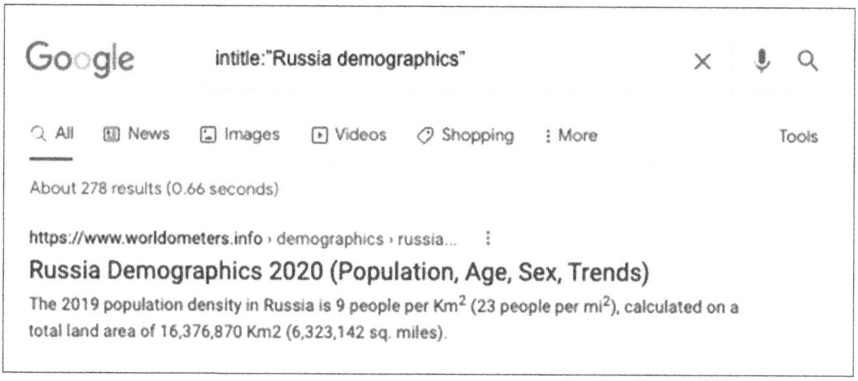

Fig. 3.20 Google search results for *intitle:"Russia demographics"* (Google and the Google logo are trademarks of Google LLC)

Fig. 3.21 Google search results for *intitle:"Russia's demographics"* (Google and the Google logo are trademarks of Google LLC)

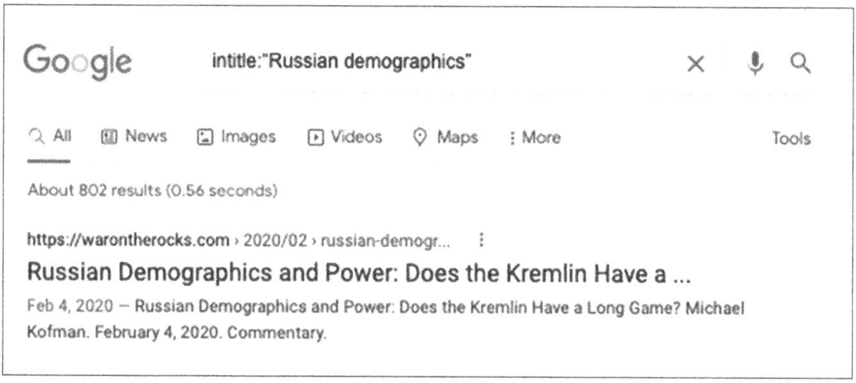

Fig. 3.22 Google search results for *intitle:"Russian demographics"* (Google and the Google logo are trademarks of Google LLC)

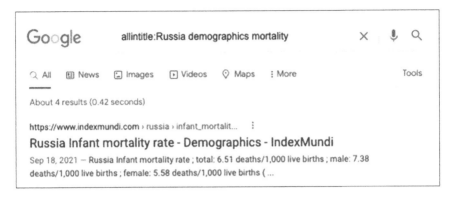

Fig. 3.23 Google search results for *allintitle:Russia demographics mortality* (Google and the Google logo are trademarks of Google LLC)

the operator does not matter. To demonstrate this, let's return to our initial brainstorm on words relating to demographics issues.

Consider the search *allintitle:Russia demographics mortality* as in Fig. 3.23. There are only four results, indicating this is a well-crafted search. It returned only results containing all three words in the title. Notice that the words are not in the order of the search. If order were important, the researcher could craft a search using the intitle: operator and the search terms in quotation marks. In this case, however, order does not matter, making the allintitle: operator the right choice.

The reason the researcher may want to search for terms only in the titles of web pages is because the titles often capture the most important themes contained on the web page. In other words, if the terms are in the title, they are likely to be the main focus of the site. This is only one way to narrow down the search results – when searching for something very specific, less is more.

For some search engines, the intitle: and allintitle: operators sometimes work with foreign character sets, too. The screen capture in Fig. 3.24 below shows results for the search *intitle:демография россия*. This search returns pages containing the Russian word for *demographics* in the title of the page, and the Russian word for *Russia* anywhere on the page (including the title, body, etc.).

Using the allintitle: operator with the same search parameters returns websites containing the Russian words for *demographics* and *Russia* both in the title of the page, in any particular order. In other words, the order of the search parameters does not matter, as long as both words are somewhere in the title of the website. Figure 3.25 shows the sample output of the search *allintitle:демография россии*, meaning *Russia's demographics*, without quotation marks. All results should contain both of these words anywhere in the title, in any order.

To return results where words must be in a particular order, use quotation marks with the allintitle: operator. For example, the search *allintitle:"демография россии"* in quotation marks will search for all words in the title of the page in the exact order as listed within the quotation marks. Figure 3.26 demonstrates how all

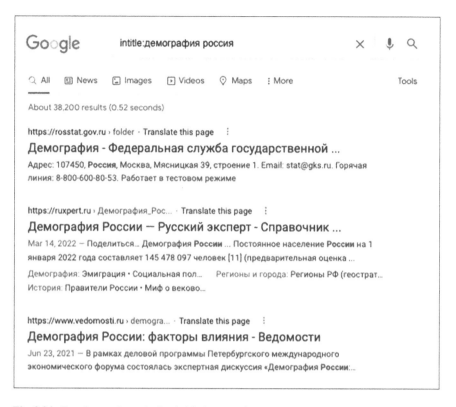

Fig. 3.24 Google search results for *intitle:демография россия*, meaning *Russia's demographics* in Russian (Google and the Google logo are trademarks of Google LLC)

results contain both words in order in the title, and that these results differ greatly from the results in the previous searches.

Also, in the example in Fig. 3.26, notice how the words within quotation marks are separated by dashes and colons. In other words, quotation marks ignore punctuation. Consider this when crafting searches using advanced operators with quotation marks.

The intitle: and allintitle: operators work in other search engines, too, but not all. They work in Bing, DuckDuckGo, and Yahoo, among others. The results may still differ greatly, though. Consider the results for the search *allintitle:демография россия* in Bing, as shown in Fig. 3.27. The top results in Bing do not come from the same sources as they did in the same Google search, even though the search parameters are exactly the same. The number of search results also varies greatly between Google and Bing: this search in Google returned 463 results, and only 60 results in Bing. The researcher is left to explore the remaining differences.

On the other hand, the intitle: and allintitle: operators do not work in MillionShort, for example. In StartPage and DuckDuckGo, only the intitle: dork works. In Baidu, the intitle: dork only appears to work in certain languages, such as Chinese and English; it does not function properly in Russian.

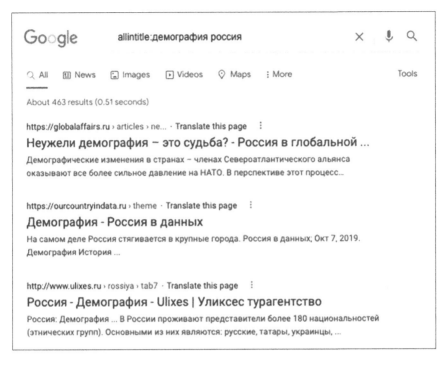

Fig. 3.25 Google search results for *allintitle:демография россия*, meaning *Russia's demographics* in Russian (Google and the Google logo are trademarks of Google LLC)

3.4 Discovering Website Content with intext:, allintext:, inbody:, +, and −

The *intext:* and *allintext:* operators search for websites containing the specified key terms in the main text (body) of the page. The key difference between the two is that the intext: operator will only look for the term directly after the operator. The allintext: operator will look for all key terms after it. Similar to the intitle: and allintitle: operators, spaces and quotation marks change the behavior of these search operators. The intext: and allintext: operators may also return pages that contain the specified key word(s) in the title, but only if those words are in the body of the website, too.

First, consider the search *intext:Russian demographics literacy* as in Fig. 3.28. This search will return any website containing the word *Russian* in the body of the page, and the words *demographics* and *literacy* anywhere on the page. This means that the words *demographics* and *literacy* need not be in the text of the page: they may also be found in the title, links on the page, or even within the page's URL. Consider the first result from knoema.com. This result contains the words *literacy* and *Russian* in both the text and the title of the page. At first glance, the word *demographics* does not appear in the text or the title.

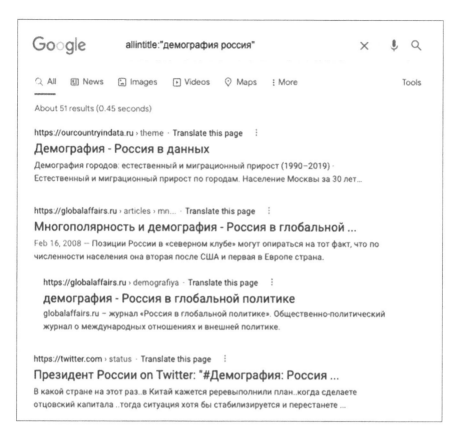

Fig. 3.26 Google search results for *allintitle:"демография россии"*, meaning *Russia's demographics* in Russian, with quotation marks (Google and the Google logo are trademarks of Google LLC)

Why would google return this website in the results for this search? Clicking on the link for the result reveals that the page does not have the word *demographics* on the page, either. Still, there must be some reason that Google would return this result with the given parameters of our search. Viewing the Web Inspector in the web browser and searching for the word *demographics* reveals that the image files used on the page contain the word *demographics* in the image files. Despite the word *demographics* not being visible on the website, Google included this search result. It is important to realize that search engines often behave this way while crafting search parameters and interpreting results.

Another important consideration is the use of quotation marks with the intext: operator. When used with quotation marks, the intext: operator will not search for each word individually and in any order. Instead, it will return the exact words in the exact order and with the exact spelling within the quotation marks. Consider the search in Fig. 3.29 below. Google's search engine will only return web pages

Fig. 3.27 Bing search results for *allintitle:демография россия*, meaning *Russia's demographics* in Russian © Microsoft 2021

containing the words *Russian*, *demographics*, and *literacy* all in a row and spelled exactly so. There are no results returned for this search, likely because this is not a sensical phrase.

When using quotation marks with the intext: operator, the researcher should use common vernacular to capture meaningful phrases. Here, a search such as that in Fig. 3.30 may be more appropriate. This search uses language that is more likely to appear in text because it is a complete phrase rather than a list of key words.

If the researcher would still rather conduct a key word search where word order does not matter, the allintext: operator will perform this task more effectively. The allintext: operator will return results that contain every word following it in any order. Consider the search *allintext:Russian demographics literacy* as in Fig. 3.31. These results all contain all key search terms in the text in any order on the page.

To demonstrate the relationship between the intext: and allintext: operators, consider the search *intext:Russian intext:demograhics intext:literacy* as in Fig. 3.32. This search actually is equivalent to the previous search using the allintext: operator

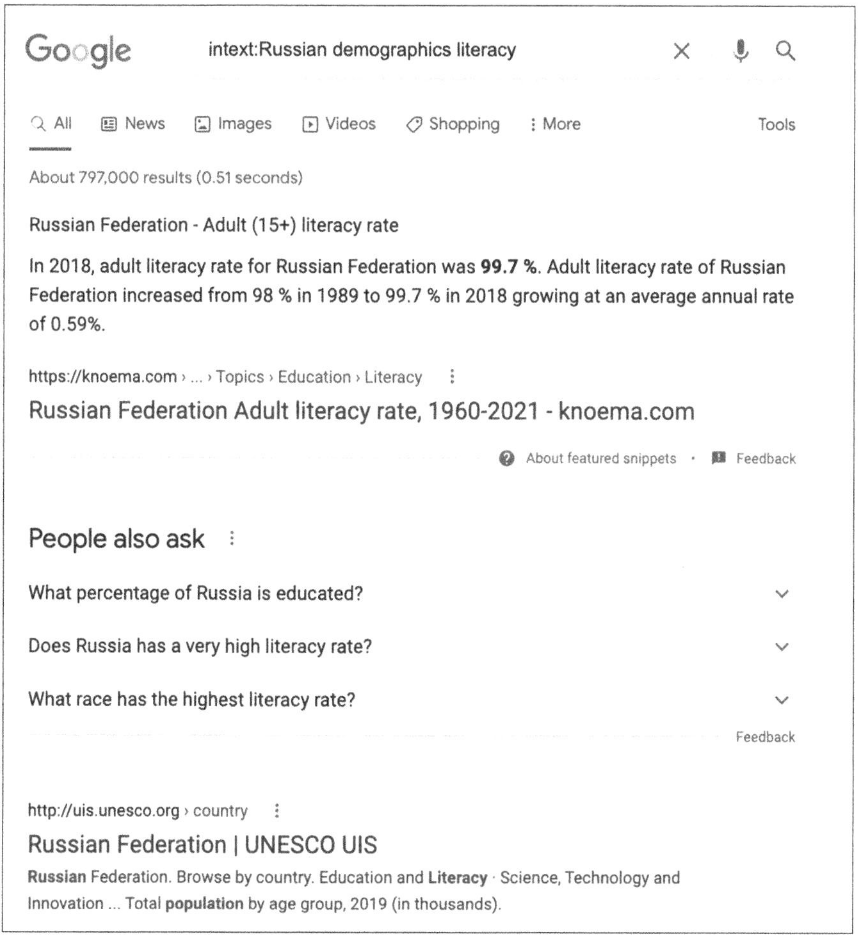

Fig. 3.28 Google search results for *intext:Russian demographics literacy* (Google and the Google logo are trademarks of Google LLC)

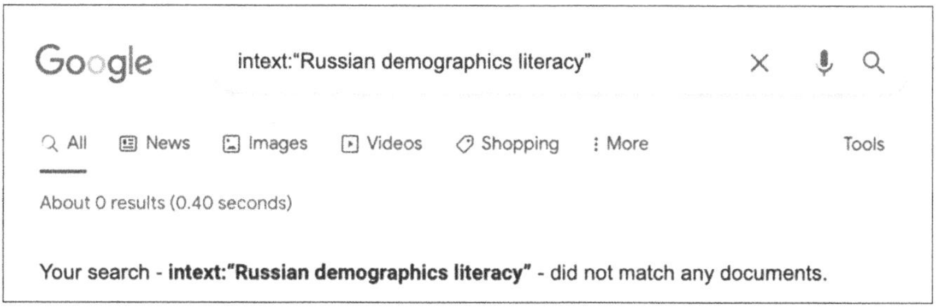

Fig. 3.29 Google search results for *intext:"Russian demographics literacy"* (Google and the Google logo are trademarks of Google LLC)

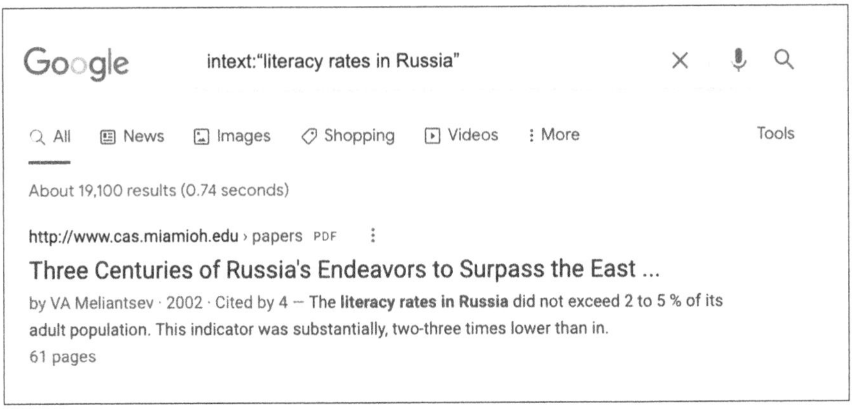

Google   intext:"literacy rates in Russia"   ✕   🎤   🔍

🔍 All   📰 News   🖼 Images   ⟋ Shopping   ▶ Videos   ⋮ More   Tools

About 19,100 results (0.74 seconds)

http://www.cas.miamioh.edu › papers   PDF   ⋮
Three Centuries of Russia's Endeavors to Surpass the East ...
by VA Meliantsev · 2002 · Cited by 4 — The **literacy rates in Russia** did not exceed 2 to 5 % of its
adult population. This indicator was substantially, two-three times lower than in.
61 pages

Fig. 3.30 Google search results for *intext:"literacy rates in Russia"* (Google and the Google logo are trademarks of Google LLC)

Google   allintext:Russian demographics literacy   ✕   🎤   🔍

🔍 All   📰 News   🖼 Images   ▶ Videos   ⟋ Shopping   ⋮ More   Tools

About 2,310,000 results (0.57 seconds)

https://www.rand.org › pubs › issue_papers   ⋮
Russia's Demographic 'Crisis': How Real Is It? - RAND ...
Life expectancy, especially among working-age males, has dropped precipitously. The **Russian**
fertility rate has declined to among the world's lowest, while its ...

https://en.wikipedia.org › wiki › Demographics_of_Rus...   ⋮
Demographics of Russia - Wikipedia
Demographics of Russia ; 1.69 migrant(s)/1,000 population (2014) · ~23.21% · ~34.73%.

https://www.cambridge.org › core › journals › article › fi...   ⋮
Financial literacy and retirement planning: the Russian case*
by L KLAPPER · 2011 · Cited by 311 — We examine the relationship between financial **literacy**
and retirement planning in Russia, a country with a relatively old and rapidly ageing population, ...
Information: Journal of Pension Economics & F...

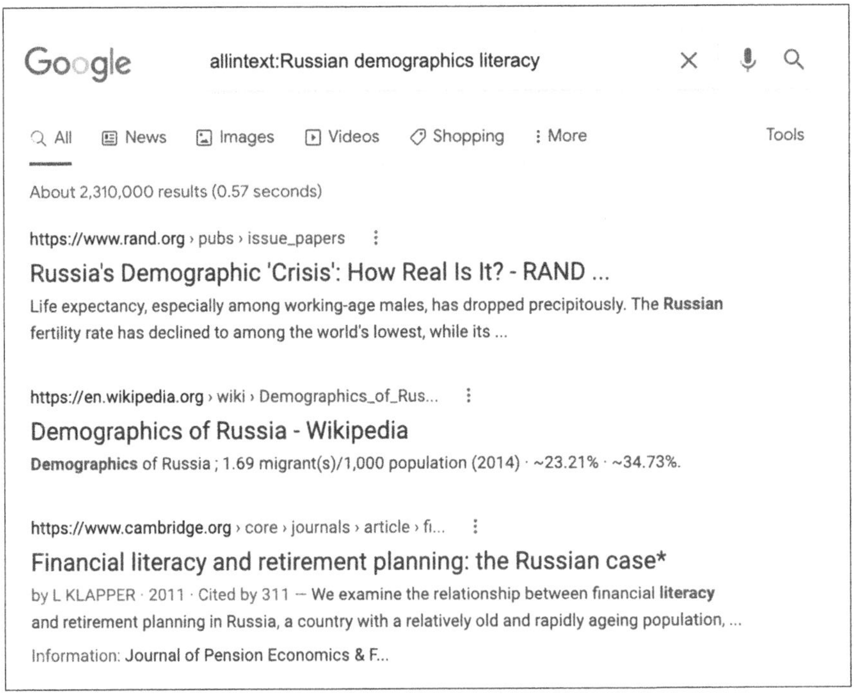

Fig. 3.31 Google search results for *allintext:Russian demographics literacy* (Google and the Google logo are trademarks of Google LLC)

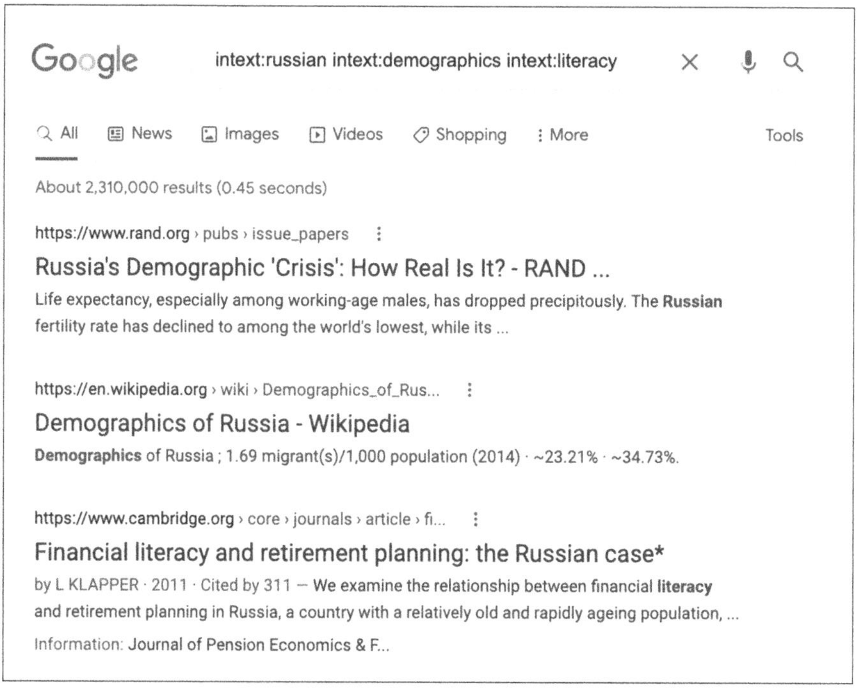

Fig. 3.32 Google search results for *intext:russian intext:demographics intext:literacy* (Google and the Google logo are trademarks of Google LLC)

[3]. This concept also demonstrates how it is possible to use multiple operators at once. This will be explained in more detail later in this section.

The intext: and allintext: operators work in Google; intext: works in DuckDuckGo. In Bing, Yahoo, and Baidu, use *inbody:* instead. In Yandex, use the + symbol to guarantee the presence of a key word or words in the body of a website.

The intext:, allintext:, and inbody: operators work with foreign characters, too. Figure 3.33 below shows the Google search results using the intitle: operator only on the Russian word for *literacy*, where the words for *demographics* and *Russia* could be anywhere on the page. Many of the top results differ greatly from the sources found in the previous English-language searches. Not only that, there are only 835 results in this search, indicating that this search is much more tailored to meet specific research goals.

Now consider a similar search in Yandex. Figure 3.34 shows an example of the Yandex search for *демография россия грамотность*, the Russian words for *demographics*, *Russia*, and *literacy*, respectively, with no special operators. This search returns 8 million results. To narrow down the number of results returned, use the "+" symbol in front of the key term(s) that must absolutely appear somewhere on the page.

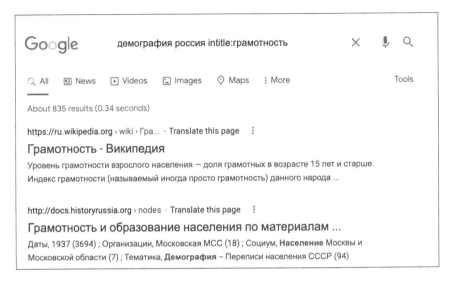

Fig. 3.33 Google search results for *демография россия intitle:грамотность*, the Russian words for *demographics*, *Russia*, and *literacy*, respectively (Google and the Google logo are trademarks of Google LLC)

Figure 3.35 demonstrates the use of the "+" symbol. This example yields only 2,000 results. While the top results appear to be largely the same across both searches, the search filters out many results that may have otherwise been irrelevant to the researcher [4].

Similarly, the minus symbol before a key term or operator omits certain results from the list. This can be very helpful if certain sources are dominating the list of results, making it difficult to examine the relevant results. For example, Wikipedia often appears within the first 10 results of many simple searches. While Wikipedia serves a particular purpose in the research process, it is not good practice to cite Wikipedia as a reputable source. If the researcher were interested in filtering out all Wikipedia pages and pages referencing Wikipedia, it would be possible to do so with the minus symbol. The search in Fig. 3.36 shows the top result for the search *Soviet demographics* as a measure for comparison.

The search for *Soviet demographics* above returns 13.4 million results, the first one of which is a Wikipedia reference. Now consider the same search minus the key term *Wikipedia*. Figure 3.37 shows these results, of which there are only 7.47 million. As it turns out, nearly half of the results were attributable to Wikipedia: either they were a Wikipedia page themselves, referenced a Wikipedia site, or contained the word Wikipedia somewhere on the page.

The *-wikipedia* addition to the search above locates pages containing the Wikipedia key term anywhere. This includes the title, text (or body), URL, links, etc. There are other ways to use the minus symbol that are discussed later in this section. The researcher is left to explore the foreign-language capabilities of other search engines and features using the intext: and inbody: search operators using their own key terms.

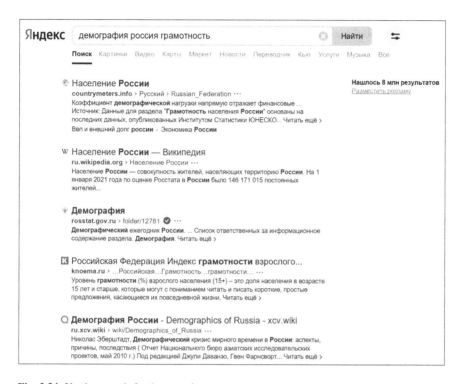

Fig. 3.34 Yandex search for *демография россия грамотность*, the Russian words for *demographics*, *Russia*, and *literacy*, respectively © 2015–2022 YANDEX LLC

3.5   Locating URLs with inurl:, allinurl:, and url:

The *inurl:*, *allinurl:*, and *url:* operators search for websites whose URLs contain certain keywords or keyword phrases, with some exceptions. URLs mostly contain Latin characters – however, there are plenty of exceptions, and some websites use foreign scripts in the URL. Different web browsers search for URL contents differently, which we will explore in this section.

In comparison with the other search operators explored thus far, the inurl: operator is more discrete in that its search results can be less apparent in their relevance to the researcher. Some websites will contain certain key terms in the URL that closely relate to the topic of the webpage but do not exist in the title or contents of the page. Some URLs contain key terms that allude to the existence of a web page within a larger domain or a certain function within the larger site. This is why it is important to consider adding a search for key terms within the URL into any research strategy.

To see how URL searches behave, consider the Google search for *inurl:russia demographics* in English as shown in Fig. 3.38. This search will return websites whose URLs contain the word *Russia*, and whose page contains the word

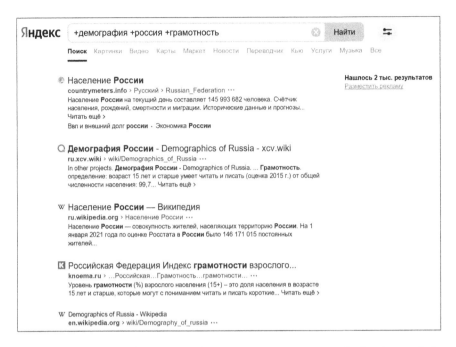

Fig. 3.35 Yandex search for *+демография +россия +грамотность*, the Russian words for *demographics*, *Russia*, and *literacy*, respectively © 2015–2022 YANDEX LLC

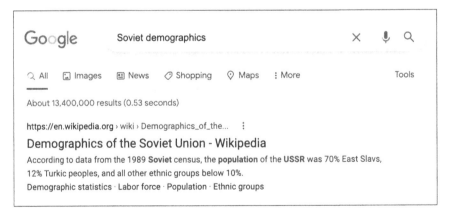

Fig. 3.36 Google search results for *Soviet demographics* (Google and the Google logo are trademarks of Google LLC)

demographics anywhere on the page. The URLs for the top three results, listed below, demonstrate how this search function works. All three examples contain the word *Russia*, but only the third contains the word *demographics*. Actually, it contains the word demography, but it still fits the requirements of the search. This is

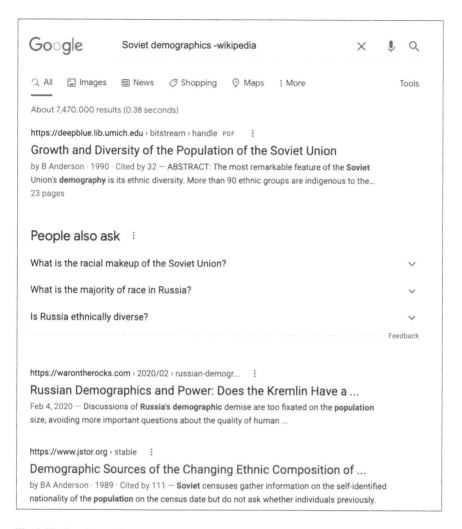

Fig. 3.37 Google search results for *Soviet demographics -wikipedia* (Google and the Google logo are trademarks of Google LLC)

because the URLs returned did not have to contain *demographics* at all. The word *demographics* should be somewhere else within the web page.

Result #1: https://worldpopulationreview.com/countries/russia-population
Result #2: https://www.worldometers.info/world-population/russia-population/
Result #3: https://foreignpolicy.com/2022/01/03/russia-demography-birthrate-decline-ukraine/

It is unlikely for the URL of a website to contain the word *Russia* without the website having something to do with Russia. However, the same is not true in reverse: there are clearly websites from previous searches that have been about

Russia that have not contained the word *Russia* in its URL. Otherwise, there would have been results in the thousands, rather than the millions.

URL-specific searches will also include special characters. This is common because URLs cannot contain spaces. The previous search demonstrate how URLs often contain dashes or underscores to separate words to make the URL easier to read. For example, the top result included the exact wording *russia-demographics*, which may also exist in other URLs. If the researcher was interested in websites on Russia's demographics, there may be some URLs containing this exact wording. Figure 3.39 shows the results for the Google search *inurl:russia-demographics* with a dash between the two words.

The top three results attest to how this search function works: each of the top three results contains the exact phrase *russia-demographics* with a dash:

Result #1: https://www.worldometers.info/demographics/russia-demographics/
Result #2: https://www.newyork-demographics.com/russia-demographics
Result #3: https://www.ohio-demographics.com/russia-demographics

The searches in Figs. 3.38 and 3.39 differ from each other in that all websites returned must have the exact phrasing *russia-demographics*, and therefore must contain the word *demographics*, too. While this search likely eliminates some relevant results, it also provides a manageable list of results that the researcher may actually be able to view. It is important to understand that these 94 results are a subset of the results from previous searches with broad parameters. These specific searches for key terms in the URL, for example, are intended to bring results to the top that would otherwise be thousands or tens of thousands of results down the list.

Since a search like this limits the results greatly, it may also be wise to conduct a search with the words inverted: that is, conduct the search *inurl:demographics-russia* to see if the results differ. Figure 3.40 shows the top results of this search.

The URLs belonging to the top three results are listed below. The second and third results contain the exact phrasing *demographics-russia* with a dash between them, and the first result contains the phrasing *demographics/russia* with a slash. In this case, it appears that Google returned a result with another symbol between the two words, but they are still in the same order.

Result #1: https://www.worldometers.info/demographics/russia-demographics/
Result #2: https://www.newgeography.com/content/007386-demographics-russia-belarus-and-ukraine
Result #3: https://www.wilsoncenter.org/event/health-and-demographics-russia-and-the-consequences-for-russian-society-and-policy

Most of the time, the order of the key terms will be of little or no importance to the researcher. When word order is unimportant, use the *allinurl:* operator. This dork will include every word that follows, even with spaces. Consider Fig. 3.41 that shows the top results of the search *allinurl:russia demographics*. The results of this search may include pages whose URLs contain the words *Russia* and *demographics* anywhere and in any order in the URL.

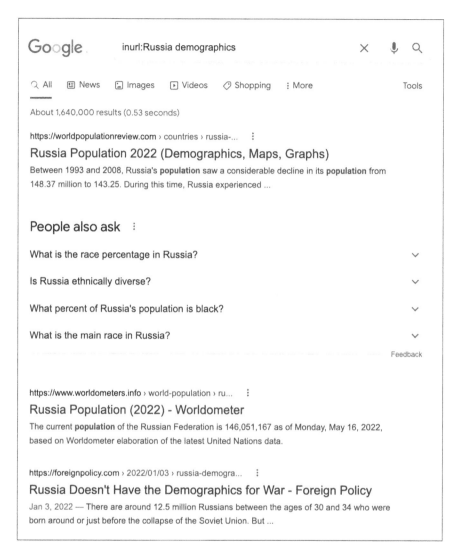

Fig. 3.38 Google search results for *inurl:Russia demographics* (Google and the Google logo are trademarks of Google LLC)

The top results of the search are shown in Fig. 3.41 above. As promised, each result contains the words *Russia* and *demographics* in the URL:

Result #1: https://www.worldometers.info/demographics/russia-demographics/
Result #2: https://www.statista.com/topics/5937/demographics-of-russia/
Result #3: https://www.newgeography.com/content/007386-demographics-russia-belarus-and-ukraine

The allinurl: dork works with other operators, including AND and OR. If the researcher were interested in discovering web pages whose URLs contained either

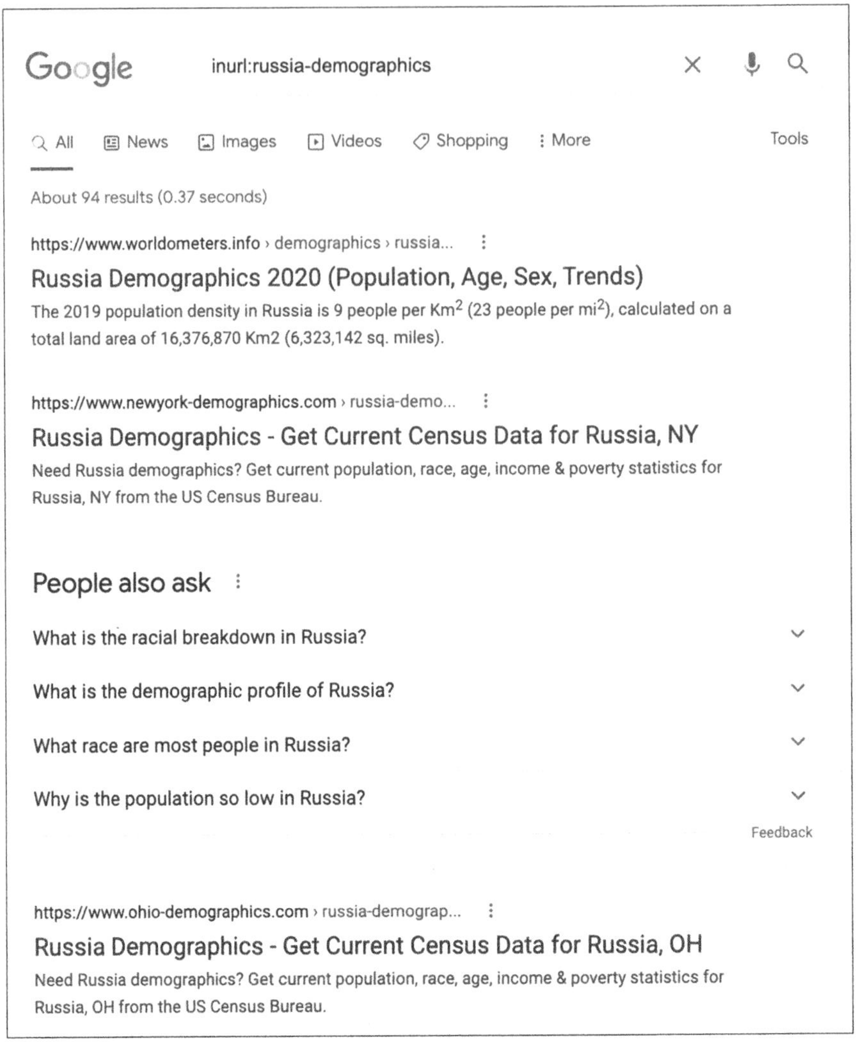

Fig. 3.39 Google search results for *inurl:russia-demographics* (Google and the Google logo are trademarks of Google LLC)

Russia, *Russian*, or *Russias*, it is possible to use the OR operator with parentheses to contain them. Figure 3.42 shows the top results for the search *allinurl:Russia OR Russian OR Russias) demographics*. All URLs returned contain one of the three spellings of Russia and *demographics*. The URLs for the top four results are listed below: together, they present all three spelling variations returned in this search.

Result #1: https://warontherocks.com/2020/02/russian-demographics-and-power-does-the-kremlin-have-a-long-game/

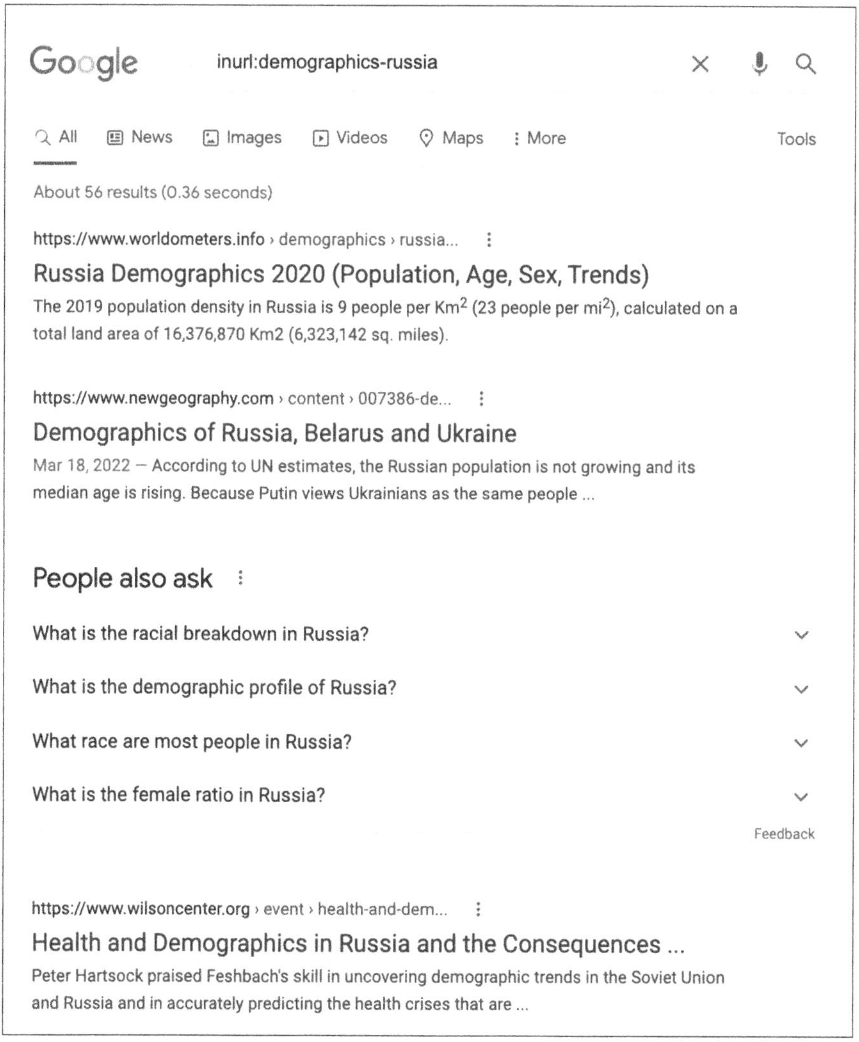

Fig. 3.40 Google search results for *inurl:demographics-russia* (Google and the Google logo are trademarks of Google LLC)

Result #2: https://www.statista.com/topics/5937/demographics-of-russia/
Result #3: https://www.worldometers.info/demographics/russia-demographics/
Result #4: https://daviscenter.fas.harvard.edu/insights/russias-discouraging-demographics-shouldnt-change-us-approach

The inurl: and allinurl: dorks work with foreign characters, too. While most websites are in English characters, even websites that host foreign-language content, some web administrators choose to use foreign characters in their URLs. This makes it more challenging to discover their resources, because these websites do not

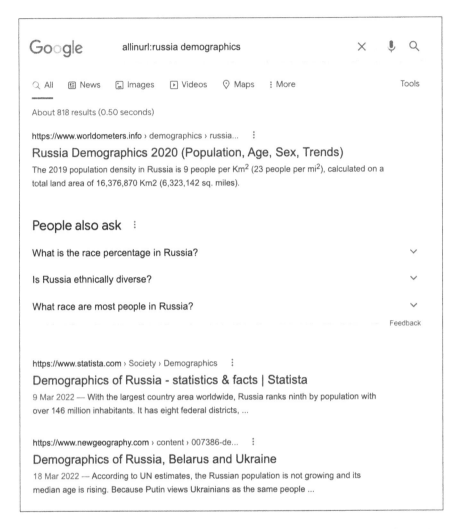

Fig. 3.41 Google search results for *allinurl:russia demographics* (Google and the Google logo are trademarks of Google LLC)

usually appear near the top of any English-language search. Figure 3.43 shows the top results of the Google search for *allinurl:демография россия*, the Russian words for *demographics* and *Russia*. All the results contain the Cyrillic text or Cyrillic-encoded text in the URL. The top three URLs are listed below:

Result #1: https://pikabu.ru/tag/демография,россия

Result #2: https://mayaksbor.ru/search/?tags=Демография%2CРоссия

Result #3: https://i.irklib.ru/cgi/irbis64r_61/cgiirbis_64.exe?LNG=&Z21ID=&
    I21DBN=IBIS_PRINT&P21DBN=IBIS&S21STN=1&S21REF=&S21FMT=F
    ULLW_print&C21COM=S&S21CNR=500&S21P01=0&S21P02=0&S21P03=

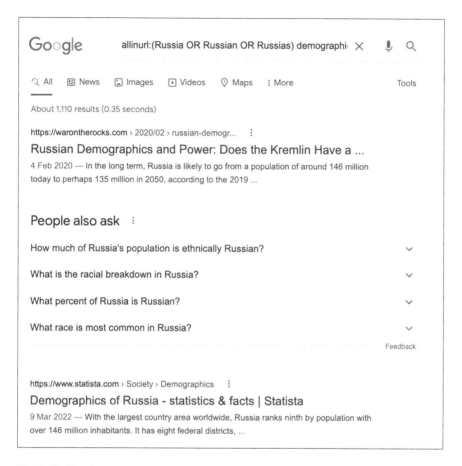

Fig. 3.42 Google search results for *allinurl:(Russia OR Russian OR Russias) demographics* (Google and the Google logo are trademarks of Google LLC)

S=&S21STR=%D0%94%D0%B5%D0%BC%D0%BE%D0%B3%D1%80%D
0%B0%D1%84%D0%B8%D1%8F%20%2D%2D%20%D0%A0%D0%BE%
D1%81%D1%81%D0%B8%D1%8F%2C%2020%20%D0%B2%2E%20
90%2D%D0%B5%20%D0%B3%D0%B3%2E%3B%2021%20
%D0%B2%2E%20%D0%BF%D0%B5%D1%80%D0%B2%D0%BE%
D0%B5%20%D0%B4%D0%B5%D1%81%D1%8F%D1%82%D0%B8%D0
%BB%D0%B5%D1%82%D0%B8%D0%B5

Notice how all of these results differ greatly from the results from all previous searches conducted using English words and characters. Additionally, there are only 2,450 results. So again, this is not a common occurrence. This is why it would be wise for the researcher to conduct both the English-language and target-language searches, even for URL keywords.

The third result does not contain the Cyrillic-text, but rather, contains Cyrillic-encoded text. The string of characters is encoded using MARC 21 specifications [5]. The character strings each map to a character in the Russian alphabet:

%D0%94 = Д
%D0%B5 = Е
%D0%BC = М
%D0%BE = О
%D0%B3 = Г
%D1%80 = Р
%D0%B0 = А
%D1%84 = Ф
%D0%B8 = И
%D1%8F = Я
%20%2D = Space Dash
%2D%20 = Dash Space
%D0%A0 = Р
%D0%BE = О
%D1%81 = С
%D1%81 = С

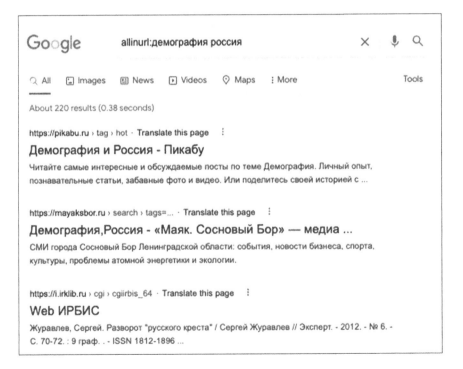

Fig. 3.43 Google search results for *allinurl:демография россия*, the Russian words for *demographics* and *Russia* (Google and the Google logo are trademarks of Google LLC)

%D0%B8 = И
%D1%8F = Я

…

And so on.

The inurl: operator works in DuckDuckGo [6],StartPage [7], and Baidu [8], but allinurl: does not work. Instead, Yandex [9] and Bing [10] use the *url:* operator. In Yandex, the url: operator will accept a full URL and return the results available from the URL. It will not search for key terms within the URL as do other search engines. The url: operator in Bing only identifies if the search engine has indexed the specified website or not. Yahoo also does not have a URL keyword search feature.

3.6 Discovering Online Documents with filetype:, ext:, and mime:

The *filetype:* operator searches for documents of a specific filetype that are within main content of the webpage. The *ext:* operator is similar in that it searches for documents of a specific filetype, however it searches for the filetype of the document based on the extension specified in the URL. Often times, the URL contains the extension of the file contained on the page, so many results will be the same when using either operator. The distinction is important to understand the output of the results based on a given search. It can also be an important consideration if the researcher is conducting a very targeted search on a particular website, because each website administrator may structure the URLs of their web pages differently.

Unlike the operators explored so far, the filetype: and ext.: operators are often used in conjunction with other search terms. Consider the search *Russian demographics filetype:pdf* as shown in Fig. 3.44. This will return all websites that

Fig. 3.44 Google search results for *Russian demographics filetype:pdf* (Google and the Google logo are trademarks of Google LLC)

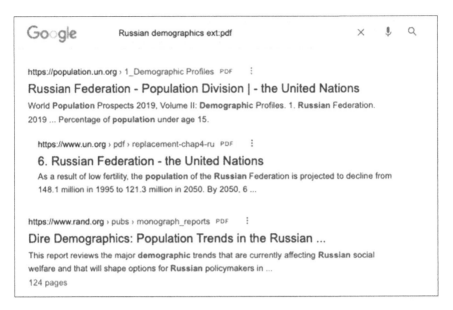

Fig. 3.45 Google search results for *Russian demographics ext:pdf* (Google and the Google logo are trademarks of Google LLC)

contain the words *Russian* and *demographics* anywhere on the page; however, the page must also be in .pdf format. At first glance, it is easy to see that all results are .pdf files. The top result is an article by Rand with the URL: https://www.rand.org/content/dam/rand/pubs/monograph_reports/2007/MR1273.pdf. The second result is another .pdf article with the URL: https://population.un.org/wpp/Graphs/1_Demographic%20Profiles/Russian%20Federation.pdf. Even though this search used the filetype: operator, the .pdf filetype is contained within these URLs. This is the case with many of the results from this search.

Now consider the same search using the ext: operator. As mentioned previously, many of the results will be the same for these two searches due to the common practice of including the page's filetype in the URL. Not all web authors use this practice, however. In the example shown in Fig. 3.45, using the ext: operator returned nearly 10 million fewer results. This means there were many websites that did not follow this naming convention. The key takeaway here is that the researcher should conduct both searches to ensure they are discovering the exact results they seek.

Another way of looking at this issue is by considering that all websites may be of a certain filetype, but their extension in the URL may differ. If the filetype and extension operators serve different purposes, it means that the filetype and extension of a website may be the same, or different. For example, a website written in HTML can contain a .pdf file. The search *Russian demographics filetype:pdf ext:html* as shown in Fig. 3.46 demonstrates this subset of results.

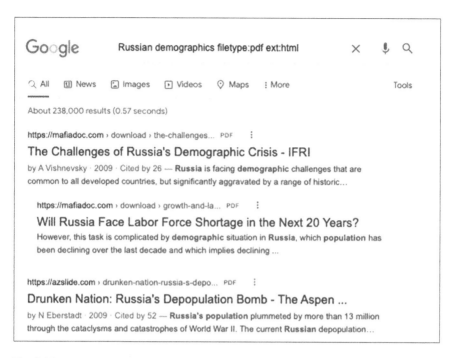

Fig. 3.46 Google search results for *Russian demographics filetype:pdf ext:html* (Google and the Google logo are trademarks of Google LLC)

It turns out there are 251,000 such websites written in HTML that contain the key words *Russian* and *demographics* that contain a .pdf file. The first result from the website moam.info has the following URL: https://moam.info/the-challenges-of-russias-demographic-crisis-ifri_5b445f6c097c4779678b458d.html. This website is a .pdf file embedded into a website (written in HTML, as many websites are). The URL does not contain the .pdf extension, but it does contain the .pdf file on the page. This file appears to be a finished report that may be of value to the researcher looking to cite a formal report on the topic of Russian demographics.

It may be beneficial to search for particular filetypes to narrow down certain products on a topic. As in the previous example, .pdf files are usually finished products and reports. To find presentations on a subject, search for PowerPoint (.ppt) files. The researcher can also further narrow down the search results by specifying image or audio file types within the search parameters. Google supports dozens of filetypes, but not all search engines index the same filetypes. A list of some of the well-known filetypes that Google supports includes: Adobe files including .pdf; website languages including .htm and .html; Microsoft Office files including .xls and .xlsx, .doc and .docx, and .ppt and .pptx; Open Office products including .odp, .ods, and .odt; text files containing programming language text including .c, .cs, .java., .py, and others; image files including .jpeg and .png; and audio files including .mp4 [11]. Yandex only supports the following filetypes: .pdf, .rtf, .swf, .doc, .xls,

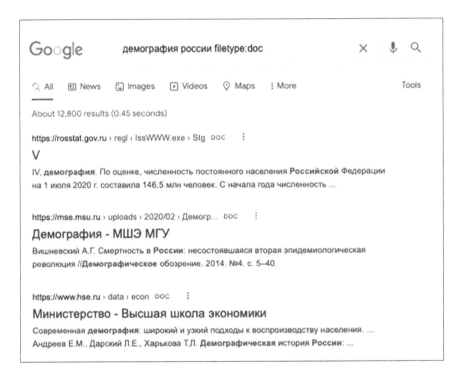

Fig. 3.47 Google search results for *демография россии filetype:doc*, the Russian phrase for *demographics of Russia* (Google and the Google logo are trademarks of Google LLC)

.ppt, .odt, .ods, .odp, and .odg [12]. Some search engines have not published lists of supported filetypes, but upon further investigation, clearly support the most popular filetypes. The best thing to do in this case is try to search for the desired filetype and explore the results.

The filetype: and ext: operators are used only with the Latin-character filetype extensions. However, it is still possible to conduct keyword searches in other languages along with the filetype: and ext: operators. Consider the search using the Russian phrase for Russian demographics as shown in Fig. 3.47. The search returns all .doc files containing the specified phrase. Notice how all results are .doc files and how the results are all in Russian.

Since the example used throughout this chapter uses a Russia-specific example, let's continue to explore searches in Yandex. In Yandex, the filetype: and ext.: operators do not work. Instead, Yandex supports the mime: operator. Consider the same search as the one above, this time using the mime: operator in Yandex (see Fig. 3.48). Notice how the top few results differ greatly. This is yet another good reason to conduct the same searches in multiple search engines.

It is also possible to use AND and OR with filetype: and ext: operators. Consider the example in Fig. 3.49 below of the search *(russian demographics OR демография*

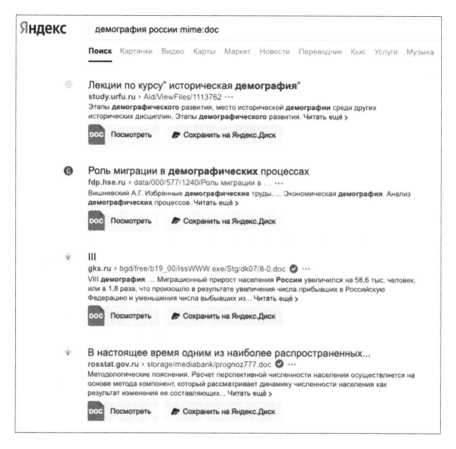

Fig. 3.48 Yandex search results for *демография россии mime:pdf* © 2015–2022 YANDEX LLC

россии) filetype:pdf, this time using DuckDuckGo. All results contain either the English or Russian terms, and all results are in .pdf format. This will work in any other search engine where the OR and filetype: operators also work.

It is also possible to search for results that are either one filetype, or another. Use parentheses and the OR operator to list all desired filetypes. Consider the search *демография россии filetype:(doc OR ppt)* in DuckDuckGo as shown in Fig. 3.50. The results all contain the desired terms in either .doc or .ppt formats.

The filetype: operator works in Google, DuckDuckGo, Bing, Yahoo, StartPage, and Baidu; it does not work in Yandex. The ext: operator works in Google, Bing, and StartPage; it does not work in Yandex, DuckDuckGo, Yahoo, or Baidu. The mime: operator is unique to Yandex and serves the same purpose as the filetype: operator.

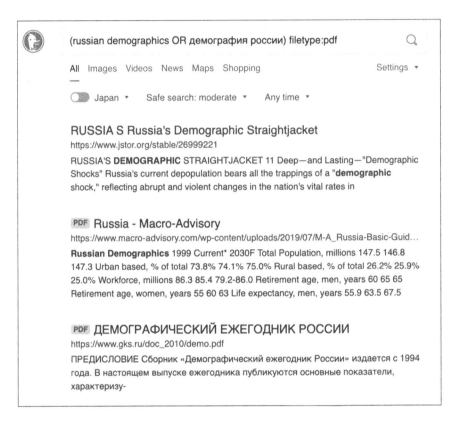

Fig. 3.49 DuckDuckGo search results for the search *(russian demographics OR демография россии) filetype:pdf* © DuckDuckGo

3.7 Searching Websites with site:

The *site:* operator searches a website for the identified search parameters. This can include key terms and can be used with other search operators. This serves as an alternate method of searching a website directly; instead of navigating to the website and conducting a keyword search on that site, it is possible to use the site: operator to locate resources on that website directly from the search engine. This can be valuable because not all individual websites are optimized to return search results; some websites do not have search capabilities at all. Since it is possible to use the site: operator with other search operators, it is possible to discover results in a way that most individual websites cannot handle or display on their own. It can also be useful in discovering permutations of websites, which this section will also explore. The site: operator works in Google, Yahoo, Bing, DuckDuckGo, Yandex, and StartPage, among others. Let's explore the functionality of the site: operator.

One entity that has published much on Russian demographics is the United Nations (UN). Let's use the site: operator to explore the contents of the UN website.

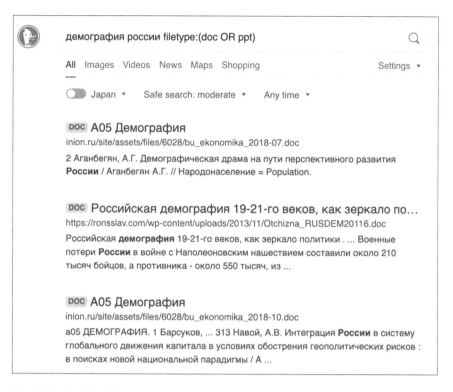

Fig. 3.50 DuckDuckGo search results for *демография россии filetype:(doc OR ppt)* © DuckDuckGo

The main website for the UN is located at the URL un.org. The first search we may conduct on the topic of Russian demographics is *Russian demographics site:un.org*, the top results of which are shown in Fig. 3.51.

All results returned from the search in Fig. 3.51 above come from the un.org website or a sub-domain: population.un.org, un.org, data.un.org, esa.un.org, etc. They also all contain the words *Russian* and *demographics* somewhere within the page. Since the UN is a global organization, it is no surprise that the UN also hosts content in foreign languages. Let's conduct the same search using the site: operator, but this time with the specified key terms in Russian, as shown in Fig. 3.52.

Figure 3.52 shows the Russian-language results for the Google search for Russian demographics on the un.org website. Again, simply changing the language of the search terms returned results that otherwise would not have appeared, let alone at the top of the list. The researcher may also notice that the un.org website has several sub-domains. Those that are apparent from this list include news.un.org and unstats.un.org, and the list continues. If the researcher were further interested in results only from the UN news or UN statistics service, the researcher could further narrow down their search to the exact sub-domain of their choice. First, to enumerate a list of all sub-domains of the site, the researcher could conduct the search *site:*.un.org*,

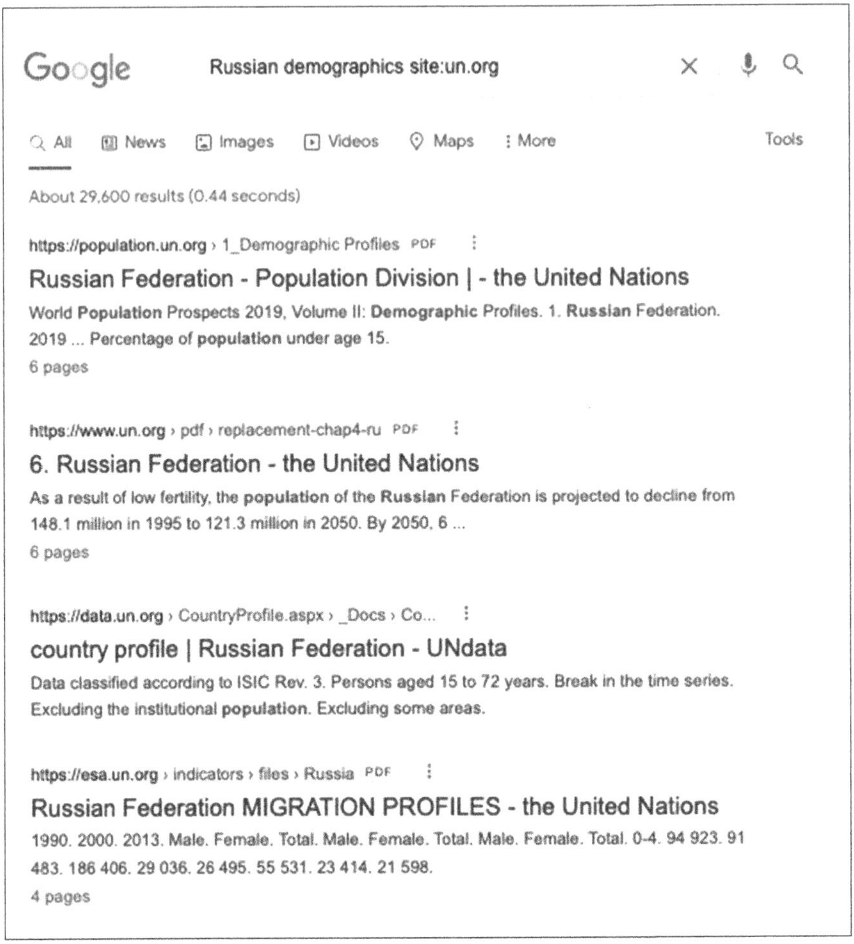

Fig. 3.51 Google search results for *Russian demographics site:*un.org (Google and the Google logo are trademarks of Google LLC)

where the asterisk serves as a wildcard for any and all sub-domains of the site. The results are shown in Fig. 3.53.

Figure 3.53 shows the top results of the search for all sub-domains of the un.org website. There are other sub-domains that do not appear in the list, too. Once enumerating the sub-domains, it is then possible to conduct the more specific search that narrows down the results to the desired resources. Consider the search *демография россии site:news.un.org* as shown in Fig. 3.54. This search returns all websites containing the Russian words *demographics* and *Russia* on the news. un.org website.

In this search, notice that all results are in Russian. Also, notice that there are only 691 results. In comparison with the same keyword search on the entire un.org

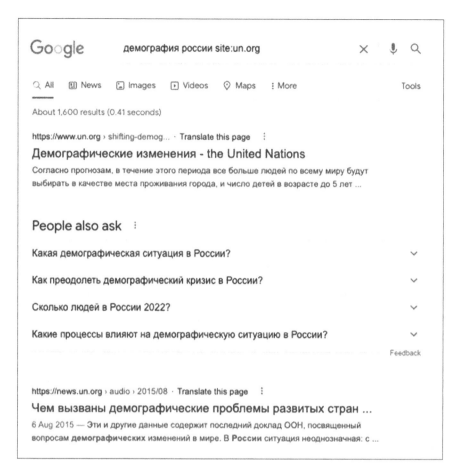

Fig. 3.52 Google search results for *демография россии site:*un.org (Google and the Google logo are trademarks of Google LLC)

website, this is significantly fewer results. This sub-domain search has filtered out all other results that may have otherwise been irrelevant. If the researcher were interested in statistical data instead, for example, they could slightly alter the search to locate resources on the data.un.org or unstats.un.org sub-domains instead. For good measure, consider the results for the same search on the news.un.org sub-domain with English keywords. Only 119 results are returned (see Fig. 3.55). As it turns out, the researcher would not have found as meaningful results by conducting the search using English terms. This may have severely limited the resources to which they had access and may have hampered the data acquisition process.

Another use for the site: operator is to filter websites with the desired TLD. This may be particularly helpful because certain online services are often associated with certain TLDs. For example, educational services are often affiliated with the .edu TLD; government services are often affiliated with the .gov TLD, and so on. Certain

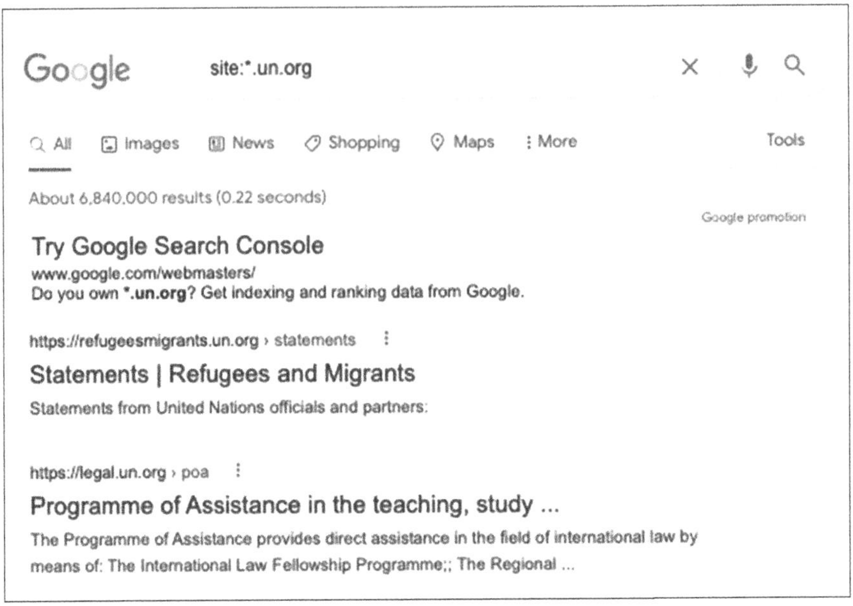

Fig. 3.53 Google search results for *site:**.un.org (Google and the Google logo are trademarks of Google LLC)

countries also use their own TLDs to host country-specific content. For example, Russian websites often use the .ru TLD, Canadian websites often use the .ca TLD, and so on. To specify the desired TLD using the site: operator, add the TLD after the colon as shown in the example in Fig. 3.56. This search will return all websites containing the specified key words for Russian demographics (in Russian) that use the .ru domain.

Upon All results returned in this search contain the Russian words for *demographics* and *Russia* anywhere on the page, on websites using the .ru TLD. This type of search is still very broad, but the initial results may provide an idea of the most popular sites with this particular TLD; with this information, the researcher can conduct a follow-up search that is tailored to the appropriate website.

So far, this section has focused on websites that use Latin-based domain names. The .org and .com domains (among others) are usually typed in Latin characters; even the .ru domain and other country-based domains use Latin characters. However, some websites use domain names that are typed in foreign characters. When conducting searches using Russian key terms and the Latin-based domain name, the results returned largely appear to come from foreign websites. However, there may still be valuable results missing. The Cyrillic-based domain for .ru is spelled .рф, which is an acronym for Российская Федерация, or Russian Federation. Using this domain rather than the Latin-based domain yields different results as shown in Fig. 3.57.

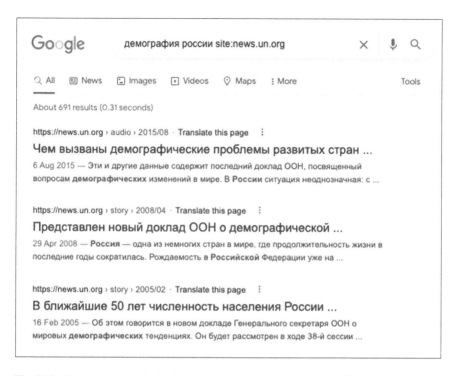

Fig. 3.54 Google search results for *демография россии site:*news.un.org (Google and the Google logo are trademarks of Google LLC)

The top results of the search above demonstrate how many websites may have been missing from all previous searches on the topic of Russian demographics. All 175,000 results contain the Russian words for Russian and demographics, and exist on the .рф domain. This search technique works in other languages and on other foreign-language domains as well. This book further explores non-Latin domains in Chap. 4, offering a list of dozens of languages and country-specific domains.

One other use for the site: operator is to filter out websites from the results. If the researcher does not care to search a website, but wants a certain website omitted from the results, it is possible to do so with the site: operator and the minus symbol. The search *демография россии -site:wikipedia.org* returns all websites containing the specified key words, as long as they are not on wikipedia.org (see Fig. 3.58).

This search differs greatly from the search conducted earlier using *-wikipedia*. Recall that this search filters out results containing the key word *Wikipedia* anywhere on the page. It does not filter the website itself, but any resource containing the word in the title, body, or URL. As a result, this search will filter out more results than the search using *-site:wikipedia.org*. This is because the search using *-site: wikipedia.org* filters out only Wikipedia pages. It may still return results referencing Wikipedia pages or containing the key term.

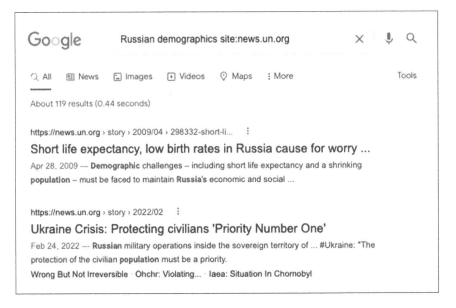

Fig. 3.55 Google search results for *Russian demographics site:*news.un.org (Google and the Google logo are trademarks of Google LLC)

Upon further inspection of the Wikipedia domain, the researcher may notice that the most commonly used TLD is the .org domain. The site: operator can also be used to see if Wikipedia uses other domains beside the .org TLD. This is used in conjunction with the wildcard, or asterisk symbol. The search *site:wikipedia.* -inurl:org* returns all Wikipedia sites that do not use the .org TLD. Figure 3.59 shows the top results from this search.

This search is a great example of how multiple operators can be used at once to produce meaningful results. Notice that Wikipedia actually uses other TLDs besides .org, even though the .org is the most commonly used. The researcher can use this knowledge to conduct subsequent searches on targeted domains, or create filters that omit other pages.

One additional example discussed in this section involves a search engine not yet discussed in this book: Naver. Naver is a South Korean search engine made especially for South Koreans. It hosts many services similar to the other search engines discussed already, including news, online dictionary and translator, and more. Naver's search engine also supports the site: dork, which is the reason it is discussed here. If the researcher were interested in learning about Korean demographics instead of Russian demographics, it would be best to search Naver instead of Google or Yandex. Figure 3.60 below shows a sample search for the Korean phrase for *Korean demographics*, searching the site kiep.go.kr. This website belongs to the Korean Institute for International Economic Policy, a great place to get started on thorough academic research on the topic.

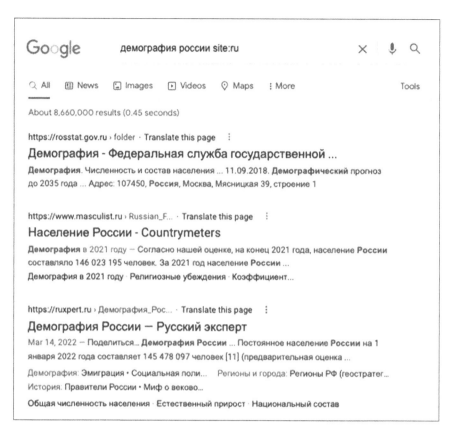

Fig. 3.56 Google search results for *демография россии site:ru* (Google and the Google logo are trademarks of Google LLC)

The researcher should continue to test these search operators in other search engines to see how they function in other contexts. As demonstrated in this section, the site: operator has several applications for foreign-language and region-specific research, and it works well across various search engine platforms. The researcher is left to explore the capabilities of this powerful operator on their own research topics.

3.7.1 Impact of Website Development Best Practices on Foreign-Language Research

When researching online, a researcher of foreign language materials must understand the web developer's approach to website development and management. Web administrators *should* follow certain best practices if they want people from certain countries or who speak certain languages to discover their content. Though these

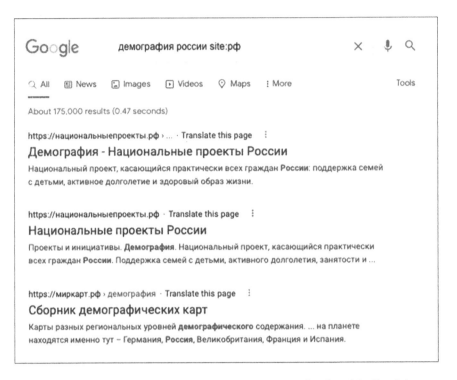

Fig. 3.57 Google search results for *демография россии site:рф* (Google and the Google logo are trademarks of Google LLC)

best practices are not required, they are common practice. Even when web developers do not use these best practices, the researcher must be aware of the inconsistencies. These best practices (or lack thereof) offer clues into how to better discover these sources with structured and targeted searches. There are two main types of websites that are of interest to the foreign-language researcher: multilingual and multiregional. Multilingual websites have content in multiple languages, and multiregional websites target users based on their geographic location in the world [13]. Many websites do both simultaneously. As a result, this section discusses both types together.

Consider the website that has the option to toggle between multiple languages. The website has multiple versions of the site that are identical, with the only difference being the website is in a different language. This is a multilingual website. Google's recommendation is to alter the URL so that each version of the website is distinct. This is important to consider when conducting a search, because the website returned will likely be in the language of the search. Search engines can also detect the language of the searcher's computer, and may present certain results based on these settings. For example, search results for English search terms are more likely to return the English language version of a website that has multiple languages. A computer whose default language settings are in English may also be more likely to return English language results. It will be more likely to return the

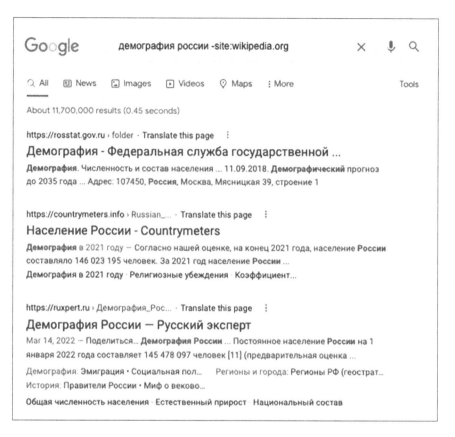

Fig. 3.58 Google search results for *демография россии -site:*wikipedia.org (Google and the Google logo are trademarks of Google LLC)

Spanish version of that same website if the search terms are in Spanish and the host computer language settings are set in Spanish.

Similarly, consider a website that sells products internationally. Some products may only be available for purchase in certain regions of the world. To ensure that customers can only purchase items available for delivery in their region, the web administrator should create a special version of that website that is accessible by people presumed to be from that region of the world. When the customer searches online for the store, the web browser can detect where the customer is from based on their IP address and smartly redirect them to the website that is most relevant to them. These are multiregional websites. It is easy to see the likelihood that a multi-regional website would also be available in a language associated with that region of the world – or, in many cases where people of a particular region speak several languages, the website, too, will be available in multiple languages.

The reason this is so important for the foreign language researcher is because the researcher may be interested in the web content of versions other than the one the

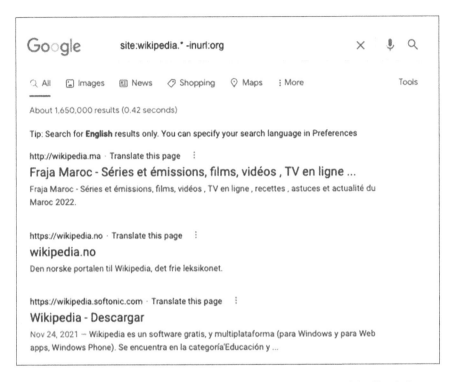

Fig. 3.59 Google search results for *site:wikipedia.* -inurl:org* (Google and the Google logo are trademarks of Google LLC)

search engine believes is most relevant. Search engines assume that the version it presents to the user is the most relevant one to the user based on the searcher's search language and geolocation. It takes extra work and specially-crafted searches to tell the search engine that the researcher is actually interested in other results. For example, a researcher located in Canada who speaks French may be interested in French news stories in France. This researcher would have to take special search measures to ensure the news resources returned from their search are the ones they seek.

These measures are search engine specific, and also depend on the web developer's preferences and settings when they created the website. The researcher's first step is to understand how the web developer prepared the website's language and region features. Once the researcher understands this, they can then tailor their searches with the methods discussed in the later sections of this book to craft meaningful searches that return exact results.

Google recommends one of three methods for web developers to specify alternate language and region versions of a site: HTML tags, HTTP headers, or Sitemaps. These methods use language and region-specific elements that indicate the website is in a particular language or located in a particular region. HTML tags specify that text on a website written in HTML code is in a certain language or region. HTTP

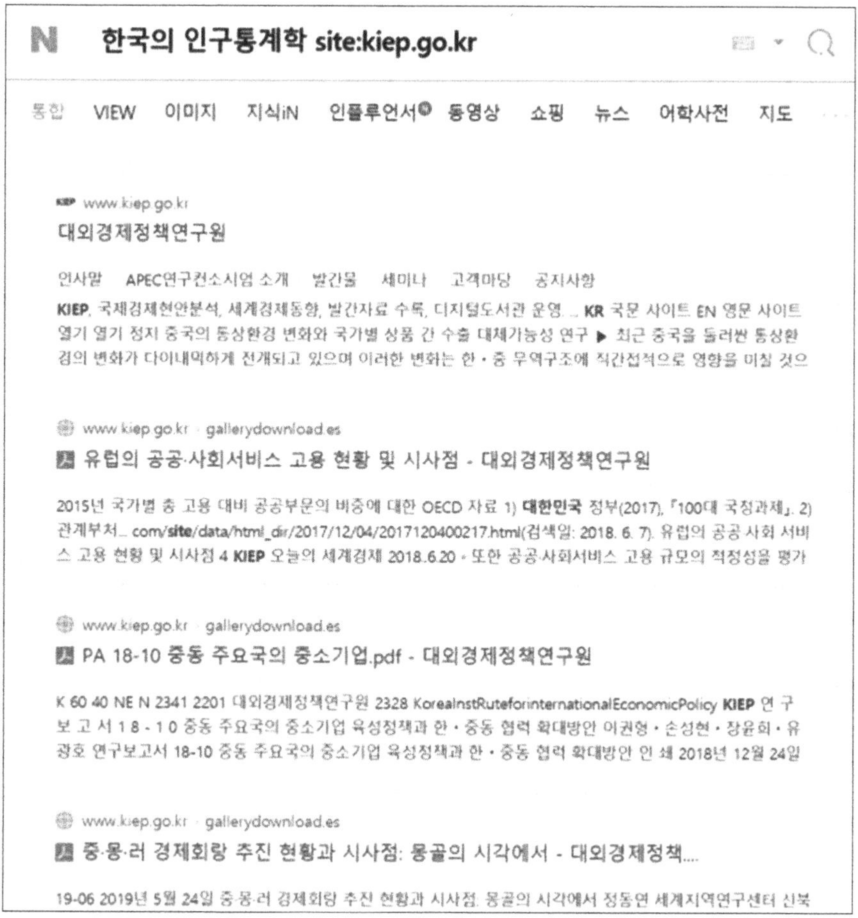

Fig. 3.60 Naver search results for **한국의 인구통계학** *site:kiep.go.kr*, the Korean phrase for *Korean demographics* © NAVER Corp

headers serve the same purpose, but for resources online that are written in code other than HTML, such as web-hosted .pdf files. Sitemaps are lists of URLs contained within the specified website that contain further details about that website, including language and region information. These methods are not required to create multilingual and multiregional websites, however they are highly encouraged to help the search engine optimize the results of searches [14]. As far as the foreign language researcher is concerned, the elements used in each of the three methods are very similar: they all use the *hreflang* tag, just in a different location in the page's code.

The *hreflang* tag specifies the language of the text contained on the website, and sometimes the region [15]. These are contained under the <link> attribute when used as an HTML tag. When this method is used, each language version of the site will have their own hreflang tag, followed by the URL of the site. This is where the web developer has the freedom to specify how they would like to denote the syntax of the URL:

```
<link rel="alternate" hreflang="lang_code" href="url_of_page" />
```

It is best practice for each alternate version of the website to contain the ISO standard language or country code for that language or country. These codes are governed under ISO 639-1 and − 2, and ISO 3166-1 Alpha 2. The ISO 639-1 standard format is a digraph for the language, and − 2 is for the trigraph [16]. The ISO 3166-1 Alpha 2 format is a code for the country or region [17]. These are the same for any of the three recommended methods: HTML tags, HTTP headers, or Sitemaps. The web developer may choose to use only one of these, or may use them together. The benefit of this is to increase the chances that the version of the website returned in the search will contain the most relevant version to that person. The best way to demonstrate how this phenomenon works is through an example.

Consider the Underarmour website, which is available in dozens of languages [18]. The front-facing website makes each language and country version easily accessible on its location navigator page. It is also possible to discover lists of URLs for various language and country codes on the robots.txt pages, which are discussed more in detail later in this book. For now, the URLs associated with the .eu domain are listed at https://www.underarmour.eu/robots.txt:

```
https://www.underarmour.co.uk/en-gb/
https://www.underarmour.de/de-de/
https://www.underarmour.de/en-de/
https://www.underarmour.es/es-es/
https://www.underarmour.es/en-es/
https://www.underarmour.fr/fr-fr/
https://www.underarmour.fr/en-fr/
https://www.underarmour.it/it-it/
https://www.underarmour.it/en-it/
https://www.underarmour.nl/nl-nl/
https://www.underarmour.nl/en-nl/
https://www.underarmour.eu/de-at/
https://www.underarmour.eu/en-at/
https://www.underarmour.eu/en-be/
https://www.underarmour.eu/en-dk/
https://www.underarmour.eu/en-pl/
https://www.underarmour.eu/en-pt/
https://www.underarmour.eu/en-se/
https://www.underarmour.eu/fr-be/
https://www.underarmour.eu/nl-be/
```

The above URLs refer to hreflang tags in the HTML of the websites. Similarly, each one has its own Sitemap. The digraphs immediately following "Underarmour."

represent the domain. The digraph immediately following the slash represents the language code, and the digraph following the dash represents the country code. For example, the second URL using the .de domain, language, and country code in the list is likely for German shoppers in Germany who speak German. On the other hand, the third URL using the .de domain with the EN language code and DE country code is likely for German shoppers in Germany who speak English. What is the target demographic for the other websites in the list?

The reader may notice that the first URL in the list is unlike the others. In this case, the web developer used a different URL format for the website intended for English-speakers in Great Britain. This is because the .co.uk domain is common specifically for websites intended for this demographic. This is another reason the researcher must pay such close attention to URLs and web development basics: each developer has the freedom to customize their website and formatting the way they see fit. Upon further inspection, it is possible to see that versions of the same website made for other regions of the world besides the European Union follow a different format. For example, Australia and New Zealand's versions contain the following formats:

```
https://www.underarmour.com.au/
https://www.underarmour.co.nz/
```

These give clues into how other versions of the Underarmour website may be formatted. To discover other versions that may also use the .com and .co domains along with a country-specific domain, it is possible to use a search technique called *dorks*. Dorks are specific instructions the researcher can use to specify where certain terms or attributes may exist on a website. These are discussed extensively in the following chapter; however, it is appropriate to introduce the *site:* dork here to demonstrate URL formatting and website discoverability. The *site:* dork returns results containing specific references from the specified website. This dork also accepts wildcards, which allow any letter or number combination to exist in its place.

For example, the Google search for *site:underarmour.* * will return all websites whose URL is of the form "Underarmour." followed by any domain type. This reveals the foreign country versions of the Underarmour website that are also of this form. Notice the first three results of the search as shown in Fig. 3.61. The .cz domain is for the Czech Republic, the .id domain is for Indonesia, and the .cl is for Chile. These are only the first three results. The researcher may also notice that the Indonesian website displays English text rather than Indonesian. The researcher is encouraged to attempt this search on their own and explore these websites. Check the URL: what clues exist that the website is intended for English-speakers in Indonesia?

Recall the other forms of the Underarmour website that used the .com and .co domains, followed by a country code. These websites should also be somewhere in the search results of the previous search, but they may be buried tens of thousands of results down the list. To search for these results separately, conduct the two separate searches *site:underarmour.com.* * and *site:underarmour.co.* * as in Figs. 3.62 and 3.63, respectively. Notice how the number of results from each of these searches

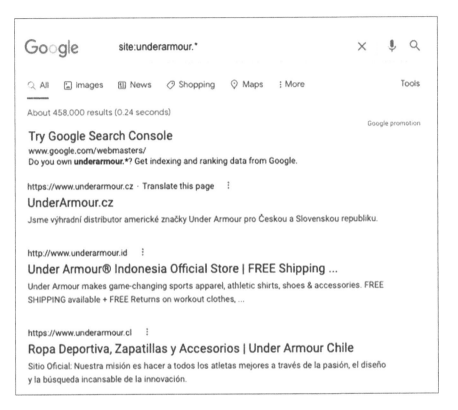

Fig. 3.61 Google search results for *site:underarmour.** (Google and the Google logo are trademarks of Google LLC)

is much smaller than the search for *site:underarmour.**. This is because these searches are much more specific, returning only a subset of the websites discovered in the first search.

As mentioned previously, web developers do not always follow the same rules. Web developers have the freedom to implement language and country coding as they see fit for their specific website. Once the researcher discovers a particular website of interest to their research, the next step is to understand how the website is structured and organized. This helps the researcher tailor their subsequent searches for information on that website. The above search techniques worked for the Underarmour website because this is how that website's URL is structured. This may not work for other websites that are structured differently.

Sometimes, the website will specify the language elsewhere in the URL, or not at all. For example, the University of Luxembourg's website is available in French, German, and English. The URLs for each of these websites are:

French: https://wwwfr.uni.lu/
German: https://wwwde.uni.lu/
English: https://wwwen.uni.lu/

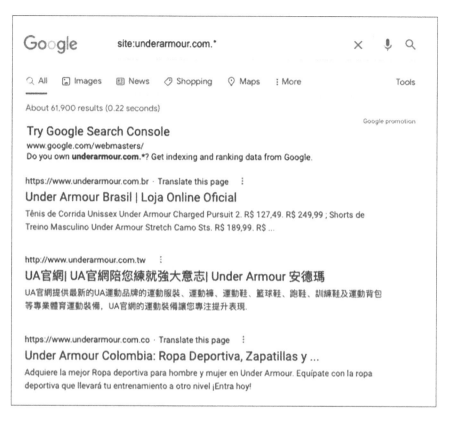

Fig. 3.62 Google search results for *site:*underarmour.com.* (Google and the Google logo are trademarks of Google LLC)

Unlike the Underarmour example, the language designator is sitting immediately with the "www" portion of the URL. Not only that, there is only a language designator in this URL: there is no country or region code. While this URL format is relatively uncommon, it is an example of how web developers have the freedom to designate their language and/or region settings based on their desired results.

On the other hand, a country code should not be used by itself. This is because it is common for the people of a country to speak several languages. As a result, there are no default languages assigned for a country [19]. So in our previous example, it is possible for a website to use only the language code DE for German without a country designator altogether. This depends largely on the web developers' goals and intended audience.

For more on how Google manages website languages and regions, see the developer documentation at https://developers.google.com/search/docs/advanced/crawling/managing-multi-regional-sites and https://developers.google.com/search/docs/advanced/crawling/localized-versions.

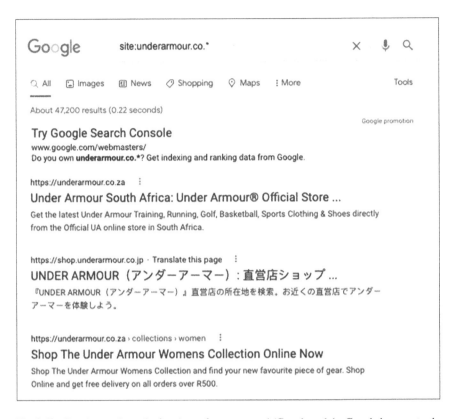

Fig. 3.63 Google search results for *site:underarmour.co.* * (Google and the Google logo are trademarks of Google LLC)

While Google and Yandex support hreflang indexing, Bing does not. Instead, Bing encourages web developers to use HTML tags for foreign language material to be discoverable in its search engine [20]. Bing web developer documentation advises the use of the "content-language" meta tag in the <head> section, along with the ISO standard digraphs previously mentioned. For example, the header may look as follows:

<meta http-equiv="content-language" content="de-de">

This would be for a website in German made for users physically located in Germany. There is also the option to specify the region using the locale element:

<meta property="og:locale" content="de_DE"/>

Bing also gives the option to specify the language and region in the <html> or <title> elements; however, Bing advises against using the "content-language" tag in addition to the <html> and <title> elements. Here's an example directly from Bing documentation [21]:

<html lang="de-de">

<title lang="de-de">

The problem here is that web developers may not implement proper language and country coding for every search engine. As a result, the website that contains the researcher's desired results may appear in the search results conducted in one search engine, but may not appear in another. This all depends on how the web developer of that website prepared the foreign language coding. Knowing this, the researcher must assume that the web developer of the site (that they may not know in advance) has only partially coded their site properly. The researcher would be wise to conduct their searches in multiple search engines based on the structure of how that browser calls language and region settings.

Consider the search for restaurants in the Czech Republic. Ideally, the Czech restaurants that have websites in the Czech language will have the proper HTML tags to make it easy for the researcher to discover them. To demonstrate this requires the introduction of another dork. The *meta:* operator allows the researcher to specify attributes specified in a website's meta tags. This requires the use of parentheses around the attributes. The researcher can also specify key search terms in conjunction with the <meta> attribute.

So, to search for Czech restaurants whose websites are written in the Czech language (and properly specified as such in the <meta> tag), first look up the language and country code for Czech language and Czech Republic, respectively. The Czech language code is CS and the country code for Czech Republic is CZ. Next, using an online translator, find the Czech word for *restaurant* [22]. With this information, our search parameters are: *restaurace meta:(cs-cz)*, the results of which are shown in Fig. 3.64.

Notice there are 15,200 results. Upon further inspection, only some of the top results point to Czech restaurants, but the ones that do not point to services where one might discover more restaurants.

Meta tag searches are unique to Bing. They do not work in Google, DuckDuckGo, Yahoo, or other search engines.

3.8   Locating Links to Websites with link:

The *link:* operator returns websites that contain a linked URL to the specified domain. Many websites have links to other websites. Any clickable link from the specified website will be included in results using the link: operator. This can be helpful when searching for resources that cite or link to a particular resource of interest. This section will use the example of the American think tank, Rand Corporation. Figure 3.65 shows the results of the search for all websites containing the key words *Russian* and *demographics* that also link to any page on the rand.org website.

All results shown contain the specified key terms on websites that contain links to rand.org. Not surprisingly, many Rand articles also link to themselves, which is

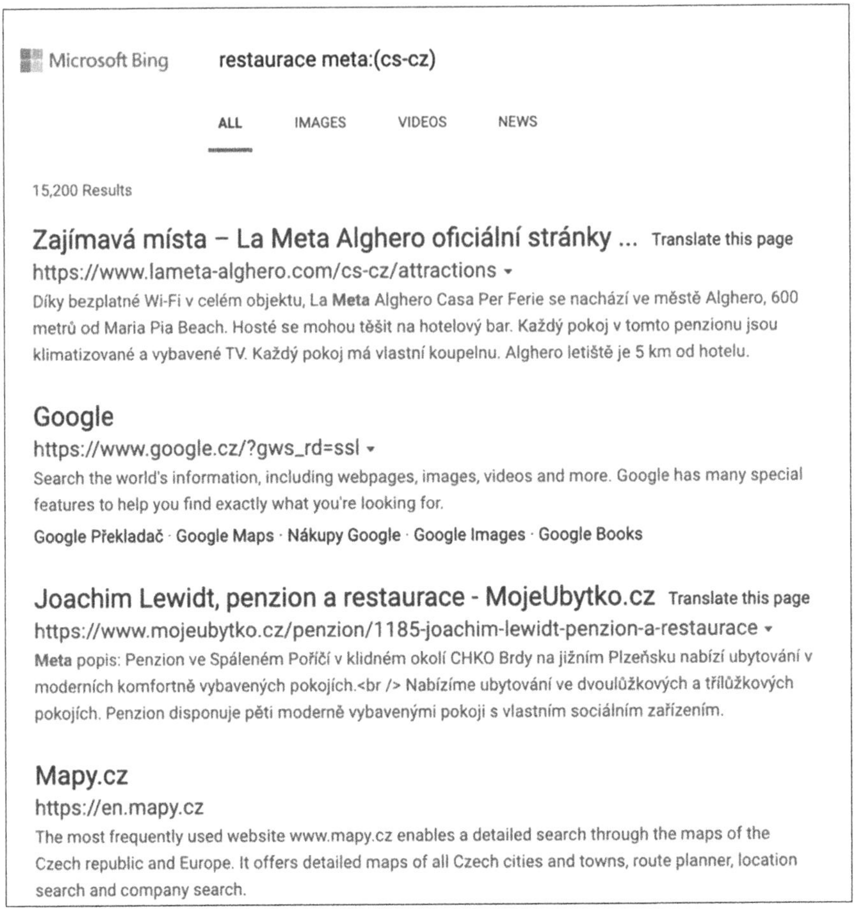

Fig. 3.64 Bing search results for *restaurace meta:(cs-cz)* [23] © Microsoft 2021

the reason so many results from this search are from the rand.org website itself. To eliminate these results from the search, it is possible to use two dorks at once, along with the minus sign explored earlier. Recall that the minus sign will exclude certain results from a search. Additionally, the site: operator will include results from a specified website. As a result, adding *-site:rand.org* to the end of the search will return all websites containing the desired key terms that link to rand.org, excluding rand.org. Figure 3.66 demonstrates the results of this search.

None of the results from the search above are from the rand.org website, however, they all contain links to the rand.org website somewhere on the page. Again, this may be helpful when trying to discover related resources, or resources that also cite a resource that is of interest to the researcher.

The link: operator only works in Google; it does not work in StartPage, Yahoo, Bing, DuckDuckGo, or Baidu. So, it may be reasonable to start the search for linked sites in Google, and then continue the research in the appropriate search engine.

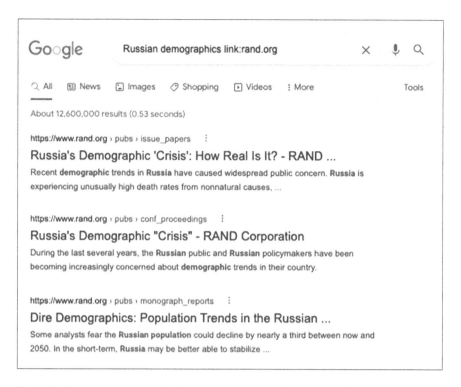

Fig. 3.65 Google search results for *Russian demographics link:*rand.org (Google and the Google logo are trademarks of Google LLC)

3.9   Discovering Related Websites with related:

One very useful tool is the related: operator, which returns the home pages of websites related to the specified site. This is particularly helpful when searching for alternate sources similar to the one the researcher already knows. Recall the example using rand.org. Rand Corporation is a prominent American think tank that publishes analytic pieces and finished reports on global national security issues. There are dozens of other think tanks that do similar work. If the researcher had exhausted their research on Rand products, they may be able to discover websites belonging to similar think tanks using the related: operator.

Figure 3.67 shows the top results for the search *related:rand.org*. Notice that there are about 32 results, which is a manageable list of websites for further exploration. The related: operator is unique to Google; it does not work in any other search engines. Even in Google, it does not work on every website. Still, it is worthy of trial and error.

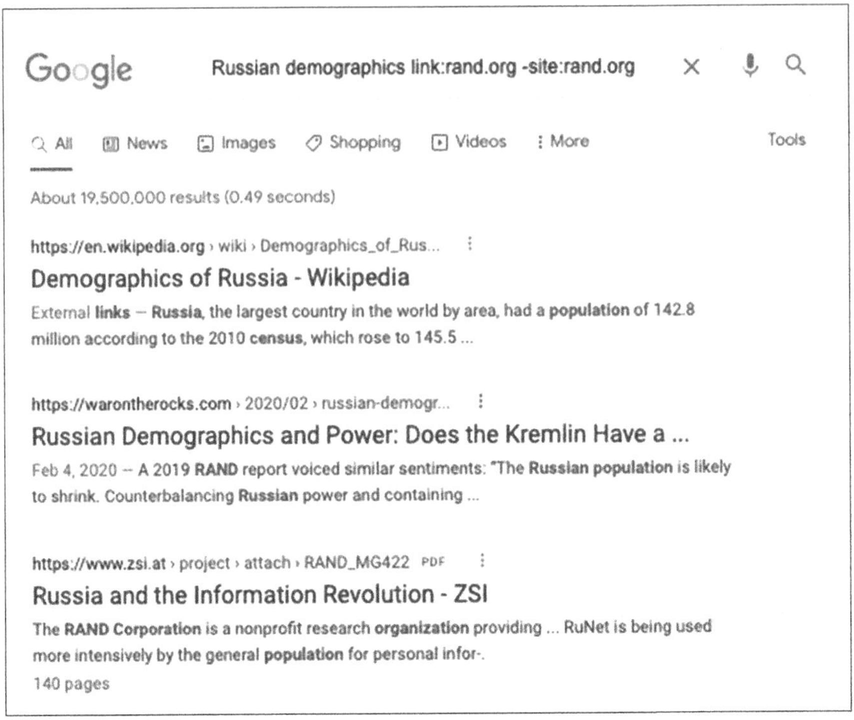

Google Russian demographics link:rand.org -site:rand.org ✕ 🎤 🔍

🔍 All 📰 News 🖼 Images 🛒 Shopping ▶ Videos ⋮ More Tools

About 19,500,000 results (0.49 seconds)

https://en.wikipedia.org › wiki › Demographics_of_Rus... ⋮
Demographics of Russia - Wikipedia
External **links** — **Russia**, the largest country in the world by area, had a **population** of 142.8 million according to the 2010 **census**, which rose to 145.5 ...

https://warontherocks.com › 2020/02 › russian-demogr... ⋮
Russian Demographics and Power: Does the Kremlin Have a ...
Feb 4, 2020 – A 2019 **RAND** report voiced similar sentiments: "The **Russian population** is likely to shrink. Counterbalancing **Russian** power and containing ...

https://www.zsi.at › project › attach › RAND_MG422 PDF ⋮
Russia and the Information Revolution - ZSI
The **RAND Corporation** is a nonprofit research **organization** providing ... RuNet is being used more intensively by the general **population** for personal infor-.
140 pages

Fig. 3.66 Google search results for *Russian demographics link:*rand.org *-site:*rand.org (Google and the Google logo are trademarks of Google LLC)

3.10 Specifying Search Language with lang: or language:

The *lang:* or *language:* dork allows the researcher to specify the desired language of all search results. This feature only works if the website's author has properly coded their website with the proper language codes, which is why this book recommends conducting searches using keywords in the target language first. In most cases, searching for a key term in a language that does not match the language code yields less useful results; the lang: and language: dorks function best when used with key words in the language matching the language code used with the operator. As previously demonstrated throughout this section, searches using key words in the target language already yields results in the target language, even when the lang: or language: operators are not in use. Nevertheless, a discussion of dorks pertaining to foreign language research cannot omit this operator.

The lang: and language: dorks do not currently work in Google, StartPage, or Baidu; however, they do work in DuckDuckGo, Bing, and Yandex. In DuckDuckGo and Bing, use the language: operator, and in Yandex, use the lang: operator. The

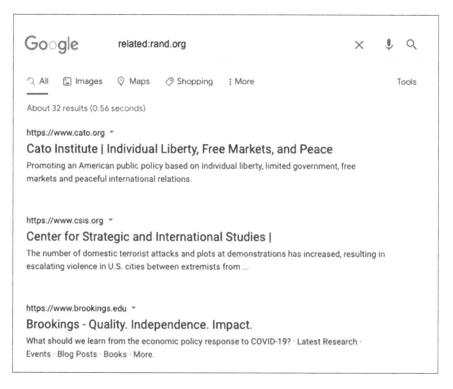

Fig. 3.67 Google search results for *related:*rand.org (Google and the Google logo are trademarks of Google LLC)

language codes used are those consistent with the ISO 639 standard, which is the international standard for language and country codes published by the International Organization for Standardization (ISO). Some common codes are listed in Table 3.1, however a complete list is available online by searching for the ISO 639 standard.

Since the current topic is related to Russian demographics, let's conduct a search using the lang: operator in Yandex. Ideally, the search *Russian demographics lang:ru* should return results on the topic of Russian demographics only in the Russian language, even though the search terms are in English. Figure 3.68 shows that most, but not all results, are in Russian. The sixth result, which is a Wikipedia page, is in English. The URL of the site even contains the English language code EN. Upon further inspection, the page does contain some Russian-language text, even though the page is written primarily in English. This is the likely reason this website is included in the results.

Another possible reason that the English-language version of the Wikipedia page appears in the list of results for this search is because the key search terms are in English. When the key terms and the language code do not match, this confuses the search engine. This is apparent in the results of the same search using the

Table 3.1 List of common ISO 639 language codes [24]

Language	Code
English	en
Spanish	es
Arabic	ar
Chinese	zh
Russian	ru
French	fr
German	de
Korean	ko
Farsi	fa

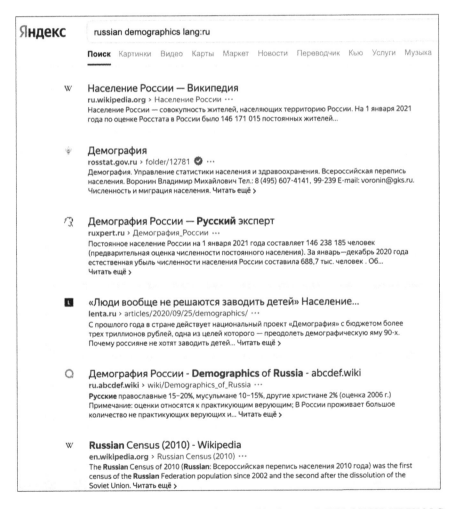

Fig. 3.68 Yandex search results for *Russian demographics lang:ru* © 2015–2022 YANDEX LLC

Fig. 3.69 Yandex search results for *демография россии lang:ru* © 2015–2022 YANDEX LLC

Russian-language search terms (where the search terms and language code both match). Figure 3.69 shows the top results of this search.

Another distinction between these two searches is the number of results returned. The number of results returned from the search using English-language terms was 3 million; the number of results returned from the search using Russian-language terms was only 36,000. It appears that there are so many more results in the first case because the search containing the English-language key terms and the Russian-language code returned all websites containing the English and Russian-language text. In other words, any website written in English that also contains any Russian-language text will also be included in the results. These results are omitted from the second search, which is why there are such fewer results returned. Each search has its own value: conduct whichever search suits the needs of the research project at that time. The key takeaway is to understand how either configuration changes the results, with the goal of constructing the best search possible.

3.11   Discovering Results from a Specified Date with before:, after:, date:, and inurl:

The *before:*, *after:*, and *date:* operators narrow the results to a specified date or date range in Google only. The format for the date is YYYY-MM-DD, where YYYY represents the four-digit year, MM represents the two-digit month, and DD represents the two-digit day. It is also possible to specify the year only (i.e. by omitting the MM-DD portions). Doing so is equivalent to conducting the search YYYY-01-01, that is, January 1 of the identified year. The date: operator works in Yandex in the same format without the dashes. That is, it uses the format YYMMDD, and allows the use of wildcards. The reason date ranges are important in the foreign-language research context is because time adds additional context to the research question.

For example, Russian demographics have changed significantly over time. If the researcher were interested in narrowing search results to those that discuss Russia's demographics the decade prior to the collapse of the Soviet Union, they could specify the date range from December 26, 1981 to December 26, 1991. Figure 3.70 demonstrates that the top results were published during this time frame. Results need not be published within the specified time frame; they may also discuss the

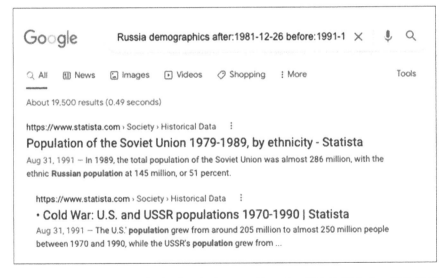

Fig. 3.70 Google search results for *Russia demographics after:1981-12-26 before:1991-12-26* (Google and the Google logo are trademarks of Google LLC)

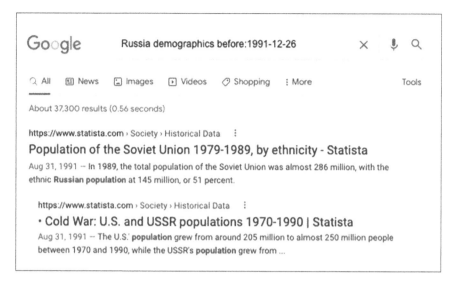

Fig. 3.71 Google search results for *Russia demographics before:1991-12-26* (Google and the Google logo are trademarks of Google LLC)

time period specified in the search. For example, an article published in 2020 that discusses Russia's demographics between 1981 and 1991 may also appear in the list of results.

It is not necessary to use both after: and before: in the same search. For example, it is possible to conduct the search *Russian demographics before:1991-12-26* with no start date for the date range. This will return all web pages containing the specified key terms before December 26, 1991. Figure 3.71 shows the top results for this search. In this case, the top few results are the same; however, the second search using only the before: operator returned more results because the search was not limited to results dated prior to 1981.

As with most other dorks discussed in this section, the before: and after: operators also work with foreign-language searches. Consider the Russian-language search *демография россии after:1981-12-26 before:1991-12-26* as shown in Fig. 3.72.

In the Russian-language search, most results are in Russian. All results appear to come from the specified time period, which was the purpose of the search.

Let's conduct similar searches, this time using Yandex [25]. The search *демография россии date:19911226* returns results containing the key terms for Russian and demographics on December 26, 1991. Figure 3.73 shows there is only one result: a Wiki page that contains historical demographics data. If this were exactly the information the researcher sought, it would be much easier to examine this one website than it would be to examine a list of millions of results.

If the one result shown from the previous search was too specific, the researcher could alter the parameters to search for all websites before or after the specified

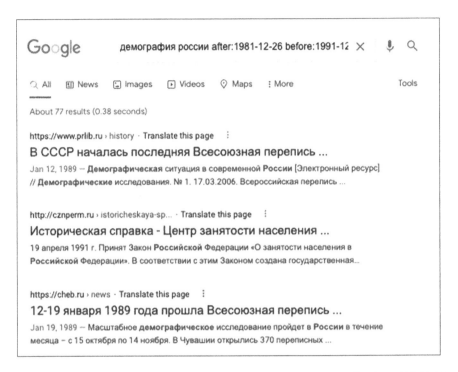

Fig. 3.72 Google search results for *демография россии after:1981-12-26 before:1991-12-26* (Google and the Google logo are trademarks of Google LLC)

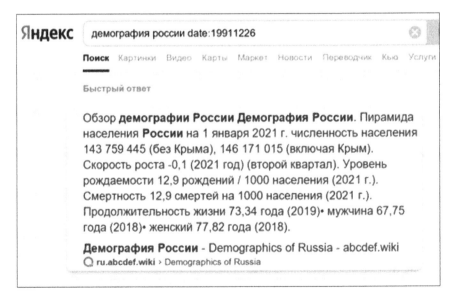

Fig. 3.73 Yandex search results for *демография россии date:19911226* © 2015–2022 YANDEX LLC

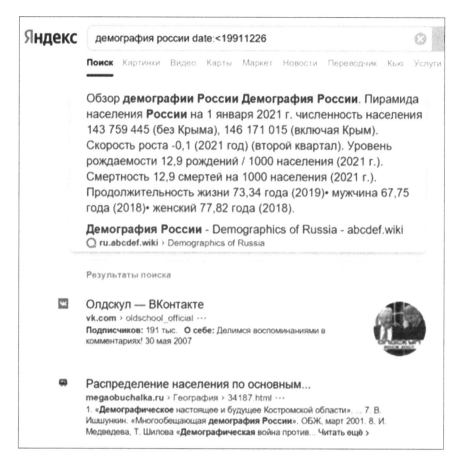

Fig. 3.74 Yandex search results for *демография россии date:<19911226* © 2015–2022 YANDEX LLC

date. To do this, add the < immediately after the colon to locate websites before the date, and > to locate websites after the date. The search *демография россии date:<19911226* returns results pertaining to Russian demographics before the collapse of the Soviet Union. Figure 3.74 shows the top few results of this search in Yandex.

Still, this search is quite broad: while there are only 11 results, depending on the topic and the date, it is easy to see that all resources before a certain date may still be too broad. When this is the case, the researcher can specify a specified date range using two dots between the dates. The search *демография россии date:19911226..20011226* returns all results on the topic of Russia's demographics within the 10 years following the collapse of the Soviet Union. There were around 2000 results, the top few of which are shown in Fig. 3.75.

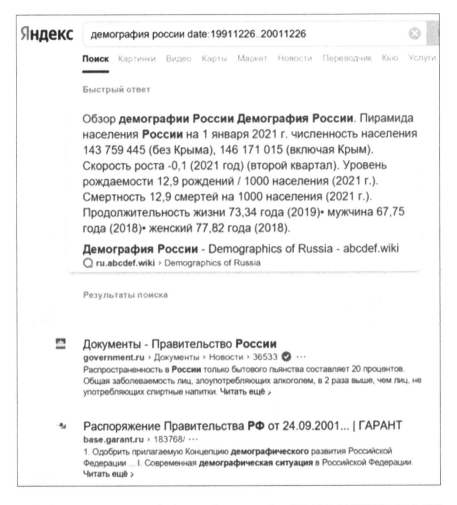

Fig. 3.75 Yandex search results for *демография россии date:19911226..20011226* © 2015–2022 YANDEX LLC

The final Yandex search introduced in this section is the use of the wildcard. When the exact day of the month does not matter, insert the wildcard (or asterisk) in place of the day. For example, the search *демография россии date:199112** will return results from the entire month of December 1991. This is equivalent to the search *date:19911201..19911231*. Figure 3.76 shows the top few results of this search, of which there are only three.

The before: and after: operators work best in Google. Yahoo has a filter below the search bar where the researcher can select a time period from the past day, past week, or past month. StartPage has a similar filter below the search bar where the researcher can select a time period from the past 24-hours, past week, past month, or past year. Bing's date-range options are similar: it also has a custom range option,

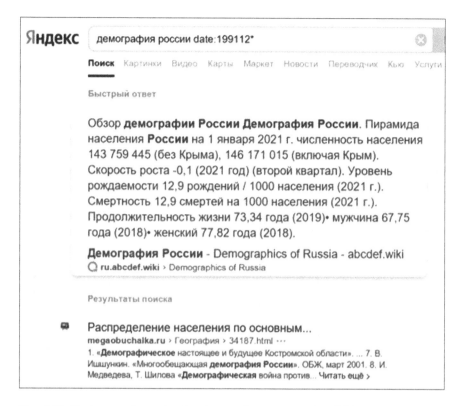

Fig. 3.76 Yandex search results for *демография россии date:199112** (© 2015–2022 YANDEX LLC)

but this only goes back as far as one year from the current date. DuckDuckGo has an option below the search bar to specify a date range, even though it is not entered directly into the search bar. Figure 3.77 below shows the custom date range option in DuckDuckGo along with the English-language search for *Russian demographics*.

Another way to locate documents from a particular date or date range is by searching the content of URLs. Often, websites that host many documents or reports, such as news outlets, organize their files and websites by inserting the date as part of the URL. So, a key word search with the operator *inurl:2008/10* may return websites published in October 2008. Let's conduct this search with the English-language key terms Russian demographics. Figure 3.78 shows the top results of this search.

Sure enough, many websites returned were published in October 2008. The URLs for the first four results demonstrate how websites such as these organize their URLs by date. The first URL is dated October 1, 2008, and the URL for the

Fig. 3.77 DuckDuckGo search for *Russian demographics* and the date range December 26, 1981 to December 26, 1991 © DuckDuckGo

article contains the year and month the article was published. The New York Times and Pew Research Center, on the other hand, include the year, month, and date of publication in the URL. The search returned these results because their URLs contained this exact structure. This is because these websites organize their articles in this fashion. The researcher will be happy to know that many web content providers organize their pages this way.

1. https://www.theatlantic.com/daily-dish/archive/2008/10/not-a-great-power/210899/
2. https://www.nytimes.com/2008/10/25/opinion/25eberstadt.html
3. https://www.nytimes.com/2008/10/13/world/europe/13russia.html
4. https://www.pewresearch.org/hispanic/2008/10/22/latinos-account-for-half-of-us-population-growth-since-2000/

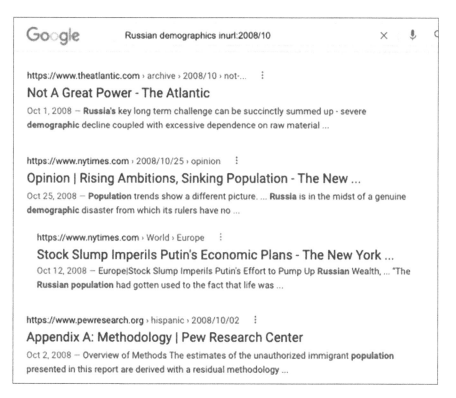

Fig. 3.78   Google search results for *Russian demographics inurl:2008/10* (Google and the Google logo are trademarks of Google LLC)

Knowing how each of these websites organizes their articles, it is possible to conduct targeted searches by date on any of these websites using the inurl: operator. This method will work in search engines that do not have robust date search capabilities, but do support a URL search operator.

3.12   Discovering Topical Books with book: and the Google Books Database

The *book:* operator suggests books relating to a specified topic and is unique to the Google search engine. This operator does not work on all key terms, and spelling and VPNs also impact the results returned. When using this operator, the researcher should be aware of spelling alternatives to their key terms and try different spellings to increase the relevancy of the results. In the context of Russian demographics, the book: operator actually returns more useful results for the key term *demography* rather than *demographics*. There are also differences in the results when using the

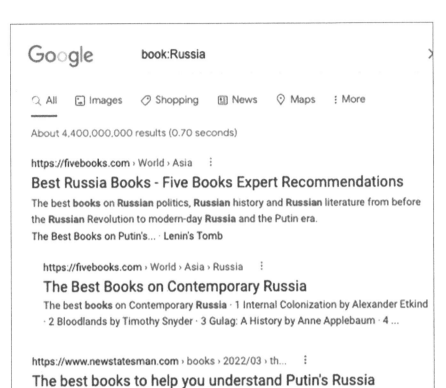

Fig. 3.79 Google search results for *book:Russia*. (Google and the Google logo are trademarks of Google LLC)

term *Russia* versus *Russian*. For example, consider the Google search for *book:Russia* as shown in Fig. 3.79. There are about 1 billion results, the top results for which are from book publishers and other websites containing information on books.

Now consider the search *book:Russian* as shown in Fig. 3.80. Google has returned a list of books along the top of the page, indicating that the search engine has indexed these books using the word *Russian*, not *Russia*. Still, it appears that Google has returned some popular fiction literature in the English language, which is still not very relevant to research on Russian demographics.

It is also possible to use the book: operator with foreign-language search terms. Consider the search *book:россия*, using the Russian word for *Russia* (the country). Some of the top books are similar as in the English-language search, but the top website does differ and some of the books in the list are also different. Still, the results are primarily in English, as shown in Fig. 3.81.

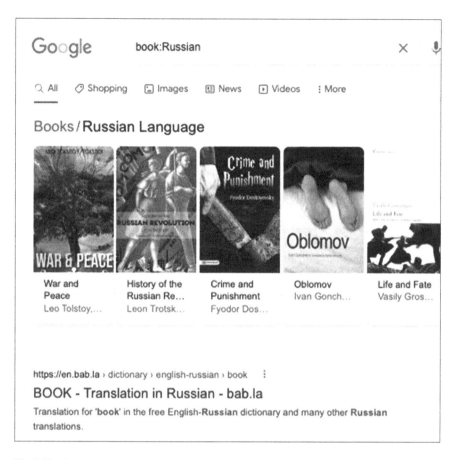

Fig. 3.80 Google search results for *book:Russian*. (Google and the Google logo are trademarks of Google LLC)

As demonstrated earlier in this book, VPNs, or Virtual Private Networks, do have an impact on results returned. The reason for this is because the Google search engine is attempting to return results it believes are most relevant to the researcher. Google will assume that a researcher physically located in the United States may not be so interested in bookstores in Moscow: this is why these results do not appear on the top of the list from searches such as those in this section. However, the same search as the one above set with a Russian VPN returns a list of bookstores in Moscow. Figure 3.82 shows the sample output from this search.

Still, none of these searches so far contained any books relating specifically to Russian demographics. Let's conduct a more tailored search to narrow the scope of books returned on this subject. There are a few ways to do this. One way is to use the book: operator with other operators. Another is to use the book: operator multiple times in the same search when the research subject contains more than one

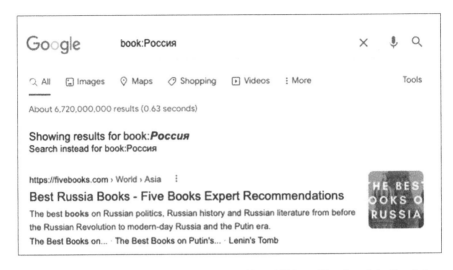

Fig. 3.81 Google search results for *book:Россия* with no VPN set. (Google and the Google logo are trademarks of Google LLC)

Fig. 3.82 Google search results for *book:россия* with a VPN located in Russia (Google and the Google logo are trademarks of Google LLC)

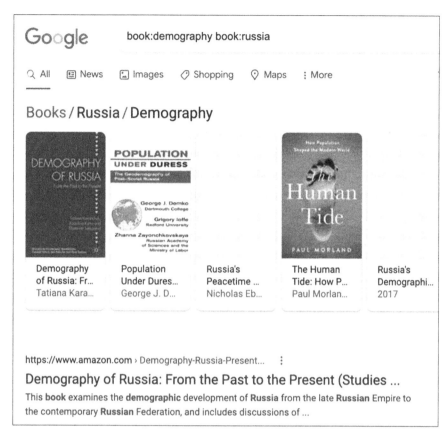

Fig. 3.83 Google search results for *book:demography book:Russia* (Google and the Google logo are trademarks of Google LLC)

word. For example, the search *book:demography* would only return books on the subject of demography in general; it would not return books specific to Russian demographics. Similarly, the search *book:Russia* would only return books on Russia in general, and it would not be likely for these books to be on the topic of demographics issues. The search *book:demography book:Russia* yields results that are more relevant to the research topic in this section (the Russia VPN now turned off). Figure 3.83 shows the top results of this search.

Figure 3.83 shows the results for the search using the book: operator twice. The top results are now much more related to the topic of Russian demographics. The "Books/Russia/Demography" label on top also indicates that this is a well-known subject in the Google Books index. Let's say the researcher were interested in Russian books on demographics published in the years leading up to the collapse of the Soviet Union. It is possible to narrow down the list of books even further by specifying the desired date range. Figure 3.84 expands upon the same search above,

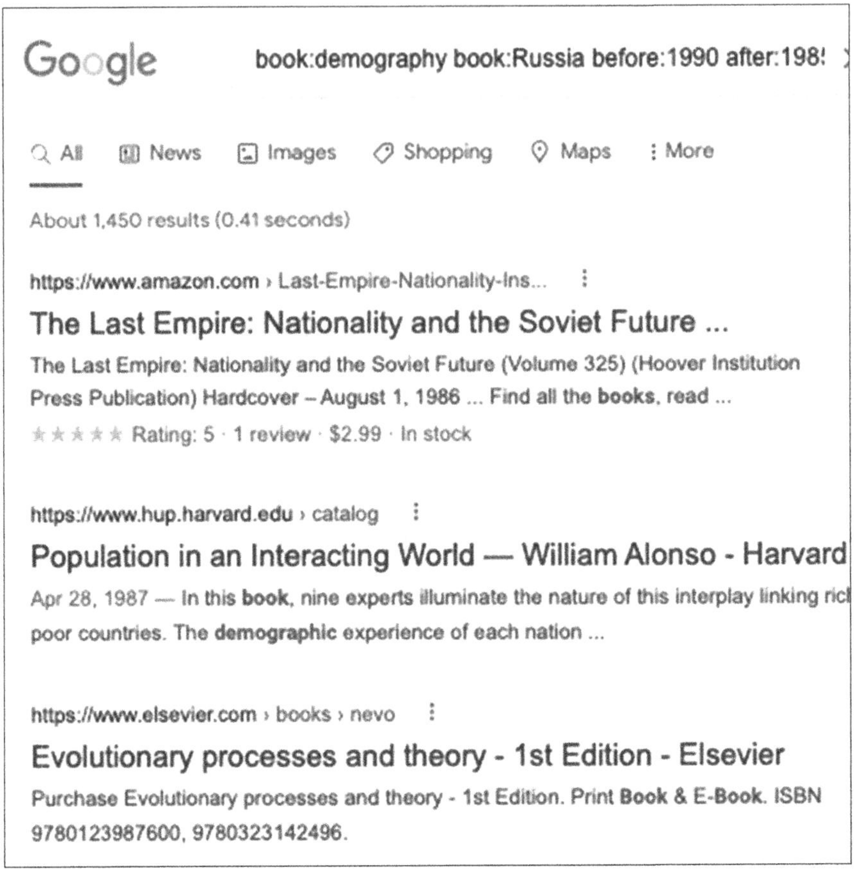

Google   book:demography book:Russia before:1990 after:198!)

Q All   ☷ News   ⌷ Images   ⊘ Shopping   ⊙ Maps   ⋮ More

About 1,450 results (0.41 seconds)

https://www.amazon.com › Last-Empire-Nationality-Ins...   ⋮

The Last Empire: Nationality and the Soviet Future ...

The Last Empire: Nationality and the Soviet Future (Volume 325) (Hoover Institution
Press Publication) Hardcover – August 1, 1986 ... Find all the **books**, read ...

★ ★ ★ ★ ★ Rating: 5 · 1 review · $2.99 · In stock

https://www.hup.harvard.edu › catalog   ⋮

Population in an Interacting World — William Alonso - Harvard

Apr 28, 1987 — In this **book**, nine experts illuminate the nature of this interplay linking rich
poor countries. The **demographic** experience of each nation ...

https://www.elsevier.com › books › nevo   ⋮

Evolutionary processes and theory - 1st Edition - Elsevier

Purchase Evolutionary processes and theory - 1st Edition. Print **Book & E-Book**. ISBN
9780123987600, 9780323142496.

Fig. 3.84 Google search results for *book:demography book:russia before:1990 after:1985*
(Google and the Google logo are trademarks of Google LLC)

this time using the before: and after: operators to narrow down the date range
between 1985 and 1990.

In the search shown in Fig. 3.84, the first book appears to be published in 1986,
the second was published in 1987, and so on. This narrowed down the list of results
greatly, making it easier to locate books more related to the desired date range.

Since Google Books is itself a service that Google provides, it is also possible to
conduct multiple keyword searches directly into the Google Books database, located
at https://books.google.com/. Figure 3.85 shows the Google Books homepage, and
Fig. 3.86 shows the top results of this search.

The search results in Fig. 3.86 are all on the topic of Russian demographics in the
English language, and the book: operator was not required at all. Google Books also
supports foreign-language search terms, as shown in Fig. 3.87.

Fig. 3.85 Google Books home page, located at https://books.google.com/ (Google and the Google logo are trademarks of Google LLC)

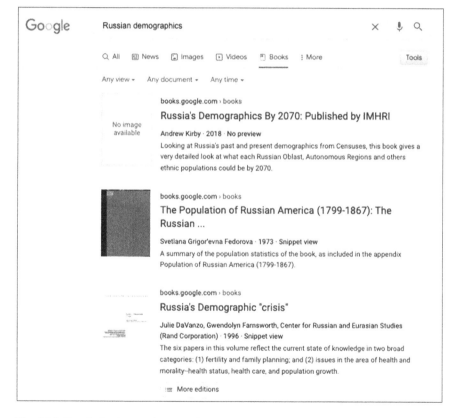

Fig. 3.86 Google Books search results for *Russian demographics* (Google and the Google logo are trademarks of Google LLC)

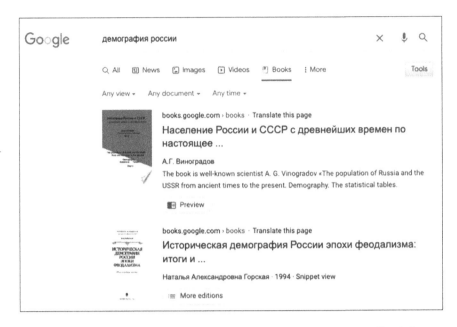

Fig. 3.87 Google Books search results for *демография россии* (Google and the Google logo are trademarks of Google LLC)

The results of the Russian-language search are also in Russian, and offer a list of completely different books. The researcher should consider both list of works in their research.

One final feature in Google Books that is the document type. Google Books separates books, magazines, and newspapers. Depending on the topic, the researcher may also be interested in discovering the content of other resources to diversify the list of references they cite in their products. Figure 3.88 shows the drop-down menu located directly beneath the search bar. Consider exploring the other features built into Google Books.

3.13 Locating Results Geographically with loc:

The *loc:* operator specifies the geographic location of the results. This differs from the *site:* operator, which only looks for the domain registration. As will be discussed in the next chapter, not all domain registrations are necessarily specific to a certain location. For example, the .com domain, which is among the most commonly used, is not necessarily associated with a country or language. Even certain domains that are associated with a certain country need be located in a certain place. This is where the loc: operator comes into play.

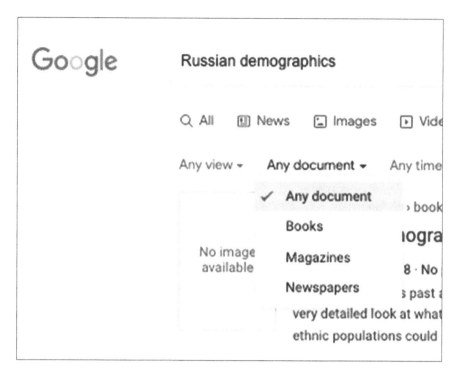

Fig. 3.88 Google Books document type feature dropdown menu (Google and the Google logo are trademarks of Google LLC)

This operator works only in the Bing search engine, which is something to keep in mind when deciding which search engine to use for a specified problem. Not all foreign-language searches require location-focused results. Still, this is another good justification to perform similar searches in various search engines.

Consider the search for real estate located in Hungary, using the English-language search term for real estate. Figure 3.89 shows how the top result is focused on prop-erties for sale in Hungary, where the geographic location of the results is focused specifically in Hungary. It just so happens in this example that some of the top results are also registered using the .hu domain, but this was not a requirement.

Now consider a similar search, this time using the country-code for Slovakia, SK, as shown in Fig. 3.90. The top result focuses specifically on real estate available in Slovakia, and demonstrates how the loc: and site: operators differ. Namely, the focus of the results is the geographic location of the search term, not the domain registration. While the domain can often be an important measure of the relevancy of certain results to a research topic, they are not the only factor. Using the site: operator may exclude certain results that would otherwise be relevant and interest-ing. In this case and many others like it, conducting both searches may be beneficial.

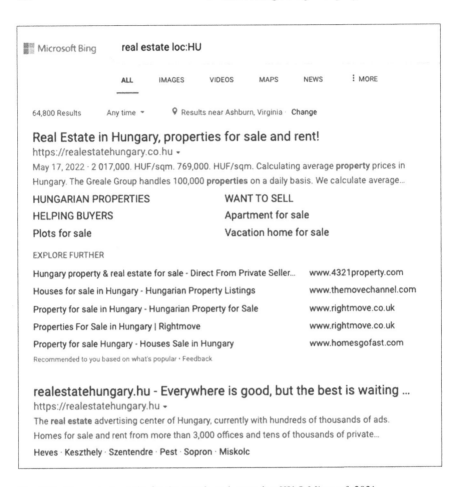

Fig. 3.89 Bing search results for the search *real estate loc:HU* © Microsoft 2021

Finally, let's conduct the similar search using the *loc:* operator and the Slovak word for real estate, *nehnuteľnosť* as shown in Fig. 3.91. When using the foreign-language word and the *loc:* operator combined, the top results tend to correlate more closely to those that a native within that country may see. This would most likely be more valuable in a search where there is a geographic nexus to the problem.

This chapter introduced some of the most useful advanced search operators in the context of several popular search engines. Next, let's discuss country-specific domains and non-Latin character domains.

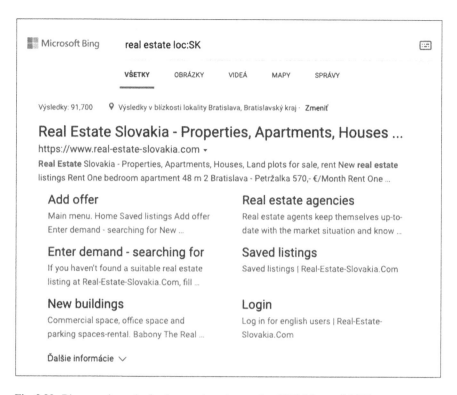

Fig. 3.90 Bing search results for the search *real estate loc:SK* © Microsoft 2021

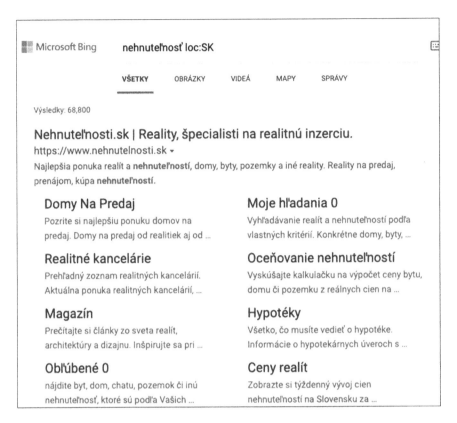

Fig. 3.91 Bing search results for the search *nehnuteľnosť loc:SK* © Microsoft 2021

Online Database References

1. "Демография [Demographics]," last modified September 3, 2020, https://en.wiktionary.org/wiki/демография.
2. Ibid.
3. This same concept will also work for the intitle: and allintitle: operators.
4. View the official documentation on Yandex text searches at https://yandex.com/support/search/query-language/search-context.html.
5. "MARC 21 Specifications for Record Structure, Character Sets, and Exchange Media," December 2007, https://memory.loc.gov/diglib/codetables/4E.html.
6. "DuckDuckGo Search Syntax," accessed May 6, 2021, https://help.duckduckgo.com/duckduckgo-help-pages/results/syntax/.
7. "Advanced Search: Which search operators are supported by Startpage?," last modified September 13, 2021, https://support.startpage.com/index.php?/Knowledgebase/Article/View/989/0/which-search-operators-are-supported-by-startpage.
8. ProgrammerSought, "Baidu search tips," accessed May 6, 2021, https://www.programmer-sought.com/article/61052619397/.
9. "Search pages and sites," accessed May 6, 2021, https://yandex.com/support/search/query-language/qlanguage.html.
10. "Advanced search keywords," accessed May 6, 2021, https://help.bing.microsoft.com/#apex/bing/en-us/10001/-1.
11. "Indexable File Formats," accessed May 6, 2021, https://www.google.com/support/enterprise/static/gsa/docs/admin/current/gsa_doc_set/file_formats/file_formats.html.
12. "Search by date, language, and file type," accessed May 6, 2021, https://yandex.com/support/search/query-language/search-operators.html.
13. "Managing multi-regional and multilingual sites," accessed May 6, 2021, https://developers.google.com/search/docs/advanced/crawling/managing-multi-regional-sites.
14. "Tell Google about localized versions of your page," accessed May 6, 2021, https://developers.google.com/search/docs/advanced/crawling/localized-versions.
15. Ibid.
16. A list of language codes (digraph and trigraph) is available at https://www.loc.gov/standards/iso639-2/php/English_list.php.
17. A list of country codes is available directly on the ISO website at https://www.iso.org/obp/ui/#search.
18. "Please Select Your Location," accessed May 13, 2021, https://www.underarmour.fr/en-fr/change-location.html.
19. "Supported language/region codes," accessed May 13, 2021, https://developers.google.com/search/docs/advanced/crawling/localized-versions#language-codes.
20. See Rachel Costello, "Hreflang," October 26, 2018, https://www.deepcrawl.com/knowledge/technical-seo-library/hreflang/.
21. "How To Tell Bing Your Website's Country and Language," March 1, 2011, https://blogs.bing.com/webmaster/2011/03/01/how-to-tell-bing-your-websites-country-and-language/.
22. For more on online translation options, see Chapter 5 of this book.
23. Search conducted with VPN set to Czechia.
24. Language codes from "ISO-639 Language Codes," accessed May 15, 2021, https://docs.oracle.com/cd/E13214_01/wli/docs92/xref/xqisocodes.html#wp1252447.
25. Syntax from the official Yandex Support website can be found at https://yandex.com/support/search/query-language/search-operators.html

Chapter 4
Country-Specific Domains and Non-Latin-Character Domains

Search engines can detect the researcher's physical location in the world based on their computer's IP address. The search engine returns results based on the researcher's geolocation, making assumptions about the results it *thinks* the researcher will most likely want to see. For example, a researcher located in New York conducting a search for "volunteer events" will see results primarily in the New York area, even if the query does not include the phrase "in New York." To see volunteer events outside of New York, the researcher will have to specify their desired location in the search query. This method will only work if the desired results are in English—if the researcher is trying to find volunteer opportunities in Estonia or Greece, for example, they should conduct a targeted search specifically on Estonian or Greek websites. One way to do this is using country-specific domains, or non-Latin-character domains.

According to the ISC's 2019 report, there are 1,012,695,272 websites online (see Fig. 4.1) [1]. Most of these do not use the standard .com and .net domains:

Sites registered with each of the above domains are largely affiliated with countries or services. Generally, Internet users are aware of the domain affiliated with their country, and they are comfortable visiting and creating websites with these domains. Sometimes, country-specific domains are a symbol of national pride.

Take for example Canada's campaign to encourage Canadians to register their websites with the .ca domain instead of .com. The campaign criticized any Canadian who wittingly registered their website using .com, .net, or another domain. The campaign showed RCMP officers pouring maple syrup—a symbol of Canada—on computers displaying the .com domain. Campaigns such as this recognize the value of affiliating websites with domains that citizens of a certain country can trust. These domains are also affiliated with certain platforms or goals, such as the .us domain, which appeals to those with "dreams to chase, ideas to share, and businesses to promote." This paints a very American image, pointing its customers to achieving the American dream by registering with the .us domain [2].

M. D. Miller, *Discovering Hidden Gems in Foreign Languages*, Terrorism, Security, and Computation, https://doi.org/10.1007/978-3-031-18479-6_4

Domain	Hosts =	All - Hosts	Dup Names	Level 2 Domains	Level 3 Domains	
TOTAL	1012695272	1077730537	65035265	4832503	121929359	
net	367709849	376265314	8555465	306335	63743254	Networks
com	171764916	193223063	21458147	2892775	23341686	Commercial
jp	74749861	74914275	164414	60402	1243484	Japan
de	44753593	44875251	121658	150103	2265608	Germany
br	36307426	36948579	641153	508	257810	Brazil
it	25103710	25159545	55835	39393	657436	Italy
fr	21101768	21216185	114417	41715	625312	France
cn	19812950	21385254	1572304	8836	23749	China
mx	17918753	19266502	1347749	2691	109655	Mexico
ar	14488605	14711480	222875	41	15419	Argentina
au	14429786	14867783	437997	77	74847	Australia
nl	12329780	12548732	218952	63913	2960981	Netherlands
pl	11240083	11305338	65255	27936	1882133	Poland
edu	10635693	10996207	360514	9044	3248976	Educational
ru	10510317	11174765	664448	86063	2625128	Russian Federation
ca	10033516	10387096	353580	38133	1085731	Canada
in	8360182	8924006	563824	12184	73387	India
tr	6922403	6943540	21137	29	7674	Turkey
tw	6780226	6852022	71796	1586	27865	Taiwan, Province Of China
co	6673396	6993222	319826	9427	32744	Colombia
za	6197417	6268058	70641	48	22616	South Africa
se	5521773	5608922	87149	12430	341231	Sweden
be	5362014	5384917	22903	21951	144671	Belgium
ch	5230569	5336918	106349	25871	1302078	Switzerland
uk	5158243	6206332	1048089	1558	108360	United Kingdom
eg	4989280	5004756	15476	39	798	Egypt
es	4497723	4520594	22871	12307	546872	Spain
fi	3980155	4001608	21453	11336	1818068	Finland
pt	3820151	3837388	17237	7294	261028	Portugal
at	3650990	3669590	18600	25815	352943	Austria
no	3422043	3450893	28850	11413	247748	Norway
th	3377426	3389538	12112	19	4607	Thailand
cl	3313332	3395473	82141	10569	66045	Chile
nz	2935395	3454503	519108	429	23237	New Zealand
cz	2913384	2937528	24144	22538	655923	Czech Republic
hu	2666466	2675428	8962	16883	501101	Hungary
gr	2384554	2388251	3697	6920	54727	Greece
arpa	2314318	3281297	966979	115	5908	Mistakes
dk	2309516	2323904	14388	11076	54452	Denmark
il	2253613	2271382	17769	25	11953	Israel
gov	2211757	2997286	785529	2291	621385	Government
sg	2131215	2143755	12540	1237	9295	Singapore
ro	2090200	2144757	54557	21436	1627126	Romania
us	1945613	2081685	136072	22928	111087	United States

Fig. 4.1 The top 44 domains by number of websites registered, according to ISC, 2019 © 2022 Internet Systems Consortium, Inc.

Many website creators prefer common domains because these are well-recognized: as a result, potential visitors are more likely to trust the source. Often, websites with less popular domains deter visitors, especially if they are affiliated with an entity foreign to them. The marketing campaign for the .us domain appeals to anyone with an interest in achieving the "American dream" online—but actually, most Americans do not associate websites using the .us domain as trustworthy and domestic websites. Actually, anyone can create a website using the .us domain, not just American citizens or businesses. This is the case with many domains: it is not always a requirement to be from a particular country to register a website with a country-specific domain. However, some countries, such as Canada, require proof of Canadian citizenship, residency, representation, or aboriginal affiliation to register a website using the .ca domain [3].

When citing sources in another language or sources affiliated with a foreign country, critics will point to the credibility of the source. To defend the use of a foreign source, it is imperative to know the rules of the domain to aid in assessing the veracity of the source. For example, in the case of the Canadian website using a

.ca domain, it is fair to say that any content on that source represents a truly Canadian view. On the other hand, content found on an American website using a .us domain may not necessarily represent American views. Know the rules and the background of each site, including the domain, before citing a website.

4.1   Narrowing Online Searches to a Country Code Top-Level Domain (ccTLD)

So now that you know the value of paying attention to particular domains, how do you search for websites specific to a domain? To narrow down a search to return only pages using one domain, use the *site:* dork, followed by the domain. For example, the search *site:hu* will return only sites that are registered using the .hu (Hungarian) domain. Figure 4.2 shows the top results of this search in Google. In

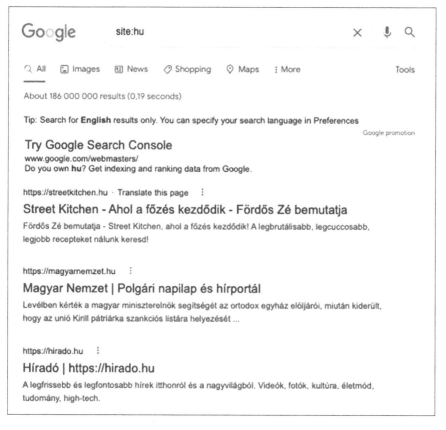

Fig. 4.2 Sample Google search results for sites using the .hu domain (Google and the Google logo are trademarks of Google LLC)

Fig. 4.3 Google search results for sites using the .hu domain and the key word *diákhitel,* the Hungarian word meaning *student loans* (Google and the Google logo are trademarks of Google LLC)

this example, the results are all on a variety of topics. Also, there are approximately 279 million results, which are too many to be useful.

It is possible to stack the *site:* operator with other operators or other key search terms to narrow down the results. For example, a researcher might be interested in discovering Hungarian websites on the topic of student loans. In this case, the search *site:hu diákhitel* (the Hungarian word for *student loan*) will return only sites using the .hu domain that contain the key word *diákhitel* on the page. Figure 4.3 demonstrates how this narrows the scope of the search.

All of the results are registered using .hu domain and on the topic if student loans. And, most of the results from the above search are in the target language. In this example, though, it was not really necessary to specify the .hu domain because Google understood that the word *diákhitel* is Hugarian. A general search for *diákhitel* without specifying the Hungarian domain will return results very similar to the search that specified the *site:hu* (see Fig. 4.4).

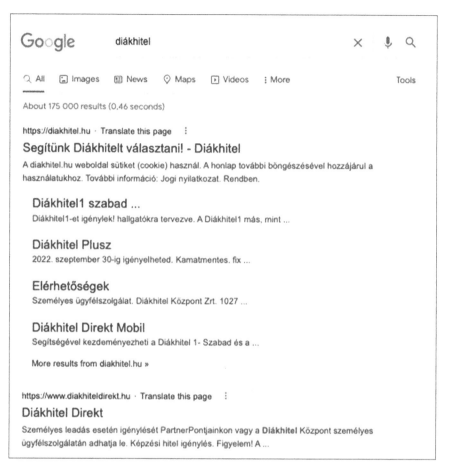

Fig. 4.4 Google search results for sites containing the Hungarian word *diákhitel* (Google and the Google logo are trademarks of Google LLC)

The distinction between the two searches is not easily apparent in the results on the first page. One way to measure the difference is in the number of results: Google returned approximately 110,000 results when specifying *site:hu*, and it returned approximately 175,000 results without specifying. In that regard, specifying the domain limited the search results drastically.

4.2   Non-Latin-Character ccTLDs (ccIDNs)

Some country-specific domains do not use Latin characters. In 2010, the Internet Corporation for Assigned Names and Numbers, or ICANN, introduced the first domain names written in other scripts. This was due to the increasing amount of information available online in various languages. Now, there are several dozen such domains, also known as ccIDNs (Internationalized Domain Names) [4].

Researchers interested in search of foreign-language resources must know how to search for sources that may be registered with a ccIDN. What follows is a list of some country-specific domains that have non-Latin aliases. Not all ccIDNs are listed here, and there are bound to be more ccIDNs registered in the future. If a researcher is interested in a ccIDN that is not listed here, it would be wise to conduct a preliminary search for the country-specific ccIDN, and copy and paste this text directly into their search parameters. Here is a list of some popular ccIDNs by country (in alphabetical order):

- Algeria: .dz. and .الجزائر.
- Arabic (no country specified): .شبكة. and .بازار.
- Armenia: .am and .հայ.
- Bangladesh: .bd and .বাংলা.
- Belarus: .by and .бел.
- Bulgaria: .bg and .бг.
- China: .cn, .游戏,. 中国,. 中國,. 公司,. 网络, and others.
- Cyrillic (no country specified):. сайт and. Онлайн.
- Egypt: .eg and .مصر.
- Georgia: .ge and .გე.
- Greece: .gr and .ελ.
- Hong Kong: .kh and .香港.

  . भारत, .இந்தியா, .ভারত, .ਭਾਰਤ, .ભારત, .ಭಾರತ, .بھارت., .ভাৰত,
- India: .in, .ভাৰত, .ಭಾರತ೦, .ଭାରତ .भारतम्, .भारोत, and .پارت.
- Iran: .ir and .ایران.
- Iraq: .iq and .عراق.
- Israel: .il and .ישראל.
- Jordan: .jo and .الاردن.
- Kazakhstan: .kz and .қаз.
- Laos: .la and .ລາວ.
- Macau: .mo,. 澳門, and. 澳门.
- Macedonia: .mk and .мкд.
- Malaysia: .my and .مليسيا.
- Mongolia: mn and. Мон.
- Morocco: .ma and .المغرب.
- Oman: .om and .عمان.
- Pakistan: .pk and .پاکستان.
- Palestine: .ps and .فلسطين.
- Qatar: .qa and .قطر.
- Russia: .ru, .рф, and .moscow/.москва.
- Saudi Arabia: .sa and .السعودية.
- Serbia: .rs and. Срб (no latin-character domain).
- Singapore: .sg, .சிங்கப்பூர், and .新加坡.
- South Korea: .kr and .한국.
- Sri Lanka: .lk, .ලංකා, .இலங்கை.

- Sudan: .sd and ‏سودان‎.
- Syria: .sy and ‏سوريا‎.
- Taiwan: .tw,. 台灣, and. 台湾.
- Thailand: .th and .ไทย.
- Tunisia: .tn and ‏تونس‎.
- UAE: .ae and ‏امارات‎.
- Ukraine: .ua and .укр.
- Yemen: .ye and ‏اليمن‎.

Google searches that specify the Latin-character domain will return different results than searches that specify the domain in foreign characters. Consider a search for *travel*, one using the Latin-character domain for Thailand and the other using the foreign-character domain as shown in Fig. 4.5.

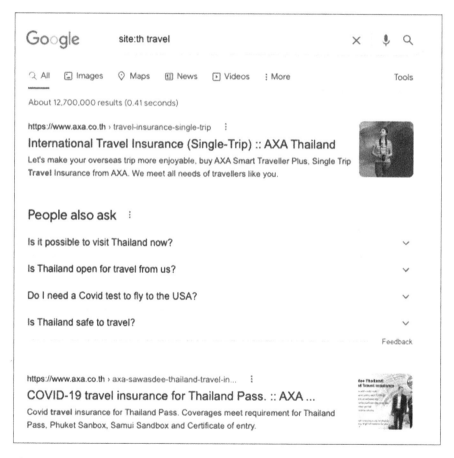

Fig. 4.5 Google search results using the .th (Thai) domain and the key word *travel* (Google and the Google logo are trademarks of Google LLC)

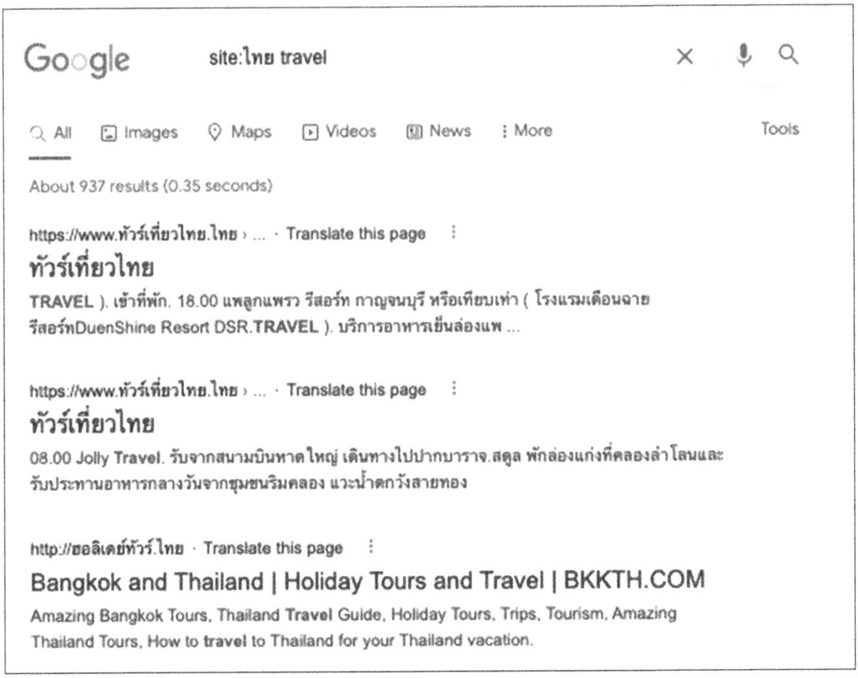

Fig. 4.6 Google search results using the .ไทย domain and the key word *travel* (Google and the Google logo are trademarks of Google LLC)

The results of the search shown in Fig. 4.5 that uses the Latin-character domain are largely in English, even though they are affiliated with Thai sources. Consider the search in Fig. 4.6 that uses the Thai-language ccIDN.

First of all, there are only 937 results from this search, whereas there were nearly 13 million results using the Latin-character domain. In this case, fewer results are better because it helps narrow the search even further and decreases the number of results the researcher must review. Not only that, it opens the aperture of search results that would not otherwise appear at the top.

4.3 Country Code Second-Level Domains (cc2LDs)

If ccTLDs specify websites affiliated with a country, then cc2LDs specify a particular enterprise or function affiliated with that country. Consider the .gov and .mil domains: these are reserved for the US government and military. As a result, foreign governments and militaries are unable to register their websites with these domains. This caused the need for cc2LDs.

Consider the domain .kh, which is the ccTLD for Cambodia. The cc2LDs under the Cambodian ccTLD are:

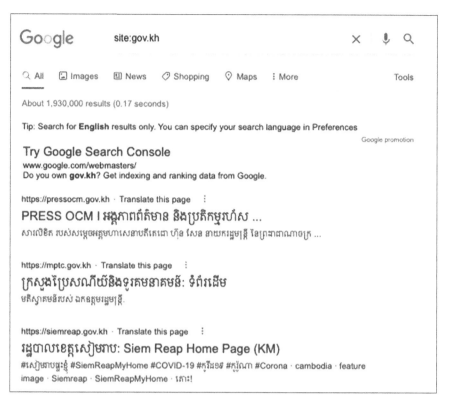

Fig. 4.7 Google search results using the *.gov.kh* cc2LD for Cambodia (Google and the Google logo are trademarks of Google LLC)

- .gov.kh
- .com.kh
- .net.kh
- .org.kh
- .edu.kh
- .mil.kh
- .per.kh [5].

This is necessary for the Cambodian government to host its own government, corporation, educational, military, and other specific services under its .kh ccTLD. Most countries have cc2LDs for this very purpose.

To narrow a search for Cambodian government sites, for example, use the search *site:gov.kh*, as shown in Fig. 4.7.

In this example, all search results possessed the .gov.kh cc2LD. To narrow the search further, this can be used in conjunction with other search terms in English or Khmer, the language spoken primarily in Cambodia. Consider the search *site:gov. kh "Ministry of Commerce"* as shown in Fig. 4.8. This should help the researcher discover the official website of the Cambodian Ministry of Commerce.

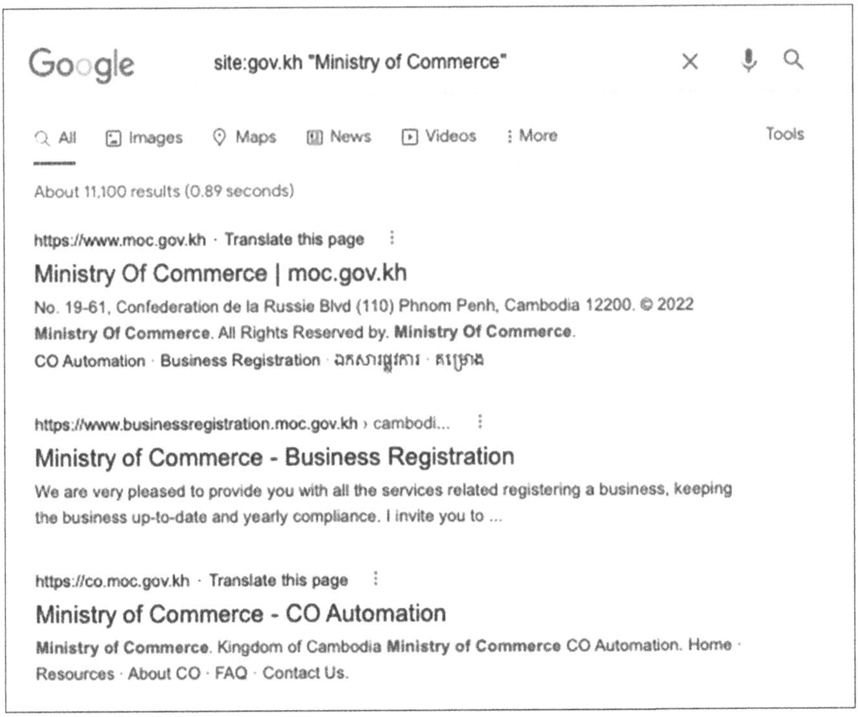

Fig. 4.8 Google search results using the *.gov.kh* cc2LD for Cambodia and the key word *"Ministry of Commerce"* (Google and the Google logo are trademarks of Google LLC)

These search methods are applicable to most country ccTLDs and cc2LDs. To discover the domain structures and foreign-character domains for the country of interest, start your search with some of the below resources.

4.4   List of ccTLD Registries

It is possible to register a site with many domains using well-known services such as GoDaddy—however, country-specific domains often have their own registry sites with useful information about domain and subdomain structures, and aliases. Here is a list of some well-known country-specific domain registry service websites to aid the researcher in identifying the cc2LDs for a specific country (in alphabetical order):

- Afghanistan: http://nic.af/ps
- Algeria: http://www.nic.dz/ (also ‏.الجزائر‎)
- Argentina: https://nic.ar/
- Armenia: https://www.amnic.net/ (also .հայ).

- Australia: https://www.auda.org.au/
- Austria: https://www.nic.at/de
- Bangladesh: http://www.btcl.gov.bd/ or http://বিডিআইএ.বাংলা (also .বাংলা).
- Belarus: https://www.cctld.by/ (also .бел).
- Belgium: https://www.dnsbelgium.be/nl
- Brazil: https://registro.br/
- Bulgaria: https://www.register.bg (also .бг).
- Canada: https://www.cira.ca/
- Chile: https://www.nic.cl/
- China: https://cnnic.com.cn/ (also .游戏,. 中国,. 中國,. 公司,. 网络, and others).
- Colombia: https://www.go.co/
- Cuba: http://www.nic.cu/
- Czech Republic: https://www.nic.cz/
- Denmark: https://www.dk-hostmaster.dk/da
- Egypt: http://www.dns.eg/ (also .مصر).
- Estonia: https://www.internet.ee/
- Finland: https://www.traficom.fi/fi/viestinta/fi-verkkotunnukset
- France: https://www.afnic.fr/ (also .paris).
- Georgia: https://nic.ge/ (also ·გე).
- Germany: https://www.denic.de/
- Greece: https://grweb.ics.forth.gr/public/ (also .ελ).
- Hong Kong: https://www.hkdnr.hk/cn/ (also .香港).
- Hungary: http://www.domain.hu/domain/
- India: https://www.registry.in/
  (also .भारत, .இந்தியா, .ভারত, .ਭਾਰਤ, .ભારત, .بھارت., .భారత్, . ভাৰত, .ಭಾರತ, .ଭାରତ .भारतम्, .भारोत, and بارت.)
- Iran: http://www.nic.ir/ (also .ایران).
- Iraq: https://www.cmc.iq/ (also .عراق).
- Ireland: https://www.iedr.ie/
- Israel: https://www.isoc.org.il/domain-name-registry (also .ישראל).
- Italy: https://www.nic.it/it
- Japan: https://jprs.co.jp/
- Jordan: https://www.dns.jo/main.aspx (also .الاردن)
- Kazakhstan: https://www.nic.kz/ (also .қаз).
- Laos: http://www.la/ (also .ລາວ).
- Lebanon: http://www.isoc.org.lb/lbdr
- Macau: https://www.monic.mo/ (also. 澳門 and. 澳门).
- Macedonia: http://marnet.mk/ (also. мкд).
- Malaysia: https://www.mynic.my/ (also .مليسيا).
- Mexico: https://www.nicmexico.mx/
- Mongolia: http://мон.мон/cgi-sys/defaultwebpage.cgi (.mn and. мон).
- Morocco: https://www.registre.ma/language/ar/a-home (also .المغرب)
- Netherlands: https://www.sidn.nl/

- New Zealand: https://dnc.org.nz/
- Norway: https://www.norid.no/no/
- Oman: http://www.registry.om/ (also عمان.)
- Pakistan: http://pknic.net.pk/ (also پاکستان.)
- Palestine: http://www.pnina.ps/ (also فلسطين.).
- Poland: https://www.dns.pl/
- Portugal: http://www.dns.pt/
- Qatar: https://cra.gov.qa/ar-QA/Services/Domains (also قطر.)
- Romania: https://www.rotld.ro/
- Russia: https://www.nic.ru/ (also .рф, .moscow/.москва, and others).
- Saudi Arabia: https://www.nic.sa/ (also السعودية.)
- Serbia: https://рнидс.срб/ (including .rs and. срб).
- Singapore: https://www.sgnic.sg/ (also .சிங்கப்பூர் and .新加坡).
- South Africa: https://www.registry.net.za/
- South Korea: https://krnic.or.kr/ (also .한국).
- Spain: https://www.dominios.es/dominios/es
- Sri Lanka: http://www.nic.lk/ (also .ලංකා and .இலங்கை).
- Sudan: http://wwe.domains.sd/ (also سودان.)
- Sweden: https://internetstiftelsen.se/
- Switzerland: https://www.nic.ch/
- Syria: https://web.archive.org/web/20130723080155/https://www.ste.gov.sy/ (also سوريا.)
- Taiwan: https://rs.twnic.net.tw/ (also. 台灣 and. 台湾).
- Thailand: https://www.thnic.co.th/th/home/ (also .ไทย).
- Tunisia: http://www.registre.tn/ar/index.php (also تونس.)
- Turkey: https://www.nic.tr/
- UAE: http://www.aeda.ae/ (also امارات.)
- Ukraine: https://hostmaster.ua/ (also .укр).
- United Kingdom: https://www.nominet.uk/ (including .uk and .gb).
- United States: https://www.about.us/
- Vietnam: https://www.vnnic.vn/
- Yemen: http://www.teleyemen.com.ye/ (also اليمن.)

Note that not all non-Latin script domains are ICANN-approved. Many applications for ccIDNs have been rejected, but this would not necessarily prevent their use. For example, in 2010, ICANN rejected Bulgaria's registration request for the Cyrillic-based ccIDN, .бг. ICANN's reason for rejecting the request was that it is too similar in appearance to Brazil's ccIDN, .br [6]. To complicate matters, there are many websites that use the disapproved .бг ccIDN. Consider the top results of the search for such websites as shown in Fig. 4.9.

This is an important consideration when conducting searches on specified domains while referencing the well-respected and internationally recognized ICANN as a source of information. The researcher may need to delve deep into the potential sources of information available in the target region and language.

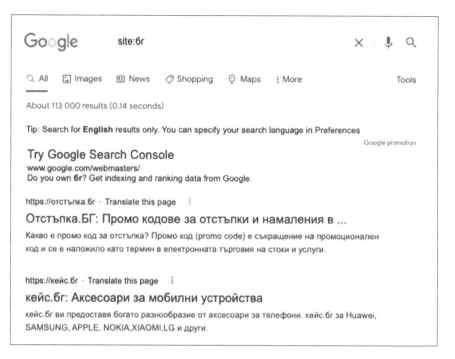

Fig. 4.9 Google search for websites using the disapproved Bulgarian ccIDN .6r (Google and the Google logo are trademarks of Google LLC)

Incorporate this background knowledge into the research methodology and literature review of your work. These types of considerations are what makes research projects unique in scope and methodology.

4.5   List of Non-Country Top-Level Domain (TLD) Registries

The purpose of this short section is to provide a list of registries for some well-known noncountry-specific TLDs as a reference only. While this book focuses largely on the country and language-specific research methods, the researcher should also be aware that there are many TLDs that are not country-specific, but are still relevant to foreign-language research. These include but are not limited to:

- .com: https://www.verisign.com/en_US/domain-names/com-domain-names/index.xhtml
- .net: https://www.verisign.com/en_US/domain-names/net-domain-names/index.xhtml
- .edu: https://net.educause.edu/
- .gov: https://home.dotgov.gov/

- .mil: http://www.nic.mil/
- .org: https://thenew.org/org-people/
- .info: https://afilias.info/
- .onion: https://www.torproject.org/
- .eu (European Union): https://eurid.eu/en/ (including .ею and .ευ, see: https://eurid.eu/en/register-a-eu-domain/guidelines-eu-cyrillic/)
- .сайт,. онлайн, ‏الجزائر‎, and other foreign-character domains: https://corenic.org/

4.6 Resources

For more online resources, visit the following websites:

- ISO3166-1–CountryCodes:https://www.iso.org/obp/ui/#iso:pub:PUB500001:en
- ICANN Accredited Registrars (List): https://www.icann.org/registrar-reports/accreditation-qualified-list.html
- World Report on Internationalized Domain Names: https://web.archive.org/web/20141210151244/http://www.eurid.eu/files/publ/IDNWorldReport2014_Interactive.pdf

Online Database References

1. While this list is a few years old already, it demonstrates how there are still many websites that exist using country-specific domains, see "Distributions by Top-Level Domain Name (by host-count)," from Internet Domain Survey, January 2019, https://downloads.isc.org/www/survey/reports/current/bynum.txt.
2. About.us main page, accessed November 18, 2020, https://www.about.us.
3. "Keeping .CA Canadian," CIRA, accessed November 18, 2020, https://www.cira.ca/ca-domains/register-your-ca-domain/requirements.
4. "Internationalized Domain Name," last modified March 12, 2021, https://icannwiki.org/Internationalized_Domain_Name.
5. "Guidelines for the online application for Domain Name System Registration (.kh)," Telecommunications Regulator of Cambodia, accessed November 18, 2020, https://www.trc.gov.kh/dns-registration/.
6. "ICANN отхвърли кандидатурата на България за домейн на кирилица "бг" [ICANN rejects Bulgaria's candidacy for Cyrillic domain "bg"]," May 19, 2010, https://www.dnevnik.bg/tehnologii/2010/05/19/903090_icann_othvurli_kandidaturata_na_bulgariia_za_domein_na/.

Chapter 5
Translation Tools and Techniques

This chapter introduces methods for translating text, websites, documents, and images. It also introduces some translator communities of interest where the researcher may turn to ask for translation assistance. Translation is an art, not a science. Many modern computer-based translator services offer translations that are good enough to generally understand the content; they may not be good enough to reproduce or publish as-is. For example, a researcher looking to use a direct quotation from a Japanese book in another language (i.e., the original text is in Japanese and the translated text will be in another language) may not find the computer-based translation worthy of publication. Instances like these may require a human translator to produce the final quotation that makes sense in the target language. In this case, the important step would be to know that this is indeed the text worth translating. This way, the researcher is asking the translator to translate the exact text they desire, and not some other text that turns out to be completely irrelevant.

So, it depends on the researcher's goals. If the researcher is only interested in understanding the content of a source, without looking to reproduce it, then computer-based translation tools may suffice. One common use is the case where the researcher wishes to learn the foreign-language word for a research term that they will use in keyword searches in an online search engine. For this use, it is perfectly reasonable to search the term in the researcher's native language, copy the translation of the term into a search engine, and then interpret the results. If the researcher is looking to translate an entire book for the sole purpose of reading the content for personal enjoyment, computer-based translation tools may also suffice. It is when the formal reproduction of text that was once in another language where human translation assistance is often required.

While this chapter recommends some tools to conduct translation of foreign text, these tools are not the only tools available. The author and Springer Nature do not endorse any of these tools, and the developers of the tools and resources mentioned in this book are not sponsors of this book. The purpose of introducing these tools here is to demonstrate the methodology for translating text in the context of a greater

© The Author(s), under exclusive license to Springer Nature Switzerland AG 2023   173
M. D. Miller, *Discovering Hidden Gems in Foreign Languages*, Terrorism, Security, and Computation, https://doi.org/10.1007/978-3-031-18479-6_5

foreign-language research project. For this, third party tools are required. The researcher is encouraged to try some of the tools mentioned here, and is also encouraged to discover more tools that support the exact research goals of the project at hand.

As mentioned previously, translation is only one small step in the foreign-language research process. The purpose of translation is to understand the meaning of foreign text in the context of a larger issue and produce meaningful analysis. This is the reason that the chapter covering translation tools and techniques appears so late in this book. Now that the researcher knows the strategic methods for discovering, interpreting, and incorporating foreign-language search results into a larger project, the researcher is now ready to interpret the content of the results.

5.1   Translating Text

Translating text involves text that the researcher is able to type, copy and paste, or alter on a computer. The distinction between this type of text and the text that exists only in an image is the resources available to aid in the translation of that text. The translation of text that does not fit into this description is discussed in the later sections of this chapter.

This section is separated into two sections: the first focuses on translation services affiliated with search engines. These usually have simple translation features, including key word and paragraph-length translations. Sometimes, these services also offer options to translate document files, which is discussed more in depth later in this chapter.

There is no single online translator that is better than the rest. Many search engines, such as those discussed earlier in this book, possess their own translator services. When possible, the best translator is the one that is created for users from a certain geographic region of the world or for speakers of a particular language. For example, the Seznam search engine will be a good choice to translate text to or from the Czech language. Google Translate may be best when looking to translate text to or from a less-common language or larger amounts of text. Sometimes, it may be wise to try multiple translators to see which services offer the most comprehensible result.

This section demonstrates the features and use cases for text translation using simple search engine translation tools, starting with Seznam.

5.1.1   Seznam Slovnik

The Seznam translator is located at https://slovnik.seznam.cz/, and is capable of translating text into Czech from English, German, French, Italian, Spanish, Russian, or Slovak. It offers a translation of the key term, synonyms, similar words, and

Fig. 5.1 Translation of the English word *translation* into Czech using Seznam Slovnik ©
1996–2021 Seznam.cz, a.s., © Lingea s.r.o

common use examples. Figure 5.1 shows a sample translation of the English word
translation into Czech using Seznam Slovnik.

It is important to consider that Seznam is limited to translations using the languages available in its drop-down menu. If the researchers were interested in finding

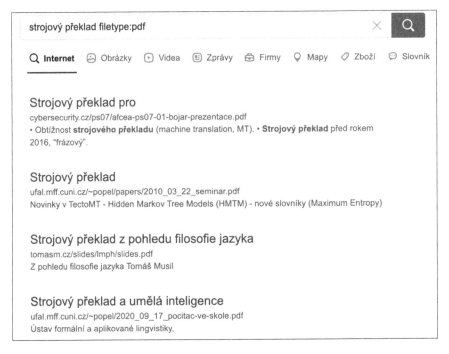

Fig. 5.2 Seznam search results for *strojový překlad filetype:pdf*, the Czech word for "machine translation" © 1996–2021 Seznam.cz, a.s

translations involving other languages, they may need to use another translation service.

With the knowledge from the results above, the researcher can conduct a tailored search using the advanced search operators introduced earlier in the book. For example, if the researchers were interested in discovering Czech-language resources on Machine Translation, they could conduct the search *strojový překlad filetype:pdf*, using one of the key terms discovered in the context section of the previous search in Seznam Slovnik. Figure 5.2 shows the top results of this search.

When the researcher has the need to translate text between two languages, where either one language is rare or there is no country-specific translation tool available, Google Translate is always a reliable choice.

5.1.2 *Google Translate*

Google Translate is located at https://translate.google.com/. It is capable of translating large amounts of text and documents to and from dozens of languages [1]. Among its many useful features includes language detection, which is of particular importance to the foreign-language researcher because of the likely case where the researcher does not know the exact language of the text they have located. Another useful feature is the foreign-character keyboards, located in the bottom right corner of the text input field. This is useful when the researcher knows the language or alphabet of the language, but does not have a keyboard installed. Figure 5.3 shows an example of the keyboard for the Nepali alphabet in Google Translate. The buttons are all click-able; the letters appear directly in the search box.

Figure 5.4 shows a sample translation of a paragraph from the Nepali Language page on Wikipedia. In this example, Google Translate correctly detected the language and produced a very clear and understandable translation of the text. In fact, the English translation of this paragraph is clear enough to cite in a formal work.

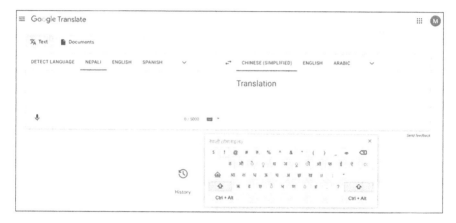

Fig. 5.3 Screenshot of the keyboard feature within Google Translate using the Nepali keyboard (Google and the Google logo are trademarks of Google LLC)

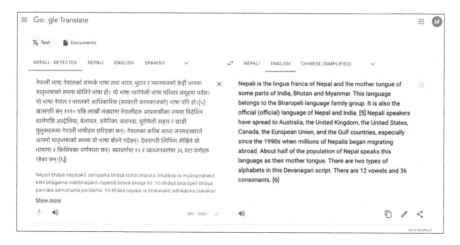

Fig. 5.4 Sample text translation from Nepali into English using Google Translate [2] (Google and the Google logo are trademarks of Google LLC)

It is also possible to translate entire documents and live websites using Google Translate. This will be demonstrated later in this chapter. Chapter 7 will discuss citations of foreign works and translations so that the researcher may properly reproduce foreign-language resources.

5.1.3 Yandex Translate

As mentioned previously, Yandex is a Russian search engine. Since Yandex is made especially for Russian computer users, it will be the best service to translate text to and from the Russian language. It has similar feature and capabilities to Google Translate: it also provides examples of usage from external sources and common use cases. It is capable of translating as much as 10,000 characters at a time, and accepts voice dictation.

To see how Yandex Translate works, let's look at an example. Figure 5.5 shows a sample translation of the word *demographics* into Russian. The large box to the right shows the translation, which the researcher may choose to copy and paste for later use. Below the search boxes, the researcher will find examples from external sources that use the word searched above. The film icon next to each sentence indicates that the example sentences are quotations from movies or television shows. Hover over each icon to see the source of the sentence. Each sentence is written in both the to and from languages, making it easy to see how the word is used in each example.

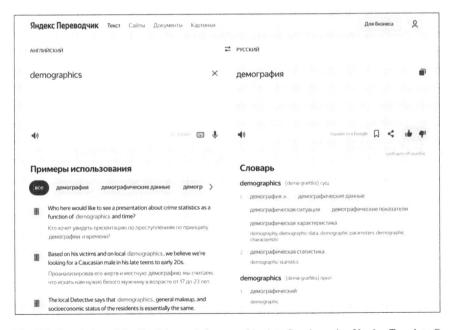

Fig. 5.5 Translation of the English word *demographics* into Russian using Yandex Translate © 2015–2022 YANDEX LLC

To the right of the sample sentences, the researcher will find sample use cases. This is particularly important for the researcher who is interested in the key term, but wants to know more about how the word is commonly used in that language. For example, the researcher may be interested in demographic data, demographic parameters, or demographic characteristic. To look up any of these phrases, simply click on each one to view the results.

It is also possible to translate entire documents, live websites, and images using Yandex Translate. This will be demonstrated later in this chapter.

5.1.4 thePashto

The aforementioned translators often work for general searches for key words and phrases in many languages. Specialized translators, on the other hand, serve a dedicated linguistic purpose. A translation service that focuses on only one language may offer better translation quality over a service that works in dozens of languages, simply because there is dedicated support for that unique service. Another consideration is the format in which results are displayed: results that show alternate uses of a word or example sentences that demonstrate the colloquial use of the word may provide context or meaning to the researcher, depending on their research problem.

The first example discussed here is thePashto (https://thepashto.com/), which specializes in Pashto-language translation. Pashto is not a very commonly spoken language, making it difficult to find resources that support Pashto translation needs online. Not only that, Pashto is a very tribal language, meaning that there are often many ways to communicate one idea. This is a risk when using a translator such as Google Translate, which will often only provide one result. If the researcher was interested in seeing other ways to say something, it would be wise to search a specialized Pashto translation tool such as thePashto. Figure 5.6 shows a sample search for the English word *translation*. It returns three different ways to say *translation* in Pashto.

If the researchers were interested in using the Pashto key term for *translation* to conduct their search, they could include all three of these terms into the search. This will return more relevant results. Figure 5.7 shows the Google search results for the search ژباړه OR ژباړنه OR ترجمه (omitting any results originating from Google.com, which brings the unique search results to the top of the list).

If the researcher discovers a Pashto word that they wish to translate into English, thePashto has the ability to search for Pashto terms. Either copy and paste the term into the search bar, or type the word into the search bar using the Pashto keyboard feature. To use the Pashto keyboard, click on the keyboard icon on the left side of the search bar. Click on the letters below to type directly into the search bar. Figure 5.8 shows the Pashto keyboard available on thePashto.

The number of resources available to look up Pashto words has increased in the last few years. Google Translate only added Pashto to the list of languages it supports in 2016. Other services, such as the next one, support Pashto translation to a limited extent.

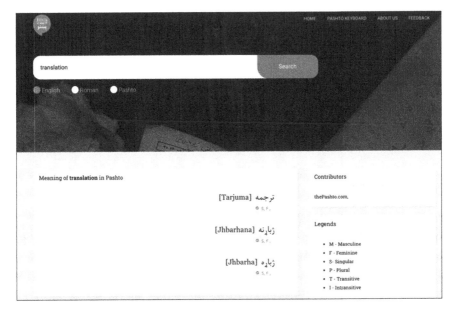

Fig. 5.6 Translation of the English word *translation* into Pashto using thePashto.com © 2021 thePashto.com

5.1.5 Glosbe

Glosbe, available at https://glosbe.com/, is an online translation service made in Poland that supports dozens of languages, even Pashto. What makes Glosbe unique is that its entries are crowd-sourced, meaning that the community of language speakers online contribute to the translations available. This means that the translations often come from native speakers who truly understand the meaning of the words; it also means that there may sometimes be mistakes. The Glosbe home page is shown in Fig. 5.9.

The content of the translation results is also unique. Like thePashto, Glosbe offers more than one translation, if available. It also provides machine translations from Google Translate, if available. Most significant, Glosbe also provides examples from websites it has searched online, serving simultaneously as a simple search engine. Figure 5.10 shows an example of the Pashto translation of the English word for *president*.

5.1.6 Naver Dictionary

As previously introduced, Naver is a South Korean search engine made especially for Korean Internet users. Besides its search engine service, Naver also hosts an online translation and dictionary service, which are particularly useful when

Fig. 5.7 Google search results for ترجمه *OR* زبانه *OR* زبایه -*site:*google.com, using three Pashto words meaning *translation* (Google and the Google logo are trademarks of Google LLC)

conducting research in the Korean language. This section showcases some of the functionality of the Naver-language services.

The Naver Dictionary service can be found at https://dict.naver.com/. This website is in Korean, making it difficult to navigate for the researcher who does not speak Korean. Upon inspection, it makes sense to try searching for a term in one of the search boxes and see what type of results it will return. Figure 5.11 shows a sample search for the English word for *president* in Naver Dictionary before selecting the enter button.

As it turns out, the search as it appears in Fig. 5.11 is a comprehensive search for the term. Many online dictionaries ask that the user specifies the target language of the translation. It is possible to select a specific language in Naver Dictionary as well, however, leaving the search as is with the left-most option selected (highlighted in blue), the search returns a comprehensive list of translations in several languages, including English, Chinese, French, Japanese, German, Vietnamese, Russian, Mongolian, Arabic, and others.

This may be very helpful to the foreign-language researcher: rather than conducting individual searches for the key term several times to obtain the translation in each language, the researcher can simply conduct the search once in Naver

Fig. 5.8 Search bar containing the Pashto word ترجمه (meaning *translation*) and the Pashto keyboard in thePashto.com © 2021 thePashto.com

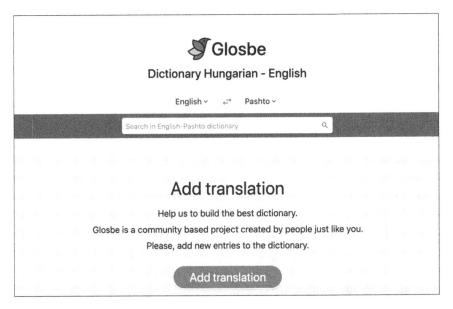

Fig. 5.9 The Glosbe home page (Printed with Permission from Glosbe)

president in Pashto English-Pashto dictionary

president ⌄ 🔊 adjective   noun   /ˈpɹɛzɪdənt/   ˈprɛ.zə.dənt   + grammar

- The head of state of a republic, a representative democracy and sometimes (in cases of constitutional violations) a dictatorship.
  +20 definitions

TRANSLATIONS **president**   [+ ADD]

⊙ ولسمشر   ⋮
   en the head of state of a republic +1 definitions
                                   en wiktionary...

⊙ اولسمشر masculine   ⋮
   en the head of state of a republic
                                   enwiktionary-...

⊙ رییس masculine   ⋮
   en the head of state of a republic
                                   enwiktionary-...

⊙ صدر masculine   ⋮
   en the head of state of a republic
                                   enwiktionary-...

Show algorithmically generated translations

President ⌄ 🔊 noun   + grammar

- An honorific for the head of state of a republic; see president (definition 1).
  +3 definitions

No translations [+ Add]

MACHINE TRANSLATIONS

🄶   ولسمشر
                                       Google translate

EXAMPLES   [+ ADD]

☑ Stem

On May 15, 2002, James Wolfensohn, the World Bank Group **President** at that time, officially reopened the World Bank Office in Kabul after 23 years of the office being closed.

۱۵ کاله وراندې په همدې ورځ (د ۲۰۰۲ کال می)، د نړیوال بانک د رییس جیمز دی ولفنسون لخوا د نړیوال بانک ګروپ دفتر په پلازمینې کابل کې په رسمي توګه بیا پرانیستل شو.

worldbank.org ⋮

Fig. 5.10 Translation of the English word *president* into Pashto using Glosbe.com (Printed with Permission)

Fig. 5.11 Home page of the Naver Dictionary, located at https://dict.naver.com/, with the English word for *president* entered in the search bar © NAVER Corp

Dictionary to obtain many translations at once. Figure 5.12 shows the results of this search in Naver Dictionary for the English word *president*.

While the primary Naver Dictionary service is primarily in Korean, the search engine does support an English-language interface, located at https://en.dict.naver.com. This interface, as shown in Fig. 5.13, suggests results as the researcher types. The default target language will always be Korean. The researcher is left to explore the capabilities of the Naver Dictionary on their own.

5.1.7 Reverso Context

Reverso is an online translation service that hosts a few unique tools in several languages. Reverso Context, located at https://context.reverso.net/translation/, accepts a key term in one language and outputs examples that demonstrate use of the term in another language. The service is available in Arabic, German, Spanish, French, Hebrew, Italian, Japanese, Dutch, Polish, Portuguese, Romanian, Russian, Turkish, and Chinese.

Dictionaries such as this are particularly important for the researcher who is looking to understand how the word is used in context, and to locate different forms of the word. As discussed previously, many foreign words come in different forms:

Fig. 5.12   Translation of the English word *president* in Naver Dictionary (showing the English and French results only) © NAVER Corp

that is, their endings change based on their part of speech, gender, and plurality. Recall the previous example of Russian demographics: words such as *demograph-ics* are often not used alone; they are used with other terms to express more mean-ingful ideas. Reverso Context can provide the perspective necessary for the non-Russian speaker to understand how this word is commonly used in speech and text.

Consider conducting your own search to see how results appear. Reverso Context will return several use cases on the top of the results, listed in the blue boxes on top. Below, it returns sample sentences in English and target-language translations of each, and highlighted the presence of the English and translated terms.

Fig. 5.13 Suggestions for the search term *translation* in the Naver English Dictionary, located at https://en.dict.naver.com © NAVER Corp

5.1.8   Wiktionary

Wiktionary is a very useful resource for conducting research on word forms, etymology, and languages spoken by region. Among all resources mentioned throughout this section, Wiktionary arguably hosts information about the largest number of languages. It is available online at https://en.wiktionary.org/wiki/Wiktionary:Main_Page. It is possible to search for any word in the Wiktionary search bar, and it accepts foreign character text as well. Figure 5.14 shows the page for the Russian word for *demographics* in Wiktionary.

Figure 5.14 demonstrates the functionality of most pages in Wiktionary. First, the page is organized by language. This is significant because, as it turns out, демография is also the Kazakh word for *demographics*. The researcher should keep this in mind when conducting searches using this word, because results may also contain Kazakh results instead of Russian. On the right, Wiktionary links to Wikipedia articles based on the word searched. Below, Wiktionary offers different forms of the word. Since *demographics* is a noun, this page shows declinations. For verbs, it would show conjugations. In other words, the researcher may encounter this word in any of these forms out in the wild.

A list of all languages in Wiktionary, along with their ISO 639-1, 639-2, and 639-3 language codes, can be found at: https://en.wiktionary.org/wiki/Wiktionary:List_of_languages. Wiktionary's All Languages page has other useful

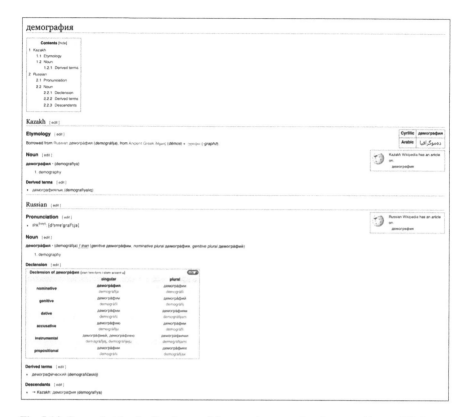

Fig. 5.14 Screenshot for the Russian word *демография*, meaning *demographics*, on Wiktionary [3] (CC BY-SA)

links, including a link to language lists by country: https://en.wiktionary.org/wiki/ Category:All_languages.

5.1.9   Linguee/DeepL Translator

Linguee / DeepL is a German translation service that offers free and paid subscriptions, accessible at https://www.deepl.com/translator. The free version offers translation of text (individual words and longer excerpts) and documents directly in the web browser. With DeepL Pro (the paid version), it is also possible to set the tone of the translation (formal or informal speech), create a glossary of terms, integrate translations with other tools, and more. DeepL also offers an API and mobile applications.

Linguee offers translations of many key terms and phrases from one language to another. It also provides related terms with the option to hear the pronunciation of the term in the target language. What makes Linguee most unique is that it will simultaneously conduct a web search for the key term in the to and from languages, effectively serving as an online search engine for both languages. The instance of the search term will appear in the from-language on the left, and the to-language on the right. Consider conducting your own search in DeepL to see for yourself.

One other convenient feature in Linguee is the unique characters that appear to the right of the search language settings: when English to German is selected on the top of the page, the four unique characters to the German language appear to the right of the drop-down menu. The researcher can click on any of these letters to add that character to the search bar. This can be particularly helpful if the researcher does not have that keyboard setup. To view the original source for the list of websites below, select the website link beneath each sample, which provides a preview of each result.

DeepL Translator will translate larger amounts of text (such as paragraphs), up to 5000 characters at a time in the free version.

5.1.10 Text Translation in Microsoft Office Products

Microsoft Office products have language translation tools built right into the functionality of the document. The translation capability is available on various Microsoft services on Windows and Macintosh operating systems, and depends on the version in use. Since the version and operating system dictates which tools are available, this section does not demonstrate these capabilities for each version and operating system. This section uses screenshots from Microsoft Office 2019 for Macintosh. Other versions are likely to be very similar.

Depending on the version and operating system, it is possible to translate text selections and entire documents in Microsoft Word, Excel, PowerPoint, Outlook, and OneNote. In Microsoft Word, Excel, and PowerPoint, this feature can be found under the Review tab. Select the Translate button. There will be an option to translate a selection or translate a document. This section will discuss how to translate a selection; the section later in this chapter will demonstrate how to translate an entire document.

Figure 5.15 shows a sample text translated from English into Urdu. Select the blue insert button below the translation to insert the text directly into the Microsoft Word document. After inserting this text into the document, it is possible to copy and paste it for use elsewhere, for example, in online searches.

This functionality is also available in other Microsoft Office products. In Microsoft Outlook, the translate tool is located under the Home tab. It is also possible to translate small sections of text in email by highlighting the text and right-clicking. For more on translation capabilities within Microsoft Office, visit: https:// support.microsoft.com/en-us/office/translate-text-into-a-different-language-287380e4-a56c-48a1-9977-f2dca89ce93f. For more on translation capabilities in Microsoft Outlook, visit: https://support.microsoft.com/en-us/office/translator-for-outlook-3d7e12ed-99d6-406e-a453-b9db0d9653fa.

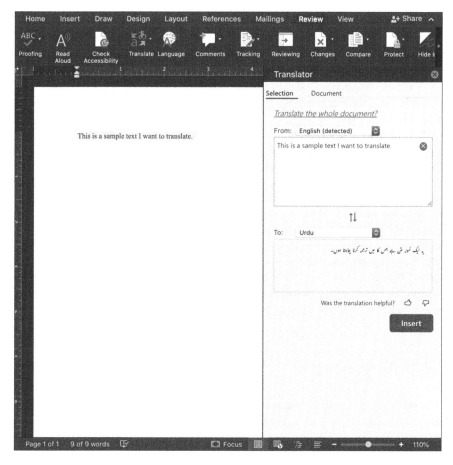

Fig. 5.15 Sample selected text translated directly in Microsoft Word © Microsoft 2021 (Used with permission from Microsoft)

5.2   Translating Live Websites

Throughout the research process, it is likely that the researcher will encounter websites that contain content in languages they do not speak. For smaller amounts of text, it may sometimes be easy to copy and paste individual words into online translators. When the researcher is interested in reading a longer research article that sits directly on a live website, it may be easier to translate the entire web page. This section introduces some resources available for translating entire websites. These are certainly not the only websites available to do so.

5.2.1   Google Translate

It is possible to translate entire websites using Google Translate. To do so, navigate to the "Websites" tab on the top of the page and paste the URL of the website into the text box. When ready, select the blue arrow to the right. Figure 5.16 shows an example using the Finnish-language Wikipedia page for *Media Suomessa*, meaning *Mass Media in Finland*.

The translation of the website will be opened in a new tab. The to and from languages must be correct, otherwise the translation will not be successful. Figure 5.17 shows the aforementioned Wikipedia page translated from Finnish into English.

The new tab presents the translation of the website. It is even possible to interact with the website within the translation: doing so will load and translate the new page in the same tab. View the original text by hovering over the translated words. Try translating a website in Google Translate to see for yourself.

It is also possible to translate a website directly from the Google search results. When the Google search engine is able to translate a website, a link containing the phrase "Translate this page" will appear to the right of the URL. Clicking on this link will open the translation of the website in a new tab. Figure 5.18 shows the top result with the "Translate this page" link available.

5.2.2   Naver Papago

The Naver search engine's translation service, called Papago, supports text and website translation to and from Japanese, Spanish, Russian, Vietnamese, Hindi, Korean, Chinese, French, Portuguese, Thai, English, German, Italian, and

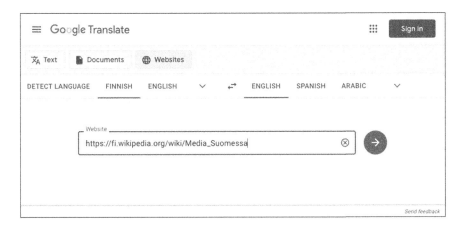

Fig. 5.16 Translating a live website in Google Translate (Google and the Google logo are trademarks of Google LLC)

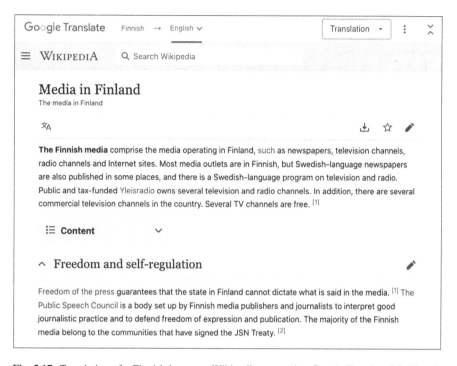

Fig. 5.17   Translation of a Finnish-language Wikipedia page using Google Translate [4] (Google and the Google logo are trademarks of Google LLC)

Fig. 5.18   Google search results for *Suomalaisia uutisia*, meaning *Finnish news* in Finnish (Google and the Google logo are trademarks of Google LLC)

Indonesian. The tool is available at https://papago.naver.com/. Since Naver's primary customer base is the Korean-speaking community, it makes sense to use Naver Papago when translating to or from Korean.

Figure 5.19 shows the Naver Papago translation interface. To translate text, enter the words in the box on the left side; the translation will appear on the right. Or, to translate a website, enter the URL in the box below. Figure 5.20 shows an example with a link to an article from Naver News.

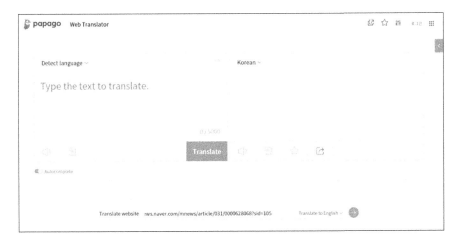

Fig. 5.19   The Naver Papago Web Translator © NAVER Corp

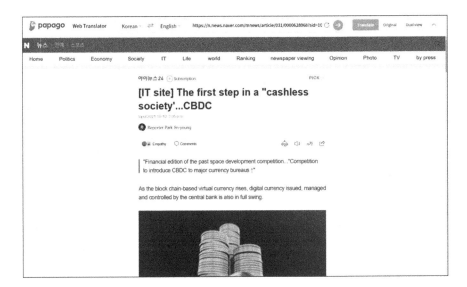

Fig. 5.20   Translation of a news article from Naver News using Naver Papago [5] © NAVER Corp

To translate the website, click on the green arrow to the right. Figure 5.20 shows the English translation of the original website, which was in Korean.

5.2.3 Yandex Translate

The last website translation service discussed in this section is Yandex Translate. Yandex Translate can translate websites in a similar manner as Google Translate, and supports dozens of languages. Yandex Translate will recognize the URL text as a link to a website, and provide the hyperlink to the translated page in the translated results. To access the website translation, click on the link on the right. Figure 5.21 shows an example of a URL for a Wikipedia article from Russian to English.

This raises the question: why not simply navigate to the English-language version of the web page directly in Wikipedia? After all, Wikipedia offers different language versions of many of its web pages natively within the Wikipedia website. This is true, however, the content of many of the various language versions of Wikipedia pages actually differs greatly. In other words, the English-language version and the Russian-language version of the Wikipedia pages for the *Population of Russia* actually contain some different content and resources. The method of using an external translation tool helps the researcher view the content that is intended for the Russian-speaking customer.

Figure 5.22 shows the translation of the Wikipedia page for the Population of Russian, translated into English using Yandex Translate. Notice that the translator did not translate the Wikipedia logo in the top left corner. Nevertheless, the translation of the main body is good quality and enables the researcher who does not speak Russian to understand this text.

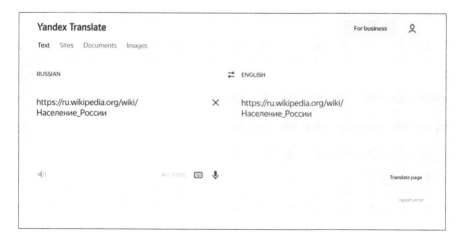

Fig. 5.21 The Yandex Translate interface with a URL from Wikipedia © 2015–2022 YANDEX LLC

Fig. 5.22 Translation of the Wikipedia page for the *Population of Russia* from Russian to English [6], translated using Yandex Translate © 2015–2022 YANDEX LLC

The key takeaway here is that there is more than one resource to achieve the translation goal. Use the tool that best serves the task at hand and the overall research goal. Now, let's discuss tools and techniques to translate documents.

5.3 Translating Documents

It will often be the case that the researcher will discover foreign-language materials that are stored in file types that are difficult to copy and paste, or not possible to copy at all. Or, the files may be so large that the translation tools discussed so far are unable to handle the text content of files of that size. Certain tools specialize in the translation of these types of files. For example, the translation of Microsoft Office documents such as Word, PowerPoint, and Excel, or Adobe PDF files may require the use of specialized tools to translate. This section introduces several services to help the researcher translate files like this. The first is DeepL Translator.

5.3.1 DeepL Translator

Introduced in an earlier section, DeepL is an outstanding tool for translating Microsoft Word and Microsoft PowerPoint files. It only supports .docx and .pptx file types; it does not support .doc, .ppt, or any other file type. The manner in which

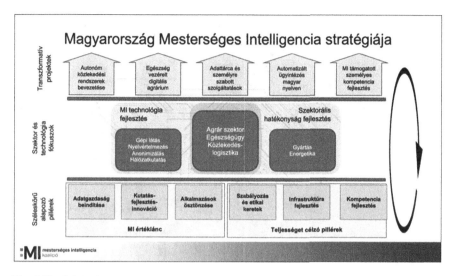

Fig. 5.23 Original presentation slide from a Hungarian-language presentation on Hungary's AI strategy [7]

it translates these types of files, however, is incredibly helpful because it maintains all formatting in a presentable manner. The DeepL interface is similar to that of Google, Yandex, and other translation services, with the original source on the left, and the translation of the source on the right. Simply upload the original source file. Moments later, the translation of the original source will be available for download.

Consider an example of a Microsoft PowerPoint slide that uses complex formatting. Figure 5.23 shows an image of a PowerPoint slide, which is written in Hungarian. Note the unique formatting and organization of the text.

The translation of the Microsoft PowerPoint slide from Hungarian into English is shown in Fig. 5.24. Not only is the translation of the text very clear to read and understand, DeepL Translator maintained all formatting from the original slide.

5.3.2   Translating an Entire Document in Microsoft Office Applications

Microsoft Word supports the translation of an entire document directly from the Microsoft application in Windows and Macintosh operating systems: no web application is required. It supports dozens of languages, too many to list here. To access this feature, navigate to the Review tab of any Microsoft Word document. Select the Translate button, and select "Translate Document." The Translator menu will appear on the right-hand side of the document. Figure 5.25 shows an example of a document ready for translation.

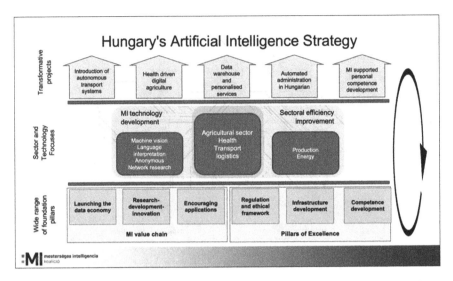

Fig. 5.24 Translation of presentation slide from a Hungarian presentation on Hungary's AI Strategy using DeepL [8]

In the Translator tab on the right, select the from and to languages. Microsoft Word will often detect the source language. In this example, the document will be translated from English to Bosnian. Click the blue "Translate" button below. The translation will appear in an entirely new Microsoft Word document. Figure 5.26 shows this new document with the text translated into Bosnian.

For the likely case where the researcher needs to translate filetypes other than Microsoft Office-supported formats, Google Translate may be one alternative.

5.3.3   Google Translate

As mentioned previously, Google Translate is able to translate documents to and from dozens of languages, as long as they are one of the following filetypes: .doc, .docx, .odf, .pdf, .ppt, .pptx, .ps, .rtf, .txt, .xls, or .xlsx. There is no limit to the number of searches the user can conduct. One of the most significant benefits to using Google Translate is the large number of languages it supports. This section uses a Microsoft Excel file containing text in Urdu as an example. Figure 5.27 shows the contents of the original file in Microsoft Excel. The middle column contains the titles of websites in Urdu. These are the titles we wish to translate.

To translate this file, navigate to Google Translate and select the "Documents" tab on the top of the screen. Upload the image and select the to and from languages. In this case, the "Detect Language" feature correctly detected the from language is Urdu. Figure 5.28 shows the Microsoft Excel file uploaded and ready to translate.

Fig. 5.25 Translating an entire document in Microsoft Word © Microsoft 2021 (Used with permission from Microsoft)

When ready, click on the blue "Translate" button below the file. The output will appear in plain text directly in the web browser; it will not download to a new file. It is still possible to copy and paste the text for use elsewhere. Figure 5.29 shows the results of the translation into English directly from the web browser.

Now, it's possible to understand these search results. Use this translated text to conduct further research or cite sources.

5.3.4   Converting Text in Google Docs and Google Drive

It is possible to extract foreign-language text from Adobe .pdf files using Google Docs and Google Drive. Once the foreign-language text is extracted, it is possible to use another translation tool mentioned throughout this chapter to translate the document. When using Google Docs, it is particularly important that the resolution of the

Fig. 5.26 Bosnian Translation of the previous document using Microsoft Word © Microsoft 2021 (Used with permission from Microsoft)

text is high: low-resolution images will contain more errors, rendering the translation of the text useless.

The example used in this section is an image from a book in Russian [9]. If the researcher was interested in knowing what this hard-copy book says, the researcher could first take a photo of the page with a camera. After uploading the image to a computer, open the image in a file viewer. Convert the image to an Adobe .pdf file, and then upload that image to Google Drive. This section describes the general process for translating a hard-copy text using Google Docs and Google Drive.

If the document to be translated is not already an Adobe .pdf file, convert it. Many image viewers have an option under the "File" menu to export an image to other file types. Figure 5.30 shows the "Export as PDF" option under the File tab in Preview on Macintosh OS.

Once the file is in the Adobe .pdf format, upload the file to Google Drive. From Google Drive, double click the file to view the file preview. Figure 5.31 shows the image preview of a page from the Russian book.

Fig. 5.27 Top 30 websites returned for the search تعمیراتی کمپنیاں, meaning *construction companies* in Urdu, conducted using Thruuu

Fig. 5.28 Microsoft Excel file uploaded into Google Translate (Google and the Google logo are trademarks of Google LLC)

On the top of the image preview, select "Open with Google Docs." This will open a new tab in Google Docs containing the text within the image. Figure 5.32 shows the sample output of the page from the book within Google Docs.

Google Docs will assess its own ability to convert the text from the image: the darker words annotate that Google believes it has more accurately detected the word in the image. Light-colored words mean that Google has doubt about its ability to accurately convert the text from the image.

Another useful tip is to use an Adobe .pdf merging tool to merge multiple pages into one document. This will save time when converting more than a few pages at once.

Fig. 5.29 Google Translate results for an Excel file from Urdu to English

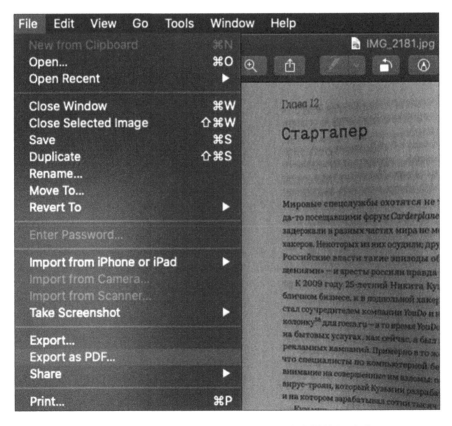

Fig. 5.30 "Export as PDF" option within Preview on Macintosh © 2021 Apple Inc.

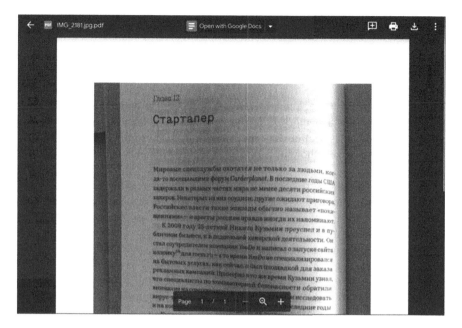

Fig. 5.31 Image preview in Google Drive (Google and the Google logo are trademarks of Google LLC)

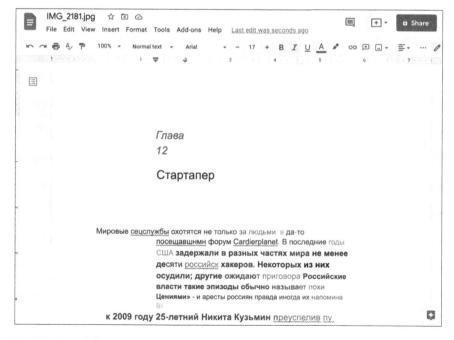

Fig. 5.32 Sample Russian text converted from an Adobe .pdf file in Google Docs (Google and the Google logo are trademarks of Google LLC)

5.3.5 Yandex Translate

In addition to its ability to translate text, websites, and images, Yandex Translate is able to translate documents to and from dozens of languages, as long as they are one of the following filetypes: .doc, .docx, .pdf, .ppt, .pptx, .xls, and .xlsx files and smaller than 5 MB in size. Yandex Translate is accessible on the Yandex Translate website by selecting "Documents" on the top menu, or at the URL https://translate.yandex.com/doc. This section uses an example of a Microsoft PowerPoint file in Norwegian. Figure 5.33 shows the third slide of the original document in Microsoft PowerPoint.

To translate the slides, drag and drop the file anywhere on the Yandex Translate interface, as shown in Fig. 5.34. Ensure the from and to languages are set appropriately, otherwise the translation will not succeed. In this case, the from-language is Norwegian, and the to-language is English.

Dropping the document into Yandex Translate automatically initiates the translation. After a few seconds, the translation appears directly in the web browser, as shown in Fig. 5.35.

Note that Yandex Translate did not include the notes beneath the slides from the original document in the translation. To understand these, conduct another translation query of the raw text by copying and pasting it in another tab.

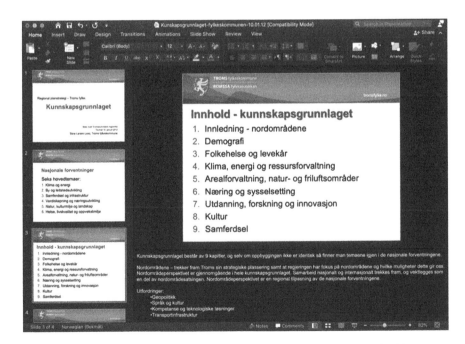

Fig. 5.33 Microsoft PowerPoint slide containing Norwegian text [10] © Microsoft 2021

Fig. 5.34 Yandex Translate interface for documents © 2015–2022 YANDEX LLC

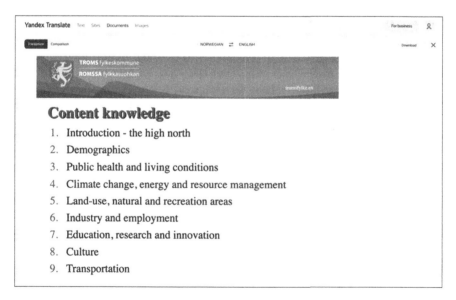

Fig. 5.35 Microsoft PowerPoint slides translated from Norwegian to English in Yandex Translate [11] © 2015–2022 YANDEX LLC

5.4   Translating Images

Translating images is usually much more difficult than translating digital text or documents, and is often not as successful. Still, there are a few free online tools today to aid the researcher with this difficult task. What makes this task so difficult, especially for the researcher who does not speak the target language, is that it is much more difficult to reproduce the text for input into a translation tool like those discussed previously. Not many of the resources discussed previously have this capability, so the researcher must look elsewhere to discover the meaning behind text in images.

Translating images uses a technology called Optical Character Recognition (OCR), which involves the conversion of the text in the image to a digital version of the text that the customer can then copy and paste for use elsewhere. Some image translators convert the text in the image to a digital format, which the reader can then copy and paste into an online translation service like those discussed previously. Other image translators will translate the text directly in the engine, emplacing the translated text over the original text. This is a personal preference and depends on the researcher's goals. This section introduces a few useful online services that demonstrate these capabilities.

5.4.1   Yandex Translate

The first OCR tool discussed in this section is Yandex Translate. Yandex Translate's OCR tool, which is available at https://translate.yandex.com/ocr, will impose the translation of the text directly onto the image. This can be very useful for the researcher to either reuse the image with the translation in the same format as the original image.

Figure 5.36 shows an image of a Danish sign, whose meaning we do not know. Without reproducing the text within this image on our own, it is possible to translate this text by placing the entire image into Yandex Translate.

Fig. 5.36 Danish sign [12]
(CC BY 2.0)

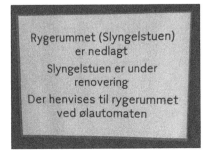

Fig. 5.37 English translation of a Danish sign using Yandex Translate © 2015–2022 YANDEX LLC (Image licensed under CC BY 2.0)

To translate the image, drag and drop it anywhere on the page. Ensure the to and from languages are correct, otherwise the image will not translate properly. Figure 5.37 shows an example translation using the Danish sign in the previous figure.

Select the "Download" button on the top right to download the image with the translated text, or select the "Open as text" button to obtain the original text without the image.

5.4.2   Google Keep

Google hosts an OCR capability, but it is not native to Google Translate. Rather, this capability can be found in Google Keep, which is a tool used primarily for keeping personal notes and reminders. Emplacing an image into Google Keep, available at https://keep.google.com/u/0/#home, provides an option to grab text from the image. While Google Keep does not translate the text, it does digitize it, making it possible to then copy and paste the text into a translation tool. Figure 5.38 shows the Google Keep interface.

To digitize the text in an image, drag and drop the image into the "Take a note…" bar on the top of the interface. The image will appear in the center. Figure 5.39 shows an example of a picture that contains Japanese text. Once the image is

Fig. 5.38   Google Keep interface (Google and the Google logo are trademarks of Google LLC)

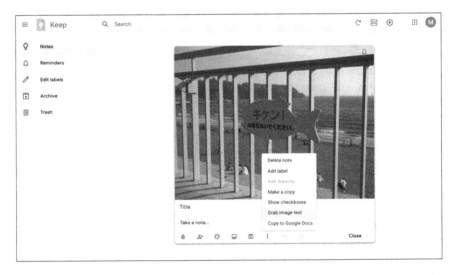

Fig. 5.39   "Grab Image Text" feature in Google Keep [13] (Google and the Google logo are trademarks of Google LLC, image licensed under CC BY-ND 2.0)

uploaded into Google Keep, select the three dots below the image. Then, select "Grab image text."

The Japanese text contained in the image appears below the image, as shown in Fig. 5.40. Now, the researcher can copy and paste the text for use as they see it.

Fig. 5.40 Japanese text grabbed with Google Keep [14] (Google and the Google logo are trademarks of Google LLC, image licensed under CC BY-ND 2.0)

5.4.3 OCR Space

OCR Space, available at https://ocr.space/, is a web-based OCR tool that takes an image or URL linking to an image (.png, .jpg, .gif, .bmp, or .pdf files only) and returns the foreign-language text; it does not translate the text. It will reproduce the image as a PDF with searchable text or will display the text directly within the tool's web interface. It provides OCR support for Arabic, Chinese, Bulgarian, Croatian, Czech, Danish, Dutch, English, Finnish, French, German, Greek, Hungarian, Italian, Japanese, Korean, Norwegian, Polish, Portuguese, Russian, Spanish, Slovenian, Swedish, and Turkish.

Figure 5.41 shows an example OCR output of an image containing Norwegian text. The text, which is now possible to copy and paste elsewhere, is returned in the text box to the right of the image. Even though OCR Space did not support images containing Norwegian-language text, it was still able to successfully provide the text by selecting Danish as the language from the drop-down menu. This is likely because the alphabets of these two languages are very similar. Now, the text is available for the researcher to copy, paste, or reproduce elsewhere.

Also consider exploring OCR Space's CopyFish tool, which is an extension built for Google Chrome, Microsoft Edge, and Firefox web browsers. It also enables the extraction and translation of text from images, videos, and PDF files. Visit https://ocr.space/copyfish for more information.

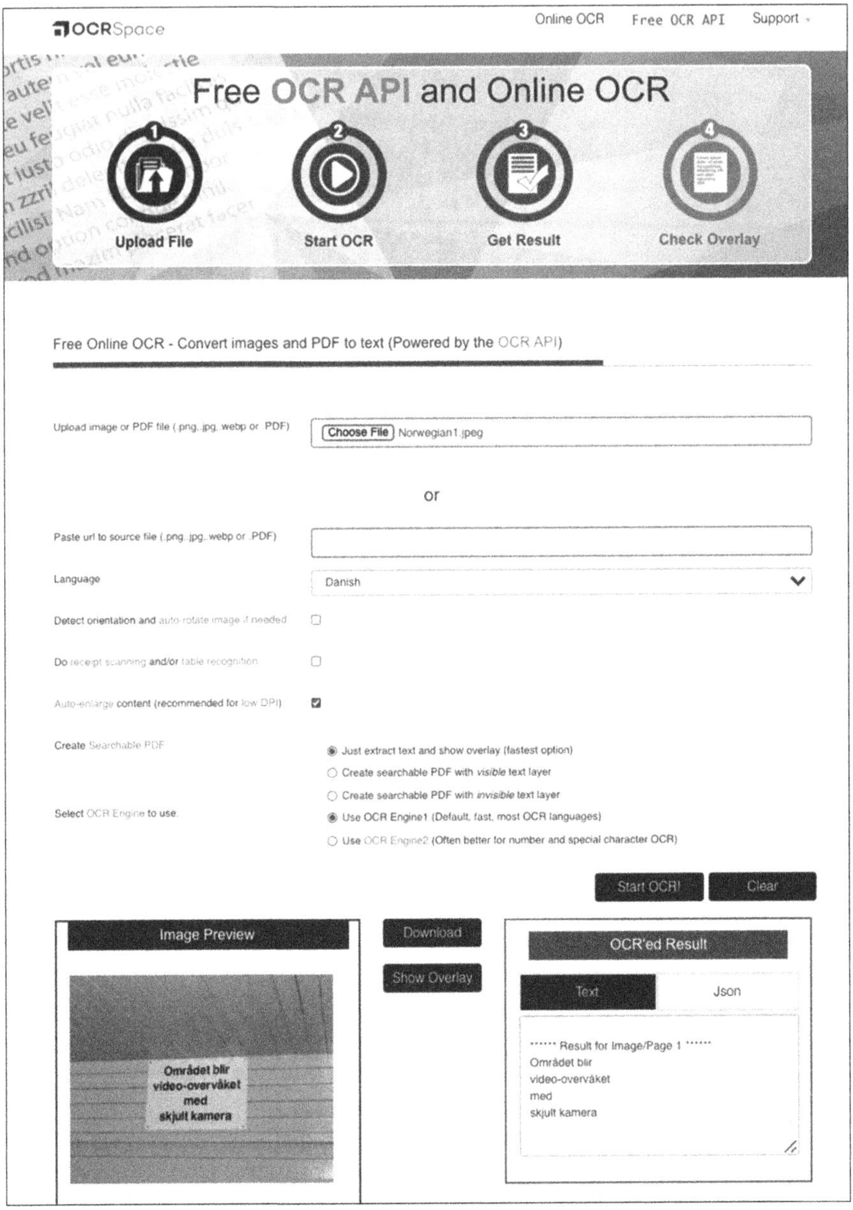

Fig. 5.41 OCR results of a Norwegian sign captured with OCR Space [15] © 2016–2021 - OCR. SPACE (Image licensed under CC BY-SA 2.0)

5.5   Translating Video

Many useful resources exist in video form. The foreign-language researcher may be interested in the content of Argentinian news reports or Icelandic films, to name a few. While it can be more difficult to understand the content of this type of resource, a thorough researcher should do their best to consider all available resources on the subject. This section introduces a few resources available to understand the content of video sources in foreign languages.

A few useful translation technologies exist online for the foreign-language researcher, both free and paid. This section discusses how to translate videos in YouTube, Veed, and Kapwing.

5.5.1   YouTube Subtitles

YouTube hosts videos in many languages other than English. Many videos have subtitle options built directly into the video, but this capability depends on the video creator. YouTube highly encourages video creators to include their own custom subtitle files into their videos to provide high-quality translations to a broader audience. This can be a daunting task, especially for a creator who does not speak the target language in which they wish to provide subtitles. One alternative is to enable auto-translated subtitles, which is a capability that YouTube offers to its content creators. This still requires the video creator to enable subtitles: if the creator does not enable subtitles, they will not be available to viewers. This section focuses on the videos that do have subtitles enabled; videos that do not have subtitles enabled (from YouTube and elsewhere) are addressed in the sections that follow.

Consider the Japanese cooking video as shown in Fig. 5.42. Subtitles, or Closed Captions, are available for this video because the "CC" button appears at the bottom of the video.

First, ensure the "CC" button is selected—a red bar will appear underneath and subtitles in the video's natural language will appear on the bottom of the video. Now, click on the settings button (shaped like a gear) to the immediate right of the "CC" button. A new dialog box will appear.

It is possible to change the subtitle language because the video creator has enabled this feature in their video. To do this, select "Subtitles/CC," where it states that the current Subtitles displayed are in Japanese, as shown in Fig. 5.43.

This video offers translations in Simplified Chinese, English, French, Italian, Japanese, Korean, Russian, Spanish, and Thai. To view subtitles in another language, select the "auto translate" option at the bottom of the list of languages, as shown in Fig. 5.43. These are computer-generated, whereas the subtitles in the listed languages may be generated from another source and my therefore be of higher quality.

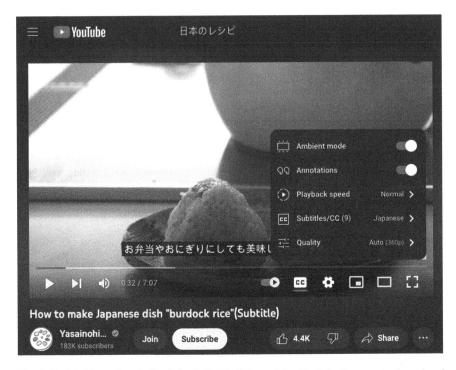

Fig. 5.42 Subtitle settings in YouTube [16] (YouTube and the YouTube logo are trademarks of Google LLC, image licensed under CC BY)

Upon selecting the "auto-translate" option, a new list of languages will appear, as shown in Fig. 5.44. This list of options is usually much longer.

Figure 5.45 shows the final result: as the video plays in Japanese, it displays corresponding Thai subtitles that correspond to the Japanese audio. The quality of the translations is usually high enough to comprehend the general message.

For those videos that do not have subtitle options enabled, the below online resources may be able to help. These tools may also work for videos that are the researcher's own work, videos that are not posted in YouTube, or videos that are not posted online at all (i.e., a video file belonging to the researcher as a video file on their personal computer).

5.5.2   Veed

Veed is an online service that offers free and paid video subtitling services, accessible at https://www.veed.io/. Visitors can create a free account that will generate subtitles for a video for free, and will accept video files in various forms from various sources. However, a paid subscription is required to download and translate subtitles.

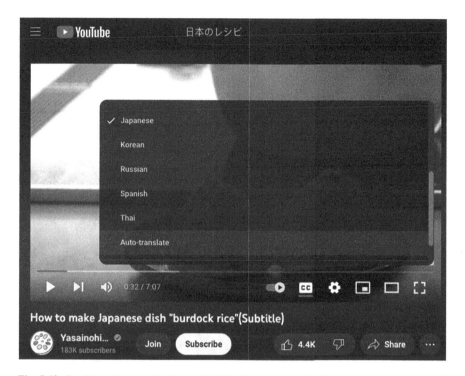

Fig. 5.43 Subtitle settings in YouTube [17] (YouTube and the YouTube logo are trademarks of Google LLC, image licensed under CC BY)

To demonstrate how Veed works, this section will use a video from a Greek cooking show. This video did not have subtitles enabled in YouTube, which means that the steps discussed in the previous section would not be available. Veed provides an alternative. From the Veed home page, as shown in Fig. 5.46, select "Create new Project" in the center of the screen.

A dialog box will invite the user to "Upload a Video or Audio File" by dragging and dropping a file, uploading from the device, uploading from DropBox, recording a video directly through Veed, or by linking from a URL from YouTube. Figure 5.47 shows these options as they appear in Veed.

Once the video is uploaded into Veed, it will open the Settings page and display each frame of the video along the bottom. In the Settings, it is also possible to play the original file, as shown in Fig. 5.48.

The next step is to add the subtitles. To add subtitles, navigate to the Subtitles tab along the left-hand side of the interface, as shown in Fig. 5.49. Select "Auto Subtitles" to have Veed generate Greek-language subtitles automatically.

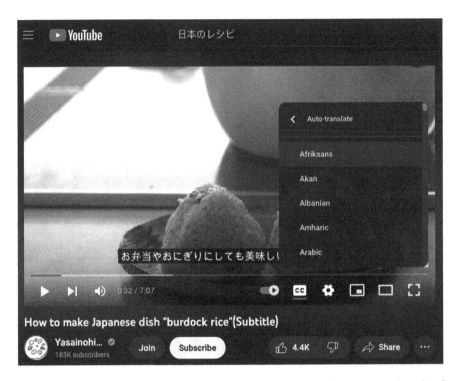

Fig. 5.44 Subtitle settings in YouTube [18] (YouTube and the YouTube logo are trademarks of Google LLC, image licensed under CC BY)

Before Veed can generate the subtitles, it still needs a little more information. As shown in Fig. 5.50, tell Veed the language it needs to detect: in this case, Greek. Then, click the "Start" button. This may take a few minutes, depending on the duration of the video.

When Veed has finished generating the subtitles, it will display them on the left-hand side of the video. It will also display them within the video on the right, and will also display the corresponding subtitle to each frame of the video on the bottom of the screen. Press the play button to watch the video with the corresponding Greek-language subtitles. Figure 5.51 shows what these subtitles look like in Veed.

Again, the free version of Veed will only allow the user to interact with the subtitles directly in the web browser. To download the video with the subtitles, translate the subtitles, download the subtitles, or download a translation of the subtitles requires a paid subscription. With a paid subscription, open the Translate tab on the top of the screen to select a target language. In the unpaid version, it is still possible to copy and paste individual lines.

Fig. 5.45 Japanese video with Thai subtitles (YouTube and the YouTube logo are trademarks of Google LLC, image licensed under CC BY) [16]

Veed also does not recognize all video links. If a certain URL is not recognized, another option is to download the video from the source and upload it as a video file into the tool. Kapwing is the next resource discussed in this section.

5.5.3 Kapwing

Kapwing is a web-based video editing service, available at https://www.kapwing.com/. Among its many capabilities include subtitling and video translation services. Kapwing asks for an email address to upload a video. After entering an email address, much of Kapwing's useful functionality is available free of charge. This section uses the video from the previous examples to show how to add English subtitles to a video in Norwegian.

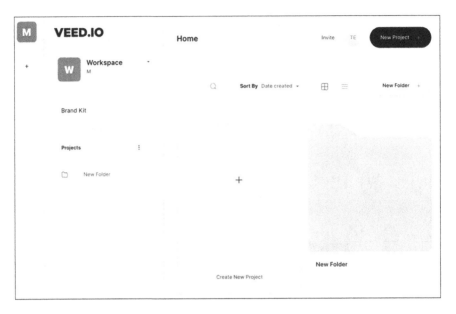

Fig. 5.46 Home page in Veed © 2021 VEED

Fig. 5.47 Upload a Video or Audio File in Veed © 2021 VEED

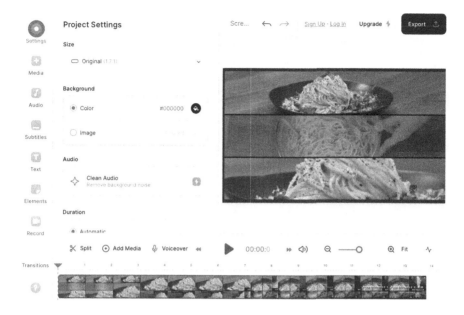

Fig. 5.48 Project dashboard in Veed © 2021 VEED (Image licensed under CC BY) [22]

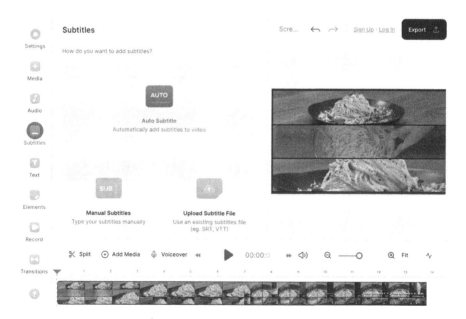

Fig. 5.49 Subtitles interface in Veed © 2021 VEED (Image licensed under CC BY) [22]

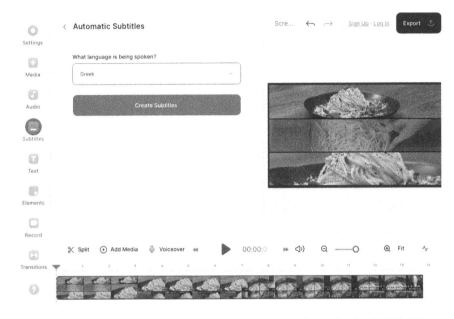

Fig. 5.50 Auto Subtitles settings in Veed © 2021 VEED (Image licensed under CC BY) [22]

Fig. 5.51 Subtitles created for a YouTube video using Veed © 2021 VEED (Image licensed under CC BY) [22]

To access the subtitler in Kapwing, click on "Subtitles" under the Tools tab, as shown in Fig. 5.52, or navigate to https://www.kapwing.com/subtitles.

The "Add Subtitles to Video" page invites the user to upload a file or link to a video online by entering its URL. Select "Choose a video" and enter the video source in the panel on the right of the workspace, as shown in Fig. 5.53.

This example uses the YouTube video located at https://www.youtube.com/watch?v=1-7fIEMxwX4 [19]. Pasting the URL into the "Paste a URL" box initiates the upload. Figure 5.54 shows the "Generate Subtitles" page with the YouTube video loaded into Kapwing.

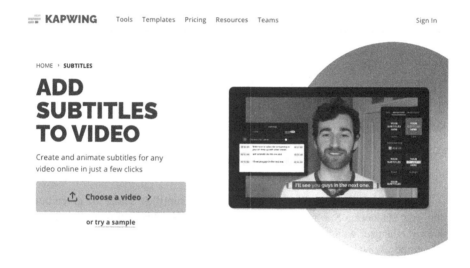

Fig. 5.52 Add Subtitles to Video in Kapwing © 2023 Kapwing

Fig. 5.53 Choose a Video in Kapwing © 2023 Kapwing

Fig. 5.54 Add Subtitles to Video page in Kapwing © 2023 Kapwing

The video is now loaded into Kapwing. To add subtitles, select the green button that says "Generate Subtitles" as shown in Fig. 5.54. This will open a dialog box that asks the user which language it should expect to find in the source video. It also asks if the user wishes to translate these subtitles into another language. Select this option, and another drop-down menu will appear where the user can select the desired target language, shown in Fig. 5.55. This video is in Norwegian, and the subtitles will be in English.

The settings in Fig. 5.55 will produce English subtitles for the Norwegian-language video. Once the languages are specified, select "Generate Subtitles" to allow Kapwing to generate the subtitles.

Figure 5.56 shows the final output: the English-language subtitles for the video, separated into small sections. To watch the subtitles on the video, click the purple play button on the top of the screen. To download the subtitles requires a paid subscription. With this method, it is still possible to understand the video well enough to interpret its meaning and cite in formal research.

5.6 Translator Communities of Interest

Sometimes, the methods discussed throughout this chapter do not work. Sometimes, external support is required. This may be because the above services do not support a certain filetype, or the automated translators available cannot capture the

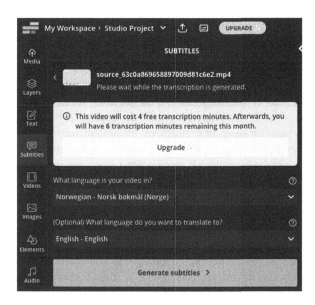

Fig. 5.55   Generate Subtitles dialog box in Kapwing © 2023 Kapwing

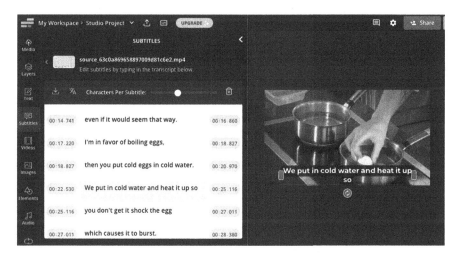

Fig. 5.56   English subtitles for a Norwegian-language video in Kapwing © 2023 Kapwing (image licensed under CC BY) [19]

colloquial nature of the source text. When this is the case, there are communities of kind experts online who are able and willing to help. These communities are incredibly helpful, but be aware that these communities often follow a certain unspoken etiquette. It is important to follow these general guidelines to enable the community to be as helpful as possible.

Generally speaking, it is the researcher's responsibility to make sure that the answer to the question does not exist elsewhere. If a respondent knows that the answer exists elsewhere, they will link to the answer and, sometimes, they may publicly shame the person who asked the question for wasting their time. It is also important to be as clear and concise as possible by stating the exact question. Ask a question that is answerable: for example, do not ask a forum to translate an entire 400-page book—this is not likely to get the desired result because the researcher does not likely need to have an entire book translated. Instead, use the resources discussed earlier in this book to determine which exact section needs translating, and provide the original text of that section. Post questions that are appropriate for the location: this will also encourage frequent users of the site to shame the poster of the question to look elsewhere. Be polite and grateful for the responses received, even if they are not the desired answer.

Following these guidelines will help the researcher get the most out of their membership in these online communities. That being said, if the reader speaks one or a few foreign languages, they are encouraged to contribute, too.

The communities of interest discussed in this section include r/translator (Reddit), Stack Exchange, and Wiktionary Tea Rooms.

5.6.1   r/translator (Reddit)

The r/translator sub-Reddit is a vast community of linguists and language enthusiasts. As of 2022, it has 125 k members who post and answer questions daily. It is a very active site, making it an excellent source to get quick answers to timely questions. The r/translator page is accessible at https://www.reddit.com/r/translator/. It does not require a username to read and search for questions already posted; however, free registration is required to ask a question or reply to someone else's post.

Figure 5.57 shows the top content of the r/translator page, including a description of the forum. On the top of the page, it is possible to conduct a key word search to see what else has already been discussed on a topic. To see the current topics of conversation, scroll down the page. Figure 5.58 shows a conversation regarding the translation of text on a mug. The asker did not know the language of origin, but within a few short minutes, the asker received a thoughtful and helpful answer from a kind Chinese-speaker.

Reddit also has sub-Reddit pages for dozens of languages, including but not limited to: r/learn_arabic, r/chineselanguage, r/italianlearning, r/LearnJapanese, r/learnpolish, and more. To see a full list of language-specific sub-Reddit pages, visit: https://www.reddit.com/r/translator/wiki/linkflair.

Fig. 5.57 Screenshot of the r/translator page on Reddit © 2021 Reddit Inc.

5.6.2 Stack Exchange (Culture and Recreation)

Stack Exchange is a collection of topical question and answer pages, ranging from complex mathematics and technology questions to special interest groups and hobbies. Within the Culture and Recreation topics includes several communities of interest specializing in individual languages. As of March 2022, there are unique pages dedicated to English, French, Japanese, German, Spanish, Chinese, Italian, Russian, Portuguese, Latin, Korean, Esperanto, and Ukrainian. Figure 5.59 shows the pages available under the Culture and Recreation section, which is available at https://stackexchange.com/sites#culturerecreation.

Figure 5.60 shows a screenshot of the Korean Language Beta site, which is a safe space to ask and answer questions pertaining to the Korean Language. This would be an acceptable place to seek translation assistance online, as long as the researcher is certain the text is in the Korean language.

Besides the pages dedicated to individual languages, there are also pages on Language Learning that may also interest the researcher who feels inspired to learn a new language.

If the researcher's language does not exist and wants to create one, Stack Exchange welcomes anyone to start a new community of interest. Visit the Area51 page, located at https://area51.stackexchange.com/, to propose a new language be added to the site.

Fig. 5.58 Conversation within r/translator regarding the translation of Chinese text on a mug [20] © 2021 Reddit Inc. (Image published with permission)

5.6.3   *Wiktionary Tea Room*

The Wiktionary Tea Room is a forum open to the discussion of word meanings, translations, and usage. Anyone with a language or translation issue is free to ask questions about any language. Like the other services discussed in this section, all replies are visible to the public and anyone can reply anonymously. All posts dating back to 2003 are visible today. The Wiktionary Tea Room is accessible at https://en.wiktionary.org/wiki/Wiktionary:Tea_room.

Fig. 5.59 Culture and Recreation Pages in Stack Exchange © 2021 Stack Exchange Inc.

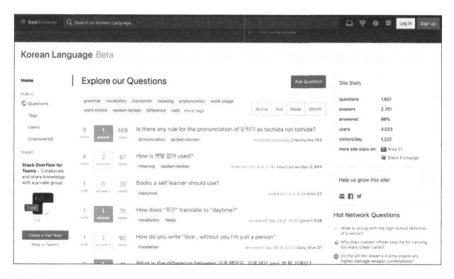

Fig. 5.60 Korean Language Community of Interest in Stack Exchange © 2021 Stack Exchange Inc. (User contributions licensed under CC BY-SA. rev 2021.10.8.40416)

Figure 5.61 shows a sample question and answer about the meaning of a Chinese character. The entire conversation between strangers is available for anyone to view, and contains useful links to other pages for reference. There is no limit to the resources and knowledge of those who may happen to stumble upon a question using one of these communities of interest.

Obsolete meanings of 気 [edit]

What exacted does 気 read & mean in s:zh:重修吳孝子廟記 and s:zh:勻皇太子即位制, or are these errors? I also found s:ko:메이지 医學語彙(疾題).djvu/7, where 気 means 氣. Crowley666 (talk) 12:22, 30 September 2021 (UTC) [reply]

@Crowley666, If you see something suspicious in classical texts over at zh-wikisource, it's most likely an error (bad OCR, electronic text of questionable provenance, mass Hans->Hant transformation out of context, etc.). The case with the last link is much more convincing because at least we have a manuscript. --Frigoris (talk) 08:24, 1 October 2021 (UTC) [reply]

@Frigoris, yes, they were copied from ctext.org by Liangent-bot. I've fixed the first one. Anyway, 気 is used as 氣 multiple times in 医學語彙(假題), but I can't find it elsewhere. I have to find a Chinese source to put it in the Chinese section. Crowley666 (talk) 14:15, 1 October 2021 (UTC) [reply]

@Crowley666, is that book a Sino-Korean glossary book? If so, you can definitely base any Chinese entry content on its Chinese part, if that meets the CFI. The reason you can't find it elsewhere is that the form is almost certainly a scribe's own hand. The CHISE⑦ somehow links the form to the Shuowen 氣, though, without explanation. --Frigoris (talk) 15:30, 1 October 2021 (UTC) [reply]

ayy s:ko:의하어(위 is my transcription project. 医學語彙 occasionally has Japanese glosses. Google web searches for some of the hanja terms (運備寒, 二日健) return mostly Korean pages. The author is unknown. 気 also appears in s:ja:日鮮日常會話. --Suzukaze-c (talk) 05:00, 2 October 2021 (UTC) [reply]

Fig. 5.61 Sample question and answer in the Wiktionary Tea Room [21] (CC BY-SA)

Online Database References

1. Google Translate is able to translate documents in one of the following file formats: .doc, .docx, .odf, .pdf, .ppt, .pptx, .ps, .rtf, .txt, .xls, or .xlsx.
2. Text from "नेपाली भाषा [Nepali Language]," accessed October 9, 2021, https://ne.wikipedia.org/wiki/नेपाली_भाषा.
3. "демография [demography]," last modified September 3, 2020, https://en.wiktionary.org/wiki/демография.
4. "Media Suomessa [Mass Media in Finland]," last modified October 24, 2020, https://fi.wikipedia.org/wiki/Media_Suomessa.
5. 박진영 [Park Jin-young], "[IT사이트] '현금없는 사회'의 첫 발걸음…CBDC [IT Site: The first step in a 'cashless society'… CBDC]," October 1, 2021 https://n.news.naver.com/mnews/article/031/0000628068?sid=105.
6. "Население России [Population of Russia]," last modified October 8, 2021, https://ru.wikipedia.org/wiki/Население_России. Available under the Creative Commons Attribution-ShareAlike License (CC BY-SA).
7. "MI Stratégia – Adatgazdálkodás [MI Strategy – Data Management]," December 9, 2019 https://www.ksh.hu/docs/bemutatkozas/hun/ost/1_nr_ost_2019_12_09.pptx.
8. "MI Stratégia – Adatgazdálkodás [MI Strategy – Data Management]," December 9, 2019 https://www.ksh.hu/docs/bemutatkozas/hun/ost/1_nr_ost_2019_12_09.pptx. Translated from Hungarian into English using DeepL.
9. The page translated in this section is from Даниил Туровский [Daniil Turovsky], *Вторжение: Краткая История Русских Хакеров [Invasion: A Brief History of Russian Hackers]* (Moscow: Individuum, 2019), 86.
10. Tromsøområdets regionråd [Tromsø Region Regional Council], "Kunnskapsgrunnlaget [Knowledge Base]," January 10, 2012, https://www.tromso-omradet.no/wp-content/uploads/2018/10/Kunskapsgrunnlaget-fylkeskommunen-10.01.12.ppt, Slide 3.
11. Ibid.
12. emme-dk, "Dagens bedste skilt på LO-skolen [Best sign at the LO school today]," accessed October 10, 2021, https://search.creativecommons.org/photos/e7bf91ec-56c1-45d5-b3b8-480bb7472e5d.
13. reikow101277, "魚のサイン [Fish Sign]," accessed October 10, 2021, https://search.creativecommons.org/photos/5e63ab26-d4fd-45fc-9b41-a8f26f3430ff.
14. Ibid.
15. Charlotteshj, "Skilt ved parkeringskælder i Oslo," accessed October 10, 2021, https://search.creativecommons.org/photos/a4053794-a3bd-4f78-a7db-7ce79eb9bed2.
16. YasainohiChannel, "How to make Japanese dish "burdock rice" (Subtitle)," January 13, 2021, https://www.youtube.com/watch?v=fB3tAv63BsY. Available under the Creative Commons Attribution License (CC BY).
17. Ibid.

18. Ibid.

19. Nasjonal digital læringsarena, "Kokt egg [Boiled egg]," March 22, 2013, https://www.youtube.com/watch?v=1-7fIEMxwX4. Available under the Creative Commons Attribution License (CC BY).

20. u/octolink and u/lexicophiliac, "[English>Japanese, Chinese] Would like this mugs statement translated. Unsure which language it is," originally posted October 8, 2021, https://www.reddit.com/r/translator/comments/q42w8s/englishjapanese_chinese_would_like_this_mugs/.

21. Crowley666, Frigoris, and Suzukaze-c, "Obsolete meanings of 気," last modified October 2, 2021, https://en.wiktionary.org/wiki/Wiktionary:Tea_room. Available under the Creative Commons Attribution-ShareAlike License (CC BY-SA).

22. Άκης Πετρετζίκης, "Αυθεντική Καρμπονάρα | Άκης Πετρετζίκης [Authentic Carbonara | Akis Petretzikis]," October 10, 2019. https://www.youtube.com/watch?v=hYaAC6zSEHE&t=4s. Available under the Creative Commons Attribution License (CCBY).

Chapter 6
Case Studies

This chapter includes a few case studies that demonstrate some of the search principles introduced earlier in this book. It provides some useful examples and methods for locating information that helps answer a unique need with a foreign-language nexus. In some cases, the foreign language need is obvious; in others, the opportunity is not clear at all.

The first case study explores the steps one might take to discover data sets from foreign sources. Just as any other source type (website, book, news service) may be biased, so too may data sets inherit biases simply due to the methods by which the data are collected. This said, the researcher may be interested in discovering data sets from sources other than those usual and familiar providers. This case study explores these possibilities using some of the advanced search operators introduced earlier in the book.

The second case study explores the steps one might take to generate a list of foreign think tanks. The ultimate goal of this exploration is to provide a stepping-off point for further search opportunities. Using simple search techniques, it is possible to make a comprehensive list of foreign think tanks from any country or region. Use this case study as an example of how to do so for any such topic.

The third and final case study investigates smart cities around the world. To do this requires the implementation of several advanced search operators at once. The searches conducted in this section build upon each other in the context of a larger question. This helps to drill deep down to the exact desired resources.

6.1 Discovering Data Sets from Foreign Sources

The modern Data Scientist might be interested to find new datasets to analyze that add a foreign dimension to their research. For example, they may have data pertaining to the GDP of America over time, which may help them answer a question such as: which natural resources contribute most to America's GDP? A more complex question may require the comparison of this data to similar data describing the GDP of Romania, or another country. The question would differ from the previous, for example: how do natural resources influence the GDP of America and Romania? Whatever the question, it is likely that the data sets that answer the second question are stored in two different databases. This section will use advanced search techniques to discover a foreign-country's data resources. First, consider the US Government site, https://data.gov. The home page for this website is shown below in Fig. 6.1.

This website contains tens of thousands of US Government datasets. The foreign-language researcher then asks: *I wonder if other countries besides the United States have a data.gov-equivalent?* First, note the URL: the US Government owns the .gov domain, so a foreign country's equivalent of the data.gov website would have the ccTLD at the end. So, to discover other a list of all foreign countries who have an official data.gov website, conduct the search *site:data.gov.** as shown in Fig. 6.2. The asterisk will cause the search to return results that contain any website where .gov is the cc2LD and .data is the 3LD.

The first three results are the website for the Taiwanese, Serbian, and Hong-Kongese data.gov websites. The answer to our initial question is certainly *yes, foreign governments do have their own data.gov equivalents.* If the researcher knows they want sources from a particular country on a particular topic, they should conduct a follow-up search on that side for particular terms or filetypes. If the researchers were interested in Serbian datasets about real estate, for example, they could conduct a search such as *site:data.gov.rs некретнина* (the Serbian word for real estate) to see if there are any datasets on the subject. Sure enough, there are about 29 results, as shown in Fig. 6.3.

Fig. 6.1 Screenshot of https://data.gov (Printed with Permission)

Fig. 6.2 Google search results for *site:*data.gov.* (Google and the Google logo are trademarks of Google LLC)

These websites come in many forms: sometimes, they contain 4LD's, too. To see if any of these sites contain lower-level domains, it is possible to broaden the search by conducting the search *site:*.data.gov.** as shown in Fig. 6.4.

The above search in Fig. 6.4 will include sub-domains for .data.gov that also contain a country ccTLD at the end. Notice how many results, there are 3.5 million results, all in random order. If the researchers were interested in datasets from the United Kingdom, for example, they could specify the ccTLD with the 4LD wildcard by conducting the search *site:*.data.gov.uk* as shown in Fig. 6.5.

The results of the above search contain websites of the form *.data.gov.uk, which offer even further opportunities for tailored research. Note that there are significantly fewer results (there are still too many results, which would warrant the addition of more search terms to narrow down the exact type of data sought).

Another important consideration is that there may be websites not containing some form of "data.gov" in the URL. In other words, there must be websites that contain useful datasets that do not originate from governments. Some of these sites may contain other TLDs. To discover other sites that may not be official government websites, but that are likely to be data-focused in content, consider the search *site:*. data.** as shown in Fig. 6.6.

Fig. 6.3 Google search results for *site:*data.gov.rs *некретнина*, the Serbian word for real estate (Google and the Google logo are trademarks of Google LLC)

Notice how the results shown in Fig. 6.6 contain websites that do not necessarily contain the .gov domain, although results further down on the page also contain variations of the data.gov website. It will be worthwhile to explore each of these sites for key terms in English and foreign-character alphabets.

Another nuance the researcher might notice as they continue to conduct targeted searches for datasets is that the URLs often contain the word "dataset" or "datasets." This was apparent in the search in Fig. 6.7 for *site:data.gov.rs некретнина*, for example. This is a great opportunity to conduct a search using the key word "dataset" and the .rs domain, to see if there are any datasets that exist on Serbian websites that are on other websites besides https://data.gov.rs. After all, this is only one website, and there may be others. If there are no other Serbian websites that meet these parameters, it is good to know that, too. So, let's conduct the search *site:rs inurl:datasets некретнина*.

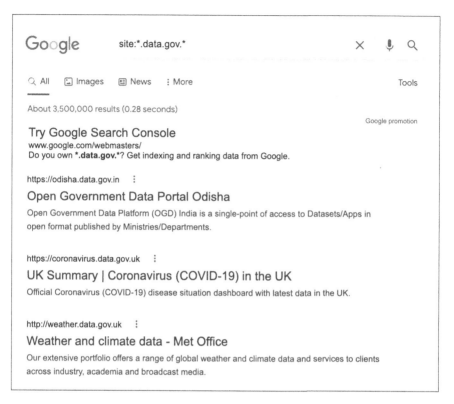

Fig. 6.4 Google search results for *site:*.data.gov.* (Google and the Google logo are trademarks of Google LLC)

In this case, there were no results returned when searching for the term *dataset* in the URL, but there were two results when searching for the term *datasets*. It would have also been possible to conduct the search to include websites that contain both the word *dataset* or *datasets* by adding an OR statement. Consider the search *site:rs inurl:(dataset OR datasets) некретнина* as shown in Fig. 6.8.

The above search included results containing the keyword "dataset" or "datasets" on any Serbian website—and look, there are new Serbian websites to explore that may contain datasets that did not exist on our starting website, data.gov.rs.

The researcher will also notice the results specify filetypes, when appropriate: the first two results are Excel files—meaning they may possess the .xls or .xlsx file extensions. This is important because many of the results may not contain datasets that are ready for download and analysis. For example, .pdf files may not be the type of file we're looking for here. So let's filter those results out by conducting the search *site:data.gov.rs некретнина ext:xls OR ext:xlsx* as shown in Fig. 6.9.

As expected, all the results are Excel files. It is important to specify both Excel filetypes because a search for .xls files will not return files that are of the .xlsx type.

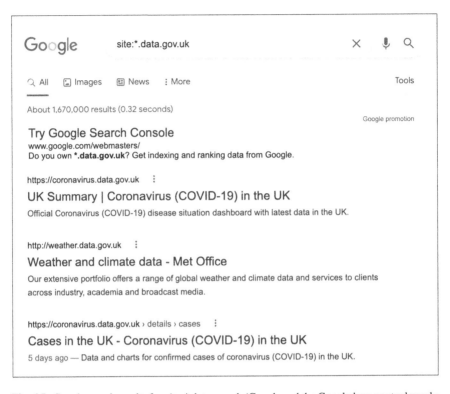

Fig. 6.5 Google search results for *site:*.data.gov.uk (Google and the Google logo are trademarks of Google LLC)

When conducting a search for datasets in general, it is important to consider the filetypes that datasets often come in. Two other common data filetypes include .csv and .json filetypes, among others. The researcher should consider exactly the type of information they are looking to find, and specify it in the search.

The last search we'll conduct in this section uses the *related:* operator. Recall that the *related:* operator returns results that are similar in theme, but different to the website in question. Consider the results of the search *related:data.gov* as shown in Fig. 6.10.

The results include other US government websites other than data.gov that may also contain datasets. For example, going to the census.gov website shows there may be some useful datasets and other data resources that may not have appeared on the data.gov website.

As seen in Fig. 6.11, the census.gov website contains other data resources that may not appear in a target search on any other website. For example, the visualizations section of the website contains interactive visualizations for which the data have already been analyzed.

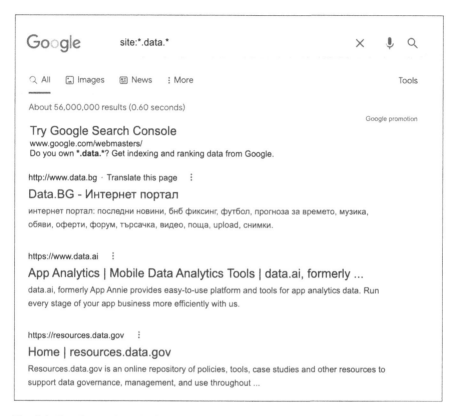

Fig. 6.6 Google search results for *site:*.data.** (Google and the Google logo are trademarks of Google LLC)

6.2   Discovering Russian Think Tanks

The academic researcher may be curious to answer question such as "What are some well-known Russian think tanks?" and "What do those think tanks have to say about XYZ subject?" Well, it is possible to answer these questions using advanced search operators.

First, let's begin by conducting a preliminary search for Russian think tanks using the key terms *Russian think tanks* and the *site: ru* operator. This will return websites that contain references to Russian think tanks and websites belonging to Russian think tanks that possess a .ru domain. Consider the search as shown in Fig. 6.12.

At first glance, the top results in the search above appear promising. However, since we conducted the search using English key terms, the results are largely in English. For example, MGIMO's top results are actually in English, even though the website is Russian. The Carnegie Endowment for International Peace is actually an American think tank that owns the .com and .ru domains for different versions of

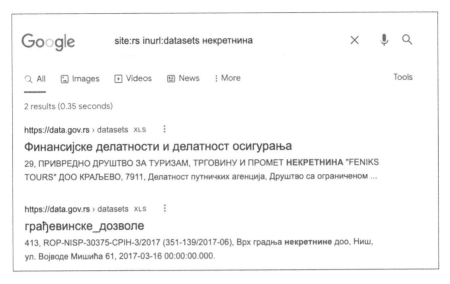

Fig. 6.7 Google search results for *site:rs inurl:datasets некретнина*, the Serbian word for real estate (Google and the Google logo are trademarks of Google LLC)

their website. These websites may be helpful and interesting, but the researcher may be more interested in websites belonging to Russian think tanks, where the resources are available in the Russian language.

The next step involves a search with Russian-character key terms. Using Google translate, it is possible to copy and paste the Russian phrase for *think tanks*, which is *мозговой центр*. Figure 6.13 demonstrates a search using the Russian-language search terms with the *site:ru* operator.

Based solely on the number of results returned, it is very unlikely that all the results returned are all Russian think tanks. The same was true for the previous search, too. Upon further inspection, it appears that the top result from ria.ru is a news article about an American think tank on a Russian news website. Exploring further, the second result is a Russian science magazine. These are not the resources we are looking for.

Consider the third website, imemo.ru. This website was also in our original search with English-language key terms (result # 6). By browsing this site and reading about the organization, it is possible to tell that this is a Russian think tank. The acronym IMEMO translates to The Institute of World Economy and International Relations.

Now, let's use the above results, along with the related: operator, to see if Google has associated any websites with imemo.ru. If the search works, we should expect it to return websites belonging to Russian research institutes on the topics of world economics and international relations. Consider the search as shown in Fig. 6.14.

The results of this search return a list of websites related to imemo.ru! It is important to note that the use of the related: operator requires a lot of trial and error. For example, it did not work on americancouncil.ru or many of the other websites

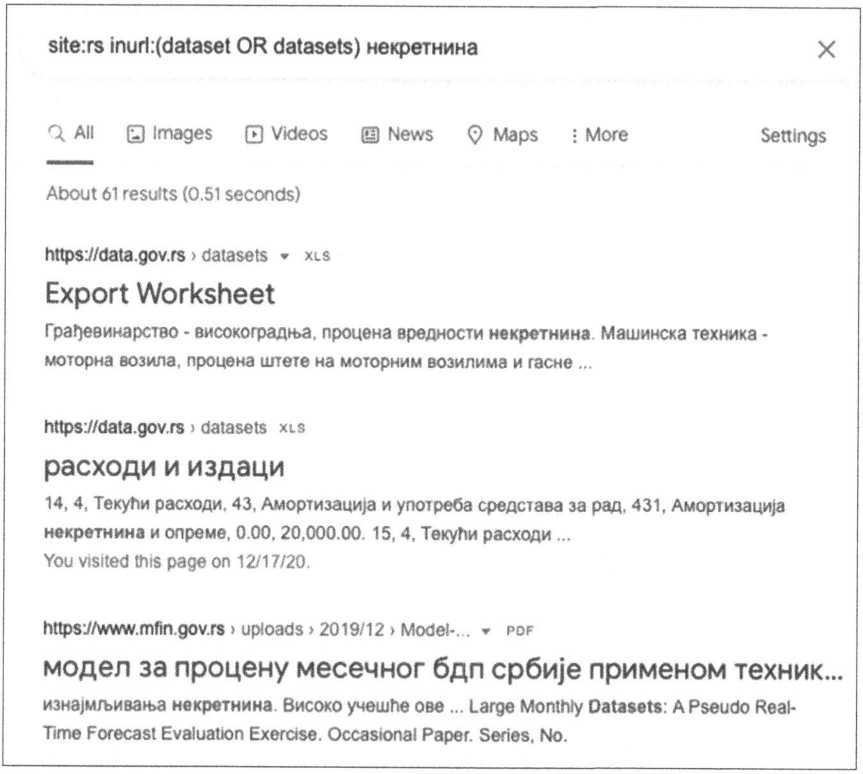

Fig. 6.8 Google search results for *site:rs inurl:(dataset OR datasets) некретнина*, the Serbian word for real estate (Google and the Google logo are trademarks of Google LLC)

returned from the original English-language search. After several searches, it is possible to see that it does indeed work for this website.

Here is a list of the associated websites and potential think tanks returned from this search. It is important to research each organization before classifying them as think tanks; however, the list is small enough to research each one and then use the desired organizations to target the search further:

(Preliminary) List of Russian think tanks related to World Economy and International Relations		
No.	Think Tank – Russian Name	Think Tank – English Name	Website URL
1	Институт экономики: Российской академии наук	Institute of Economics Russian Academy of Sciences	https://inecon.org
2	Вологодский научный центр Российской академии наук	Volgogradsky Scientific Center of the Russian Academy of Sciences	http://www.vscc.ac.ru
3	Институт экономики РАН: Отделение международных экономических и политических исследований	Russian Academy of Sciences: The Institute for International Economic and Political Studies	http://www.imepi-eurasia.ru

(continued)

(Preliminary) List of Russian think tanks related to World Economy and International Relations

No.	Think Tank – Russian Name	Think Tank – English Name	Website URL
4	Проблемы современной экономики	Problems of Modern Economy	http://www.m-economy.ru
5	Институт экономических исследований ДВО РАН	Economic Research Institute, Far East Branch, Russian Academy of Sciences	http://www.ecrin.ru/
6	Мировая экономика	World Economics	http://www.ereport.ru
7	Институт экономических стратегий РАН	Institute for Economic Strategy	http://www.inesnet.ru/
8	Международная жизнь	International Affairs	https://interaffairs.ru/
9	Высшая школа экономики	Higher School of Economics	https://www.hse.ru/
10	Институт экономики города	Institute for Urban Economics	http://www.urbaneconomics.ru/
11	Институт геополитики профессора Дергачева	Institute of Geopolitics of Professor Dergachev	http://dergachev.ru/
12	Финансовый Университет	Finance University	http://fa.ru
13	Кот Ученый	Cat Scientist	http://www.smartcat.ru/
14	Всероссийская академия внешней торговли	All-Russian Academy of Foreign Trade	http://www.vavt.ru/
15	Институт Ближнего Востока	Middle East Institute	http://www.limes.ru
16	Институт научной информации по общественным наукам	Institute of Scientific Information on Social Sciences	http://inion.ru/
17	Вольное экономическое общество России	Free Economic Society of Russia	http://veorus.ru/
18	Обучение, Образование, Исследование, Комментарии	Learning, Education, Research, Commentaries	http://www.lerc.ru/
19	Административно-управленческий портал	Administrative and Management Portal	http://www.aup.ru/
20	Финансовая библиотека Миркин	Mirkin Financial Library	http://www.mirkin.ru/
21	Институт проблем рынка Российской академии наук	Market Research Institute of the Russian Academy of Sciences	http://www.ipr-ras.ru/
22	Сибирское отделение Российской академии наук	Siberian Branch of the Russian Academy of Sciences	http://www.nsc.ru/

Google's initial estimate that there were 39 results was an overestimate: actually, there were only 23 related results, with one website no longer hosted.

Based on this list, the researcher can either continue to expand their list of think tanks by conducting similar searches using the related: operator against other known think tank websites; or, they can identify one of the resources in the list to conduct a targeted search. Let's perform the latter.

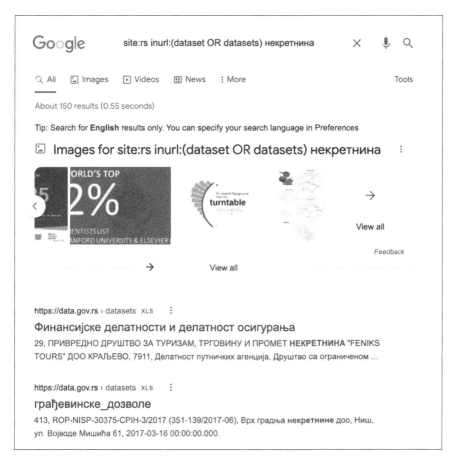

Fig. 6.9 Google search results for *site:*data.gov.rs *некретнина ext:xls OR ext:xlsx* (the Serbian word for real estate) (Google and the Google logo are trademarks of Google LLC)

Consider the Institute of Economics Russian Academy of Sciences, the first result in the previous Google search. The researcher may be interested to know what Russian think tanks and academic journals are publishing on the topic of US politics. To see if this website is hosting any information on the topic, conduct a search such as *site:inecon.org США AND политика*, where *США* is the Russian spelling of USA and *политика* is the Russian word for politics (as shown in Fig. 6.15).

The key words for USA and politics (in Russian) are bolded in the results below the search. Consider the first result, which appears to be a link to an academic journal (see Fig. 6.16).

The journal name is US – Canada: Economics, Politics, and Culture. This resource may be worth looking into further. The site contains a link to the journal's website. Visiting the website, it is possible to see that this website is more than just a journal, it is an entire Institute dedicated to US and Canadian studies, from the Russian perspective.

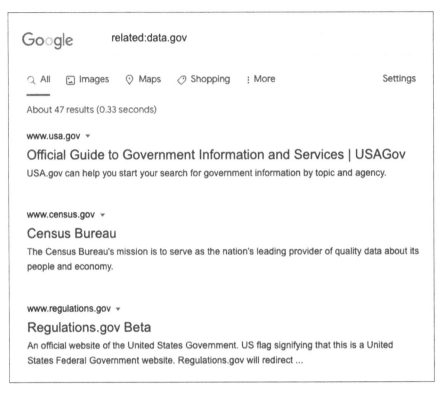

Fig. 6.10 Google search results for *related:*data.gov (Google and the Google logo are trademarks of Google LLC)

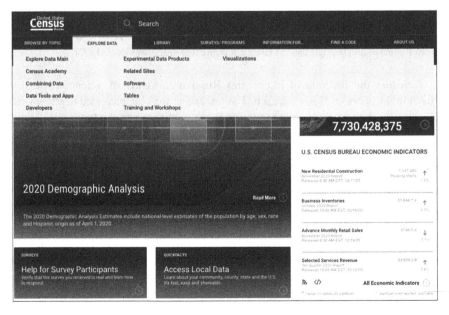

Fig. 6.11 Screenshot from the https://www.census.gov website (Printed with Permission)

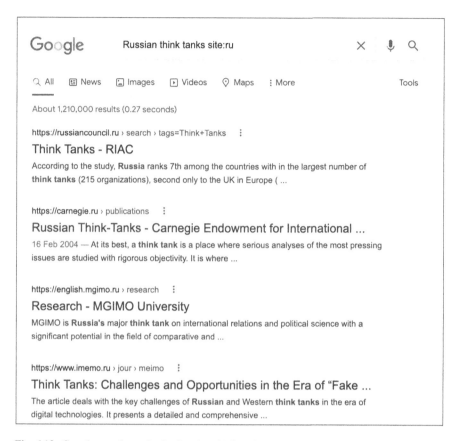

Fig. 6.12 Google search results for *Russian think tanks site:ru* (Google and the Google logo are trademarks of Google LLC)

This institution was not in our original list of think tanks. However, conducting the targeted search from another site, it led us to another valuable resource. From here, it would be possible for the researcher to conduct targeted searches against this website using the *site:* operator and key terms. The researcher is left to conduct similar searches in Yandex or other search engines. Try conducting similar searches using the Seznam search engine, and compare the results. Find videos on similar subjects and use subtitle translation tools to understand their contents. Try the same techniques discussed here to discover a list of Egyptian or Brazilian think tanks. Continue to challenge traditional research methods by looking beyond the normal scope of resources available in your native language.

6.3   Smart Cities Around the World

The term "Smart City" refers to a city that employs information and communications technologies to collect data on its population; ideally, governments use these data to provide services that have the goal of improving the overall quality of life

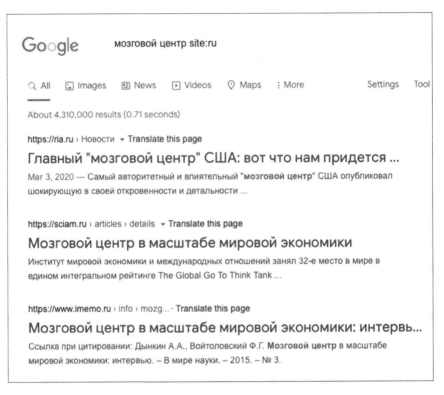

Fig. 6.13 Google search results for *мозговой центр site:ru*, with the Russian phrase for *think tank* (Google and the Google logo are trademarks of Google LLC)

within that city. A research question regarding smart cities has an inherent geo-graphic nexus: smart cities are located all across the globe, and it is reasonable to expect that there are many resources in foreign languages that discuss them. A sam-ple research question about smart cities may look something like: how do smart cities around the world use big data to drive development? To answer this question, the researcher must first compile a list of smart cities to research. With that list, conduct tailored searches specific to each smart city, using the appropriate language.

The first search a researcher might conduct is the simplest: a search for the phrase *list of smart cities around the world* in Google returns a few promising leads, as shown in Fig. 6.17.

The researcher should explore the top few results and begin to compile a list. For good measure, the researcher could try to conduct a similar search in another search engine, such as DuckDuckGo. Figure 6.18 demonstrates that the same search can return different results. Exploring these top few results from both searches, the list already contains several interesting cities to explore (in no particular order): New York, Singapore, London, Barcelona, Oslo, Toronto, Tokyo, Amsterdam, Dubai, Hong Kong, Copenhagen, Boston, Paris, Reykjavik, Berlin, Zurich, and so on.

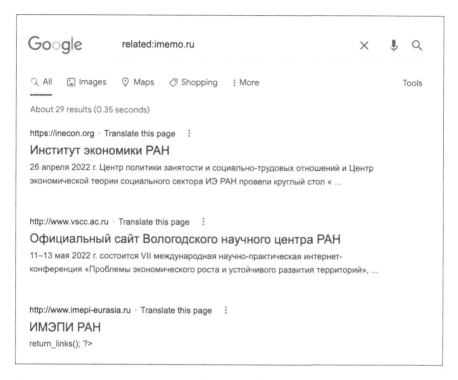

Fig. 6.14 Google search results for *related:imemo.ru* (Google and the Google logo are trademarks of Google LLC)

First, let's choose a city to use as an example: Amsterdam, the capital city of the Netherlands. The primary language spoken in Amsterdam is Dutch, and the two-letter country code for the Netherlands is NL. The Dutch word for smart city is *slimme stad*, and the phrase for big data is *grote gegevens*. The city of Amsterdam is spelled the same in Dutch as it is spelled in English. We will need all of these pieces of information to begin our search. Let's first conduct a few searches in English, then in Dutch, to see the wide variety of results and perspectives. First, consider the English-language search for *Amsterdam smart city* as shown in Fig. 6.19.

The results from the search in Fig. 6.19 for *Amsterdam smart city* return many websites containing general information about the smart city initiative in Amsterdam. The first result appears to be an official website representing the initiative, the second result appears to offer a data science analysis of Amsterdam as a smart city, and the fourth result appears to be a magazine article from MIT's Sloan Management Review. While these results are in English, they will certainly offer good context for the research. Save these for later use. Not only that, the second result links to a data set from https://data.amsterdam.nl/, a very promising resource that warrants further exploration if the researcher was interested in locating data to conduct a quantitative analysis. Still, there are over 65 million results here, which tells us this search was too broad.

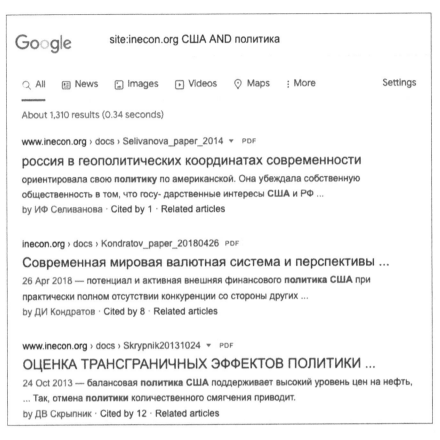

Fig. 6.15 Google search results for *site:*inecon.org *США AND политика*, the Russian words for USA and politics, respectively (Google and the Google logo are trademarks of Google LLC)

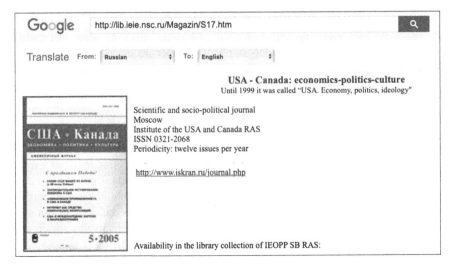

Fig. 6.16 Screenshot of the website http://lib.ieie.nsc.ru/Magazin/S17.htm (Google and the Google logo are trademarks of Google LLC)

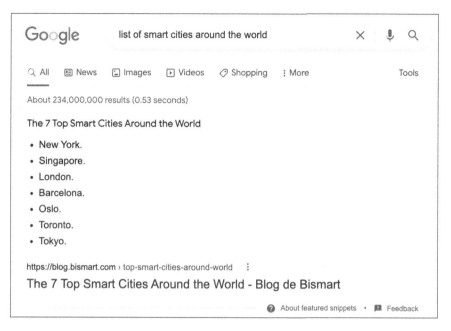

Fig. 6.17 Top result in Google for *list of smart cities around the world* (Google and the Google logo are trademarks of Google LLC)

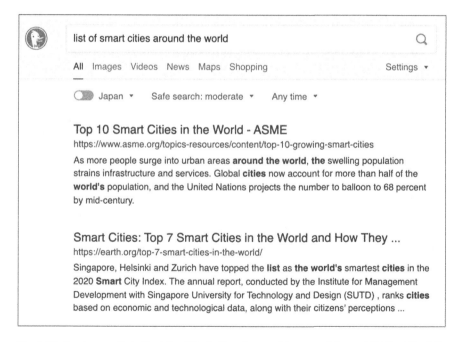

Fig. 6.18 Top two results in DuckDuckGo for *list of smart cities around the world* © DuckDuckGo

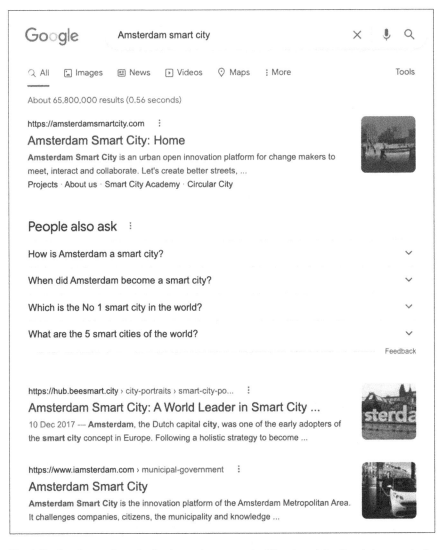

Fig. 6.19 Google search results for *Amsterdam smart city* (Google and the Google logo are trademarks of Google LLC)

Let's narrow the scope of results to just websites hosted using the .nl domain. To do this, leave the same key words and add the dork *site:nl* to the end. The top two results link to the same websites as in the previous searches, but after the third result, the results begin to differ. Figure 6.20 shows the third, fourth, fifth, and sixth results of this search. The third result appears to come from the official website of the City of Amsterdam, which will be a website worth exploring in more detail. The sixth result, from Geodan, is a Dutch technology firm that can create digital twins of cities to assess the impact of certain decisions on a smart city, such as Amsterdam,

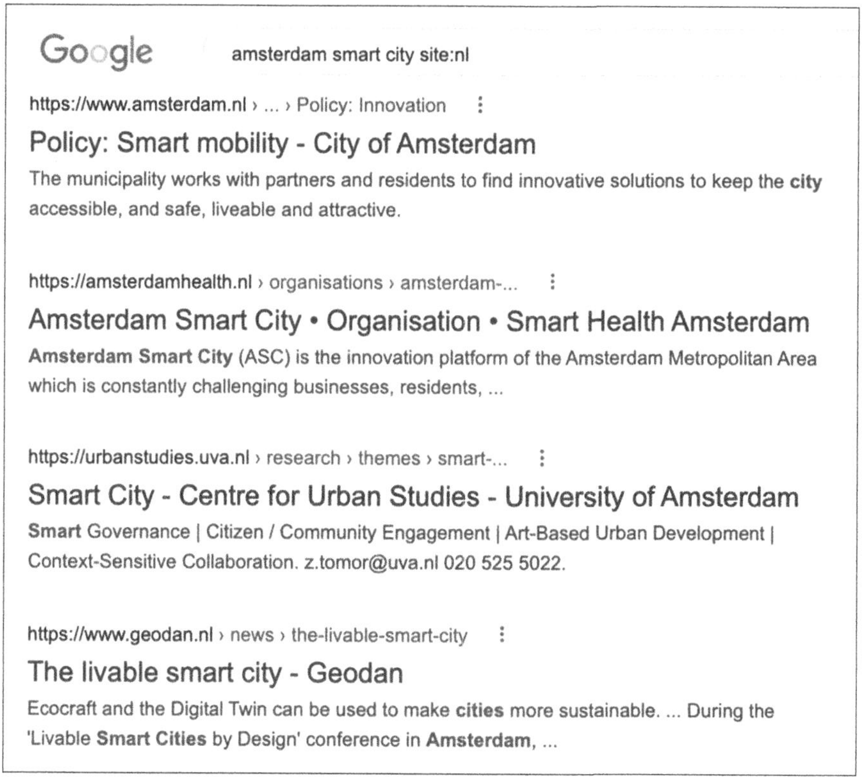

Fig. 6.20   Google search results for *Amsterdam smart city site:nl* (Google and the Google logo are trademarks of Google LLC)

using virtual reality technology [1]. This is one resource that may provide some context for our research question.

Let's further explore the official website of the City of Amsterdam to see if there are any resources pertaining to big data on this website. To do this, conduct the search *site:amsterdam.nl "big data" AND smart city* in Google. This search, shown in Fig. 6.21, returned 28 results from this website, directly pertaining to our research topic. Note that these results appear to be in Dutch; however, upon further inspection, they contain the English search terms at least once somewhere on the page.

For now, let's begin to incorporate the Dutch search terms from earlier to see what other results we may find. Figure 6.22 shows the same search as above, using Dutch terms for big data and smart city. Some of the results of the previous search also appear in this search, but there are a few hundred more results in the Dutch-language search, indicating there are a significant number of resources on this website that would otherwise not be available to the researcher only conducting their search using English-language terms.

These were the results containing these key terms on just this website, albeit, a very important website because it is the official website of the City of Amsterdam.

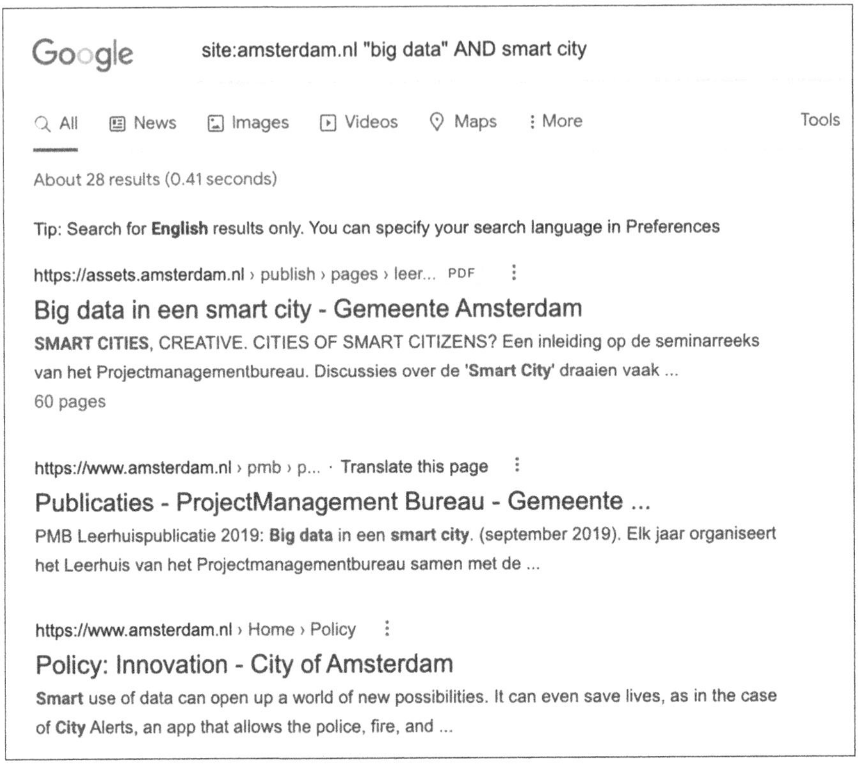

Fig. 6.21 Google search results for *site:amsterdam.nl "big data" AND smart city* (Google and the Google logo are trademarks of Google LLC)

There are, undoubtedly, other resources on other websites worth exploring. Now, let's broaden the scope of the search by locating all websites with the .nl domain, containing the Dutch words for big data, smart city, and Amsterdam. Simultaneously, let's narrow the scope by searching for only Adobe .pdf files that fit these search parameters. These results are more likely to be finalized reports or finished products (see Fig. 6.23).

It appears that many of the results returned happen to incorporate the English term for big data, despite the search using the Dutch term. This can be common when researching technical concepts in any language. The results seem to be largely relevant to the research questions, although we could conduct a search that is even more scoped to our interests.

The results in Fig. 6.24 are more likely to emphasize the smart city concept, while still mentioning big data. All are relevant to Amsterdam and originate from

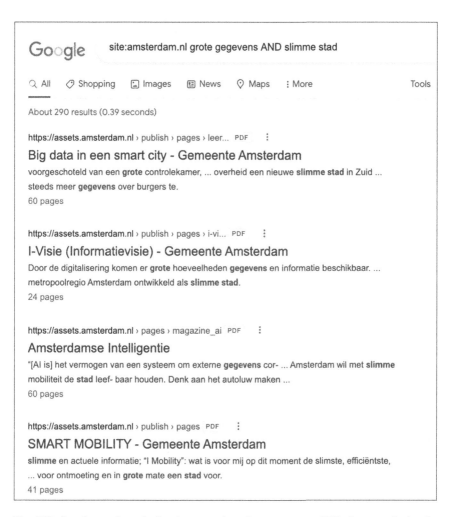

Fig. 6.22 Google search results for *site:amsterdam.nl grote gegevens AND slimme stad* using the Dutch words for big data and smart city, respectively (Google and the Google logo are trademarks of Google LLC)

Dutch websites. There are only 94 results, too, indicating that this is a good search. It also accounted for various occurrences of the Dutch or English phrase for *big data*, so as to ensure results using either phrase will be displayed.

The researcher is left to conduct other searches in the various search engines discussed throughout this book.

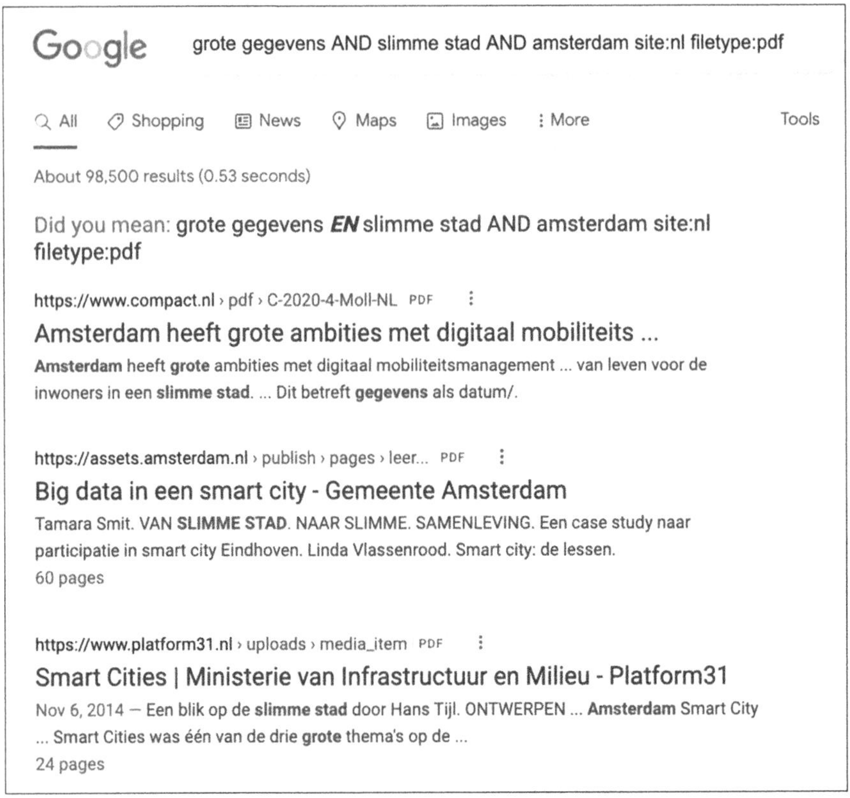

Google   grote gegevens AND slimme stad AND amsterdam site:nl filetype:pdf

Q All   ⦾ Shopping   ⊞ News   ⦿ Maps   ⊡ Images   ⋮ More   Tools

About 98,500 results (0.53 seconds)

Did you mean: grote gegevens *EN* slimme stad AND amsterdam site:nl
filetype:pdf

https://www.compact.nl › pdf › C-2020-4-Moll-NL   PDF   ⋮
Amsterdam heeft grote ambities met digitaal mobiliteits ...
Amsterdam heeft **grote** ambities met digitaal mobiliteitsmanagement ... van leven voor de
inwoners in een **slimme stad**. ... Dit betreft **gegevens** als datum/.

https://assets.amsterdam.nl › publish › pages › leer...   PDF   ⋮
Big data in een smart city - Gemeente Amsterdam
Tamara Smit. VAN **SLIMME STAD**. NAAR SLIMME. SAMENLEVING. Een case study naar
participatie in smart city Eindhoven. Linda Vlassenrood. Smart city: de lessen.
60 pages

https://www.platform31.nl › uploads › media_item   PDF   ⋮
Smart Cities | Ministerie van Infrastructuur en Milieu - Platform31
Nov 6, 2014 — Een blik op de **slimme stad** door Hans Tijl. ONTWERPEN ... **Amsterdam** Smart City
... Smart Cities was één van de drie **grote** thema's op de ...
24 pages

Fig. 6.23 Google search results for *grote gegevens AND slimme stad AND amsterdam site:nl
filetype:pdf* using the Dutch words for big data and smart city, respectively (Google and the Google
logo are trademarks of Google LLC)

Fig. 6.24 Google search results for *intext:("grote gegevens" OR "big data") AND intitle:"slimme stad" AND amsterdam site:nl* using the Dutch words for *big data* and *smart city* (Google and the Google logo are trademarks of Google LLC)

Online Database Reference

1. "The livable smart city," accessed October 12, 2021, https://www.geodan.nl/en/news/the-livable-smart-city/.

Chapter 7
Citing Foreign-Language Resources and Translations

The final step for the researcher who wishes to create written products of their own is to cite these sources. This chapter proposes a standard for formatting citations in other languages and translated works. The best way to do this is through examples. This section offers sample citations of books, translated books, websites, journals, and videos. For other citation formats, follow the prescribed guides for each citation format, following the principles demonstrated in this chapter.

As is always the case when citing works in formal research, the goal is to provide as much detail as possible. In this context, this means including the original foreign-language text, when possible. Ideally, the researcher can also provide a translation of the title to enable any reader to understand the context of that source. This chapter aims to provide a method for the researcher to do this. Not all citation formats have prescribed methods for handling foreign-language materials. The sample citations below offer a method to do so in a standardized way that is consistent with the normal formatting styles of each citation style.

To cite sources whose type is not discussed here or in a citation manual, the best rule-of-thumb is to include as much information as possible, and be consistent throughout the work. Remember, the primary reasons for providing a citation for a work in the first place are to give credit to the originating source and to make it possible for a reader to locate the information on their own.

This being said, let's begin with Turabian.

7.1 Foreign-Language Citations in Turabian

This section proposes a standardized method by which to cite foreign-language books, books translated into English from another language, foreign-language websites, journal articles, and videos in Turabian. Use this section as a guide for sources found while conducting research using the methods described in the previous chapters; use it as an inspiration for a uniformed method to cite other sources.

7.1.1 Citing Books in Turabian

Citing a book in Turabian requires the author(s), title of the book, publisher, publishing location, and year of publication. Books with titles written in foreign characters should also offer the English-language translation of the text. It should not include a transliteration (i.e., written in English as it sounds). Author name and publisher name should be translated or transliterated without including the original language text. Do not transliterate locations; instead, provide the English-language name of the location. Any additional notes should be written in English. The language of the text may be included at the end of the citation if the author deems it will be helpful to the reader.

The following is an example of a bibliographic citation of a foreign-language book (accessed online) in Turabian:

Sherbakov, A.I., M.G. Mdinaradze, A.D. Nazarov, and E.A. Nazarova. *Демография [Demographics]*. Moscow: INFRA-M, 2017. Also available at https://mgimo.ru/upload/iblock/0df/Демография%20наш%20учебник.pdf.

In the example above, the author names and publisher are transliterated, i.e., written in English characters as they sound in the original language. The city, Moscow, is provided in the English language equivalent, i.e., Moscow instead of Moskva.

The following is an example of a footnote citation of a book (accessed online) in Turabian:

A.I. Sherbakov, M.G. Mdinaradze, A.D. Nazarov, and E.A. Nazarova, *Демография [Demographics]* (Moscow: INFRA-M, 2017), 50.

Note that footnotes are denoted by a numerical superscript at the end of a sentence, and the text of the footnote is placed on the bottom of the page. This is true for all footnote types mentioned in this section (books, websites, journals, etc). Refer to a Turabian citation guide for more information on general footnote guidelines.

In the above examples, also note that the URL does contain foreign-language characters. These should not be transliterated or translated, because they will make the URL inaccessible. Also note that the book accessed online contains the URL in the bibliographic citation, but not in the footnote.

A book translated from a foreign language into English will have an English-language title, so there is no need to prepare a translation or transliteration of foreign-language text. Instead, include the translator.

The following is an example of a bibliographic citation of a translated book in Turabian:

Brandell, Gunnar. *Strindberg in Inferno*. Translated by Barry Jacobs. Cambridge, MA: Harvard University Press, 1974.

The following is an example of a footnote citation of a translated book in Turabian:

Gunnar Brandell. *Strindberg in Inferno*, trans. Barry Jacobs (Cambridge, MA: Harvard University Press, 1974), 45.

Also note that in all of the above book citations, footnotes include the page number referenced, while the bibliographic citation does not. Next, let's discuss website citations.

7.1.2   Citing Websites in Turabian

Citing a website in Turabian requires the website's author, title, date of publication or last modification, and URL. If there is no listed author, list the service providing the information (for example, if the website is a news article where the author is not listed, provide the name of the news service). If there is no date of publication or last modification, list the date of access.

The following is an example of a bibliographic citation of a website with no author listed and a date of publication provided:

RBC. "Ученый из США предупредил о сокращении населения России к концу века [Scientist from the United States warned of the decline in Russia's population by the end of the century]." September 4, 2020. https://www.rbc.ru/society/04/09/2020 /5f51dfe79a79475dda4d0a76.

The following is an example of a footnote citation of a website with no author listed and a date of publication provided:

"Ученый из США предупредил о сокращении населения России к концу века [Scientist from the United States warned of the decline in Russia's population by the end of the century]," RBC, September 4, 2020, https://www.rbc.ru/society/04/09/2020/ 5f51dfe79a79475dda4d0a76.

In both of these examples, the original foreign-language title is included in the original language, immediately followed by a translation of the title.

7.1.3   Citing Journal Articles in Turabian

Citing a journal article in Turabian requires the author(s), title of the article, title of the publication, volume, date of publication, and page number. Provide the URL in bibliographic citations if the journal was accessed online. Similar to book and website citations, provide the title of the article in the original language, immediately followed by the translation of the text. When listing the name of the publication, provide the transliteration of the title in English characters.

The following is an example of a bibliographic citation of a journal article accessed online:

Dobrokhleb, V.G. "Демографическое Старение в Аспекте Гендерных Проблем Современной России [Demographic Aging in the Aspect of Gender Problems in Modern Russia]." *Narodnonaceleniya* 23, no. 2 (January–March 2020): 5–13. https://doi.org/10.19181/population.2020.23.2.1 or http://www.isesp-ras.ru/images/narodonaselenie/2020_2.pdf.

This journal had two links, so both are provided. One was the DOI, and the other a direct link to a PDF file containing the readable version of the article. Both are provided simply for convenience and accessibility to the reader.

The following is an example of a footnote citation of a journal article accessed online:

V.G. Dobrokhleb, "Демографическое Старение в Аспекте Гендерных Проблем Современной России [Demographic Aging in the Aspect of Gender Problems in Modern Russia]," *Narodnonaceleniya* 23, no. 2 (January–March 2020): 8.

Note that the footnote citation includes a page number, in this case the page number referring to the exact information on this page. The bibliographic citation includes the entire page range of the article in the journal. Also note that the footnote citation does not include the URL, even though it is available.

7.1.4 Citing Videos in Turabian

Citing a video requires the video source, name, publication date, and duration. Also provide a URL if the video was accessed online. Provide the title of the video in original foreign-language text, along with the English translation of the title. All other aspects originally written in a foreign language, including the video source, should be transliterated. A translation of the transliterated text is optional, but not required.

The following is an example of a bibliographic citation for a video from a foreign news media outlet:

Obshestvennoe Televideniye Rossii [Russian Public Television]. "Что мешает заводить детей? [What prevents people from having children?]." July 20, 2020. Video, 39:29. https://www.youtube.com/watch?v=S6Ooo7SZLrs.

The following is an example of a footnote citation for a video from a foreign news media outlet:

"Что мешает заводить детей? [What prevents people from having children?]," July 20, 2020, Obshestvennoe Televideniye Rossii [Russian Public Television], video, 39:29, https://www.youtube.com/watch?v= S6Ooo7SZLrs.

Note how the previous two examples provide the title in the original foreign-language text with an English translation in brackets. The video source is transliterated with an English translation in brackets.

The researcher may find themselves using other citation formats. While these are similar in many ways, they also have their differences. Let's discuss Chicago formatting next.

7.2 Foreign-Language Citations in Chicago

The information required to cite a source in Chicago is largely the same, however, formatting can differ slightly. This section proposes a standardized method by which to cite foreign-language books, books translated into English from another language, foreign-language websites, journal articles, and videos in Chicago.

7.2.1 Citing Books in Chicago

Citing a book requires the author(s), year of publication, title, location of publication, and publisher. Provide the URL of the book if it was accessed online. In bibliographic citations, provide the title of the book in its original foreign-language text, immediately followed by the translation. Transliterate author names and publishers whose names are originally provided in foreign-language text. Location of publication should be provided in the English-language name; do not transliterate locations. Do not alter the URL if one is provided.

The following is an example of a bibliographic citation of a book accessed online:

Sherbakov, A.I., M.G. Mdinaradze, A.D. Nazarov, and E.A. Nazarova. 2017. *Демография [Demographics]*. Moscow: INFRA-M. Also available at https://mgimo.ru/upload/iblock/0df/Демография%20наш%20учебник.pdf.

This is largely similar to the citation using Turabian formatting, except the order of the items is altered slightly. Just like in Turabian, page numbers are also not included in bibliographic citations.

Chicago does not use footnote-style citations as does Turabian. Instead, in-text citations are used. In Chicago, citations are placed directly within the text between parentheses. Place the citation at the end of the sentence and before the period. These citations in Chicago only list the author(s), year, and page number cited. The following is an example of an in-text citation of a book accessed online:

(Sherbakov, Mdinaradze, Nazarov, and Nazarova 2017, 50).

Citing a translated book is similar to citing any other English-language book, except the name of the translator is also included. The following is an example of a bibliographic citation of a book translated into English:

Brandell, Gunnar. 1974. *Strindberg in Inferno*. Translated by Barry Jacobs. Cambridge, MA: Harvard University Press.

Just like other book citations in Chicago, the in-text citation is included at the end of the sentence within parentheses, just before the period. Include the author's last name, year of publication, and page number. The translator's name is not included. The following is an example of an in-text citation of a book translated into English:

(Brandell 1974, 45).

Next, let's discuss website citations in Chicago.

7.2.2 Citing Websites in Chicago

Citing a website in Chicago requires the website's author, date of publication or last modification, title, and URL. If there is no listed author, list the service providing the information (for example, if the website is a news article where the author is not listed, provide the name of the news service). If there is no date of publication or last modification, list the date of access.

The following is an example of a bibliographic citation of a website with no author listed and a date of publication provided:

RBC. 2020. "Ученый из США предупредил о сокращении населения России к концу века [Scientist from the United States warned of the decline in Russia's population by the end of the century]." September 4, 2020. https://www.rbc.ru/society/04/09/2020 /5f51dfe79a79475dda4d0a76.

The in-text citation requires the author's name and year of publication. If the author is not listed, provide the name of the information provider. Since websites do not have page numbers, no page number is provided. Place the citation at the end of the sentence between parentheses and before the period. The following is an example of an in-text citation of a website where no author is provided:

(RBC 2020).

In the above example, RBC is the name of the news service that provided the information referenced in the citation. This is because the referenced article does not list an author by name. Now, let's discuss journal citations in Chicago.

7.2.3   Citing Journal Articles in Chicago

Citing a journal article in Chicago requires the author(s), title of the article, title of the publication, volume, date of publication, and page number. Provide the URL in bibliographic citations if the journal was accessed online. Similar to book and website citations, provide the title of the article in the original language, immediately followed by the translation of the text. When listing the name of the publication, provide the transliteration of the title in English characters.

The following is an example of a bibliographic citation of a journal article accessed online:

Dobrokhleb, V.G. 2020. "Демографическое Старение в Аспекте Гендерных Проблем Современной России [Demographic Aging in the Aspect of Gender Problems in Modern Russia]." *Narodnonaceleniya* 23 (2) (January–March): 5–13. https://doi.org/10.19181/population.2020.23.2.1 or http://www.isesp-ras.ru/images/narodonaselenie/2020_2.pdf.

Also note in the bibliographic citation that the page range for the entire article is included, regardless of the pages referenced in the text. In-text citations in Chicago include the author's last name, year of publication, and exact page number of the information referenced. Transliterate author's names. If the author's name is not provided, use the name of the organization providing the information (for example, the news agency or academic institution providing the information). As with the aforementioned in-text citations, include the information within parentheses at the end of the sentence, just before the period.

The following is an example of an in-text citation of a journal article:

(Dobrokhleb 2020, 8).

Now, let's discuss video citations in Chicago.

7.2.4   Citing Videos in Chicago

Citing a video requires the video source, name, publication date, and duration. Also provide a URL if the video was accessed online. Provide the title of the video in original foreign-language text, along with the English translation of the title. All other aspects originally written in a foreign language, including the video source, should be transliterated. A translation of the transliterated text is optional, but not required.

The following is an example of a bibliographic citation of a video from a foreign news media outlet:

Obshestvennoe Televideniye Rossii [Russian Public Television (RPT)]. "Что мешает заводить детей? [What prevents people from having children?]." Video, July 20, 2020. 39:29. https://www.youtube.com/watch?v=S6Ooo7SZLrs.

The above example cites a source whose title and information provider are originally in a foreign language. The author's name is not provided, so the information provider's name is listed instead. The information provider's name is transliterated into English characters, and an English translation is included within square brackets. The title is included in the original foreign-language text, with an English translation immediately afterward in square brackets.

Now, let's discuss in-text citations of video sources in Chicago. Similar to the aforementioned in-text citations, the author's name and year of publication are included within parentheses at the end of the sentence, just before the period. The name should be transliterated. Do not include the exact timeframe of the information in the video.

The following is an example of an in-text citation of a video from a foreign news media outlet:

(RPT 2020).

Next, let's explore citations of foreign-language materials in APA.

7.3 Foreign-Language Citations in APA

Citing foreign-language resources in APA requires the same information as does Turabian and Chicago. One key difference is that APA does not allow foreign-character text anywhere in the citation: only provide transliterations of non-Latin scripts. For example, a source written in French, which uses a Latin-based alphabet would not be transliterated: use the original French-language title. However, a source written in Russian or Chinese should be transliterated. Additionally, titles in other languages are formatted in sentence-case: that is, do not capitalize all words in the title. Only capitalize significant words, such as the first word and proper nouns. The example in Sect. 7.3.2 (Citing Websites in APA) offers an example of this.

As does Chicago formatting, APA also uses in-text citations rather than footnotes. One minor difference is the use of commas. This will be apparent in the examples that follow.

7.3.1 Citing Books in APA

Citing a book requires the author(s), year of publication, title, and publisher. In bibliographic citations, provide the transliteration of the book title, immediately followed by the translation in square brackets. Transliterate author names and publishers whose names are originally provided in foreign-language text. Unlike in Turabian and Chicago style-citations, location of publication is not included.

The following is an example of a bibliographic citation of a foreign-language book:

Sherbakov, A.I., M.G. Mdinaradze, A.D. Nazarov, and E.A. Nazarova. (2017). *Demografia [Demographics]*. INFRA-M.

This is largely similar to the citation using Chicago formatting, except the order of the items is altered slightly and the location of publication is not included. Just like in Turabian and Chicago, page numbers are also not included in bibliographic citations. Author names are transliterated, and the title is provided in the original language with the English translation immediately after.

Like Chicago, APA does not use footnote-style citations. Instead, in-text citations are used. In APA, citations are placed directly within the text between parentheses. Place the citation at the end of the sentence and before the period. These citations in APA only list the author, year, and page number cited. Elements are separated by commas, unlike in Chicago. For books with multiple authors, list only one author, followed by "et al." Use the abbreviation "p." before the page number or "pp." before page ranges. The following is an example of an in-text citation of a book accessed online:

(Sherbakov et al., 2017, p. 50).

Citing a translated book is similar to citing any other English-language book, except the name of the translator is also included. The following is an example of a bibliographic citation of a book translated into English:

Brandell, G. *Strindberg in Inferno*. (1974). Translated by Jacobs, B. Harvard University Press.

Just like other book citations in APA, the in-text citation is included at the end of the sentence within parentheses, just before the period. Include the author's last name, year of publication, and page number. The translator's name is not included. The following is an example of an in-text citation of a book translated into English:

(Brandell, 1974, p. 45).

Next, let's discuss website citations in APA.

7.3.2 Citing Websites in APA

Citing a website in APA requires the website's author, date of publication or last modification, title, and URL. If there is no listed author, list the service providing the information (for example, if the website is a news article where the author is not listed, provide the name of the news service). If there is no date of publication or last modification, list the date of access. The order and format of the required items differs from Turabian and Chicago.

The following is an example of a bibliographic citation of a website with no author listed and a date of publication provided:

RBC. (2020, September 4). Uchyony iz USA predupredil o sokrasheny naseleniya Rossii k kontsu veka *[Scientist from the United States warned of the decline in Russia's population by the end of the century].* https://www.rbc.ru/society/04/09/2020 /5f51dfe79a79475dda4d0a76.

Note in the example above that the title of the text in both the transliteration of the original foreign-language text and the English translation provided is formatted in sentence-case: only the first word and proper nouns are capitalized. Also note the date format, which is "year, month day" order.

The in-text citation requires the author's name and year of publication. If the author is not listed, provide the name of the information provider. Since websites do not have page numbers, no page number is provided. Place the citation at the end of the sentence between parentheses and before the period. The following is an example of an in-text citation of a website where no author is provided:

(RBC, 2020).

Next, let's look at journal citations in APA.

7.3.3   Citing Journal Articles in APA

Citing a journal article in APA requires the author(s), date of publication, title of the article, title of the publication, volume, and page number(s). Provide the URL in bibliographic citations if the journal was accessed online. Similar to book and website citations, provide the transliteration of the article's original, immediately followed by the translation of the text. Titles are written in sentence-case. When listing the name of the publication, provide the transliteration of the title in English characters.

The following is an example of a bibliographic citation of a journal article accessed online:

Dobrokhleb, V.G. (January–March 2020). Demograficheskoye stareniye v aspektye gendernykh problem sovremenoi Rossii [Demographic aging in the aspect of gender problems in modern Russia]. *Narodnonaceleniya,* 23 (2): 5–13. https://doi.org/10.19181/population.2020.23.2.1   or   http://www.isesp-ras.ru/images/narodonaselenie/2020_2.pdf.

Also note in the bibliographic citation that the page range for the entire article is included, regardless of the pages referenced in the text. In-text citations in APA include the author's last name, year of publication, and exact page number of the information referenced. Transliterate author's names. If the author's name is not provided, use the name of the organization providing the information (for example, the news agency or academic institution providing the information). Use the abbreviation "p." to denote one page was referenced, and "pp." for multiple pages. Author's name, year of publication, and page are all separated with commas. As with the aforementioned in-text citations, include the information within parentheses at the end of the sentence, just before the period.

The following is an example of an in-text citation of a journal article:

(Dobrokhleb, 2020, p. 8).

Now, let's explore video citations in APA.

7.3.4   Citing Videos in APA

Citing a video requires the video source, publication date, and name. Also provide a URL if the video was accessed online. The duration of the video is not required in APA. Provide the transliteration of the video's original foreign-language title, along with the English translation of the title. All other aspects originally written in a foreign language, including the video source, should be transliterated. A translation of the transliterated text is optional, but not required.

The following is an example of a bibliographic citation of a video from a foreign news media outlet:

Obshestvennoe Televideniye Rossii [Russian Public Television (RPT)]. (2020, July 20). *Shto meshaet savodit' detei? [What prevents people from having children?]* [Video]. https://www.youtube.com/watch?v=S6Ooo7SZLrs.

The above example cites a source whose title and information provider are originally in a foreign language. The author's name is not provided, so the information provider's name is listed instead. The information provider's name is transliterated into English characters, and an English translation is included within square brackets. The title is also transliterated, with an English translation immediately afterward in square brackets. The duration of the video is not included, unlike Turabian and Chicago formatting. The type of media is also listed in square brackets.

Next, let's discuss in-text citations of video sources in APA. Similar to the aforementioned in-text citations, the author's name and year of publication are included within parentheses at the end of the sentence, just before the period. The name should be transliterated.

The following is an example of an in-text citation of a video from a foreign news media outlet:

(RPT, 2020).

Finally, let's introduce basic foreign-language citation formatting using MLA.

7.4   Foreign-Language Citations in MLA

Citing foreign-language resources in MLA requires the same information as does Turabian, Chicago, and APA. Like APA-formatted citations, MLA also does not allow foreign-character text anywhere in the citation: only provide transliterations of non-Latin scripts. However, APA differs from MLA in that titles of books, articles, and videos are written in capital-case: all significant words are capitalized.

As do Chicago and APA formats, MLA also uses in-text citations rather than footnotes. One minor difference is the use of commas. This will be apparent in the examples that follow.

7.4.1   Citing Books in MLA

Citing a book requires the author(s), year of publication, title, location of publication, and publisher. For online works, the date of last access is also required. In bibliographic citations, provide the title of the book in its original foreign-language text, immediately followed by the translation. Transliterate author names and publishers whose names are originally provided in foreign-language text. Location of publication should be provided in the English-language name; do not transliterate locations. URLs are not provided for all materials accessed online (see below for details). Instead, provide the access mechanism of the material, which is usually either print or online.

The following is an example of a bibliographic citation of a book accessed online:

Sherbakov, A.I., M.G. Mdinaradze, A.D. Nazarov, and E.A. Nazarova. *Демография [Demographics]*. Moscow: INFRA-M, 2017. Online.

In-text citations are similar to Chicago formatting. When there are three or fewer authors, list their names between commas; when there are four or more authors, list the first author and use the "et al." abbreviation. Do not use commas between the author's name and the page number(s). Place the citation between parentheses at the end of the sentence immediately before the period. The following is an example of an in-text citation for a book with four authors:

(Sherbakov et al. 50).

Citing a translated book is similar to citing any other English-language book, except the name of the translator is also included. Also include the city of publication before the publisher. Specify the access media of print or online. The following is an example of a bibliographic citation of a book translated into English:

Brandell, Gunnar. *Strindberg in Inferno*, translated by Jacobs, B. Cambridge: Harvard University Press, 1974. Print.

Just like other book citations in MLA, the in-text citation is included at the end of the sentence within parentheses, just before the period. Include the author's last name and page number. The translator's name is not included. The following is an example of an in-text citation of a book translated into English:

(Brandell 45).

Now, let's discuss website citations in MLA.

7.4.2 Citing Websites in MLA

Citing a website in MLA requires the website's author, title, date of publication or last modification, URL, and date of access. If there is no listed author, list the service providing the information (for example, if the website is a news article where the author is not listed, provide the name of the news service). For websites, list both the date of publication (if known) and the date last accessed.

The following is an example of a bibliographic citation of a website with no author listed and a date of publication provided:

"Учёный из США Предупредил о Сокращении Населения России к Концу Века [Scientist from the United States Warned of the Decline in Russia's Population by the End of the Century]." *RBC*. 4 September 2020. https://www.rbc.ru/society/04/09/2020 /5f51dfe79a79475dda4d0a76. 3 January 2021.

In the below example, 4 September 2020 is the date of publication, and 3 January 2021 is the date of last access.

When there is no known author for the cited work, the in-text citation uses the title, or a shortening of the title in the case of longer titles, instead of the author's last name. The example in this section cites a source with no author; the title is also quite long, so it is shortened for the in-text citation. Only the English translation is provided within quotations. The reader would know that this is the English translation of a foreign-language title because it is between square brackets:

("[Scientist from the United States Warned]" 2020).

Now, let's discuss MLA citations for journal articles.

7.4.3 Citing Journal Articles in MLA

Citing a journal article in MLA requires the author(s), title of the article, title of the publication, volume, date of publication, page number, access medium, and date of access (if accessed online). Similar to book and website citations, provide the title of the article in the original language, immediately followed by the translation of the text. When listing the name of the publication, provide the transliteration of the title in English characters.

As with websites, include the date of last access if the journal was accessed online. For journals accessed in print, specify "Print" after the page range; if accessed in print, no access date is required. In the example that follows, 15 March 2021 is the date of last access. Volume and issue number are written immediately after the title of the journal as a decimal in "volume.issue" format.

The following is an example of a bibliographic citation of a journal article accessed online:

Dobrokhleb, V.G. "Демографическое Старение в Аспекте Гендерных Проблем Современной России [Demographic Aging in the Aspect of Gender Problems in Modern Russia]." *Narodnonaceleniya,* 2.2 (January–March 2020): 5–13. Online. 15 March 2021.

Also note in the bibliographic citation that the page range for the entire article is included, regardless of the pages referenced in the text. In-text citations in MLA include the author's last name and exact page number of the information referenced. Transliterate author's names. If the author's name is not provided, use the title of the text (not the author's name). As with the aforementioned in-text citations, include the information within parentheses at the end of the sentence, just before the period.

The following is an example of an in-text citation of a journal article where the author's name is known:

(Dobrokhleb 8)

Lastly, let's explore video citations in MLA.

7.4.4   Citing Videos in MLA

Citing a video requires the video source, name, publication date, and duration. Also provide a URL if the video was accessed online. Provide the title of the video in original foreign-language text, along with the English translation of the title. All other aspects originally written in a foreign language, including the video source, should be transliterated. A translation of the transliterated text is optional, but not required.

The following is an example of a bibliographic citation of a video from a foreign news media outlet accessed on YouTube:

"Что Мешает Заводить Детей? [What Prevents People from Having Children?]." *YouTube*, uploaded by Obshestvennoe Televideniye Rossii [Russian Public Television (RPT)], 20 July 2020, https://www.youtube.com/watch?v= S6Ooo7SZLrs.

The above example cites a source whose title and information provider are originally in a foreign language. The author's name is not provided, so the information provider's name is listed instead. The information provider's name is transliterated into English characters, and an English translation is included within square brackets. The title is included in the original foreign-language text, with an English translation immediately afterward in square brackets.

Now, let's discuss in-text citations of video sources in MLA. Similar to the aforementioned examples, use the video's title instead of the video's creator. Provide the English translation of the title in square brackets and quotation marks, as shown below.

The following is an example of an in-text citation of a video from a foreign news media outlet accessed on YouTube:

("[What Prevents People from Having Children?]" 2020).

This concludes the chapter on foreign-language source citations. Only a few formats and media types are described here. Citations can actually become quite complicated: detail is key. Many citation formats do not have formal rules set for each citation scenario. The principles demonstrated here can be applied and extended to other citation formatting guides. The most important things to remember are: include as much information as necessary for a reader to locate the source on their own, and be consistent amongst all source citations within one document. Use your best judgment. If writing for a particular academic institution or publisher, seek guidance on preferred formats.

Chapter 8
Appendices

The appendices that follow serve as a reference guide for the researcher to begin exploring the right websites for their research problem. Recall that the same search within different directories or search engines may produce different results. It is always important to consult the appropriate resource depending on the problem at hand. These appendices focus on country and region-specific resources not discussed in detail in the main body of this book.

Also keep in mind that websites are continually changing. One day, the researcher's favorite website may disappear; with that, another new resource is created. Keep a list of your own favorite resources, continually adding to the resources listed here. Mark the ones that are no longer supported.

8.1 List of Country-Based Web Directories

This appendix contains a list of *some* country-specific web directories. This is not a comprehensive list—it is only a starting point. These URLs are likely to change over time, as people cease their support for existing directories and create new directories to meet their vision and needs.

- https://www.search.ch
- http://www.afghana.com/
- http://www.albafind.com/ (HTTP only),
- https://asia.ezilon.com/
- https://www.theeuropeanlibrary.org/
- https://indexa.fr/
- https://www.findyello.com/anguilla/ (list of lots of countries, not just Anguilla),
- https://www.eyoon.com/ (Arab Emirates),
- https://www.hayastan.com/indexen.php (Armenia),

- https://oekoportal.de/ (economically focused search portal),
- http://www.azerb.com/?i=1 (About Azerbaijan website),
- http://www.azer.com/ (About Azerbaijan),
- http://www.arabji.com/Bahrain/
- http://www.zubr.com/ (Belarus),
- http://www.annubel.com/ (Belgium),
- http://bruxelles.sharelook.be/ (Belgium),
- http://www.bolivian.com/ (Bolivia),
- http://www.achei.com.br/ (Brazil),
- http://portal.bg/index.php (Bulgaria),
- http://www.sasksearch.com/ (Saskatchewan search, Canada),
- https://www.bruncas.com/ (Costa Rica),
- http://www.greekspider.com/ (Greece and Cyprus),
- http://www.kypros.org/ (Cyprus),
- http://www.abc.cz/ (Czech Republic),
- http://szm.sk/ (Czech Republic),
- https://uzdroje.cz/ (Czech Republic),
- https://www.danskelinks.dk/ (Denmark),
- https://hvem-hvor.dk/ (Denmark),
- https://www.indexa.dk/ (Denmark),
- http://www.egyptsearch.com/ (Egypt),
- http://www.buscaniguas.com.sv/ (El Salvador),
- http://rus.log.ee/ (Estonia in Russian),
- https://www.neti.ee/ (Estonia),
- http://www.ethiolinks.com/ (Ethiopia),
- http://www.francite.com/ (France),
- http://www.sharelook.fr/ (France),
- http://www.bellnet.de/ (Germany),
- http://karokoa.com/ (Germany),
- http://www.klug-suchen.de/ (Germany),
- http://www.fouye.com/ (Haiti),
- http://timway.com/ (Hong Kong),
- https://www.megaport.hu/ (Hungary),
- http://leit.is/ (Iceland),
- https://www.indiabook.com/ (India),
- http://www.linkestan.com/ (Iran),
- https://iranmehr.com/ (Iran),
- https://www.globalirish.com/ (Ireland),
- https://www.indexireland.com/ (Ireland),
- http://www.search.ie/ (Ireland),
- http://www.mavensearch.com/ (Israel),
- http://www.attaka-navi.com/ (Japan),
- http://www.okiniiri.com/ (Japan),

- http://www.simmani.com/ (Korea),
- https://www.top.lv/ (Latvia),
- http://www.le-liban.com/ (Lebanon),
- http://www.the-lebanon.com/ (Lebanon),
- http://www.lebweb.com/ (Lebanon),
- https://www.on.lt/ (Lithuania),
- http://www.webportal.com.my/ (Malaysia),
- https://www.yellow.com.mx/ (Mexico),
- https://www.mexicoweb.com.mx/ (Mexico),
- http://www.best.sk/ (Moldova),
- https://namsearch.com/ (Namibia),
- http://nepalnet.net/ (Nepal),
- https://www.cybercur.com/ (Curacao),
- https://www.eerstekeuze.nl/ (Netherlands),
- https://www.startpagina.nl/ilse (Netherlands),
- http://www.nzpages.co.nz/ (New Zealand),
- http://yagua.paraguay.com/ (Paraguay),
- https://www.ohperu.com/ (Peru),
- https://www.alleba.com/dir.html (Philippines),
- http://katalog.gery.pl/ (Poland),
- https://www.gooru.pl/katalog/index.php (Poland),
- http://www.adresa.ro/ (Romania),
- http://www.linkuri.ro/ (Romania),
- https://www.murman.ru/ (Murmansk, Russia),
- http://www.refer.ru/ (Russia),
- http://www.ulitka.ru/ (Russia),
- http://www.best.sk/ (Slovakia),
- http://www.slovakrepublic.com/ (Slovakia),
- https://surf.sk/ (Slovakia),
- https://szm.sk/ (Slovakia),
- https://www.raziskovalec.com/ (Slovenia),
- https://www.easyinfo.co.za/ (South Africa),
- http://www.canarias24.com/ (Canary Islands),
- https://www.kaixo.com/es/directorio (Spain),
- http://www.menorcaweb.com/ (Menorca, Spain),
- http://www.lankalinksystems.com/ (Sri Lanka),
- https://sudaneseonline.com/links/ (Sudan),
- http://www.surinam.net/ (Suriname),
- http://www.inetmedia.nu/ (Sweden),
- https://www.netinsert.com/se.html (Sweden),
- https://www.furttalweb.ch/ (Switzerland),
- http://www.netstart.ch/ (Switzerland),
- http://www.kacmac.com/index.html (Syria),

- https://www.syriaonline.com/ (Syria),
- http://www.syrialinks.com/ (Syria),
- http://www.tanserve.com/ (Tanzania),
- http://www.tzonline.org/ (Tanzania),
- https://www.winoo.com/ (Tunisia),
- http://www.arabul.com/ (Turkey),
- http://www.arama.com/ (Turkey),
- http://www.turkarama.com/ (Turkey),
- http://www.brama.com/ (Ukraine),
- http://www.infoukes.com/ (Ukraine),
- http://www.uazone.net/sesna/ (Ukraine),
- http://www.abrexa.co.uk/ (UK),
- http://www.kingdomseek.co.uk/ (UK, Christian Religion),
- https://www.linkcentre.com/ (UK),
- http://www.putmyfinger.co.uk/ (UK and Ireland),
- https://www.splut.com/ (UK),
- http://www.ajdee.com/ (USA),
- https://www.azoos.com/ (USA),
- https://www.click4choice.com/ (USA),
- http://www.floridanetlink.com/ (Florida, USA),
- http://www.goguides.org/ (USA),
- https://homepageseek.com/ (USA),
- http://www.nord-amerika-suche.de/ (USA and Canada for German-speakers),
- https://scrubtheweb.com/ (USA),
- http://www.searchhippo.com/ (USA),
- https://www.whatuseek.com/ (USA),
- http://listingsus.com/ (USA),
- http://www.uruguaytotal.com/ (Uruguay),
- https://www.search.uz/eng/ (Uzbekistan),
- https://www.uzbeksites.com/ (Uzbekistan),
- https://www.viet.net/ (Vietnam),
- http://listingsus.com/us-virgin-islands/ (Virgin Islands),
- https://www.yusearch.com/ (Yugoslavia),
- https://curlie.org/ (Directory of the Web - Unspecified Country).

8.2   List of Country-Specific Domains in Major Search Engines

This appendix contains lists of country-specific domains for Google search engine, Bing, Yahoo, and DuckDuckGo. Apply your knowledge of the unique formatting used within each search engine to craft meaningful searches.

8.2.1   List of Google Domains

Google domains are of the format google (dot) <country code>. The following list of country-specific Google domains are from https://www.google.com/supported_domains:

- .google.com
- .google.ad (Andorra)
- .google.ae (UAE)
- .google.com.af (Afghanistan)
- .google.com.ag (Antigua and Barbuda)
- .google.com.ai (Anguilla)
- .google.al (Albania)
- .google.am (Armenia)
- .google.co.ao (Angola)
- .google.com.ar (Argentina)
- .google.as (American Samoa)
- .google.at (Austria)
- .google.com.au (Austria)
- .google.az (Azerbaijan)
- .google.ba (Bosnia and Herzegovina)
- .google.com.bd (Bangladesh)
- .google.be (Belgium)
- .google.bf (Burkina Faso)
- .google.bg (Bulgaria)
- .google.com.bh (Bahrain)
- .google.bi (Burundi)
- .google.bj (Benin)
- .google.com.bn (Brunei)
- .google.com.bo (Bolivia)
- .google.com.br (Brazil)
- .google.bs (Bahamas)
- .google.bt (Bhutan)
- .google.co.bw (Botswana)
- .google.by (Belarus)
- .google.com.bz (Belize)
- .google.ca (Canada)
- .google.cd (Democratic Republic of Congo)
- .google.cf. (Central African Republic)
- .google.cg (Republic of Congo)
- .google.ch (Switzerland)
- .google.ci (Ivory Coast)
- .google.co.ck (Cook Islands)
- .google.cl (Chile)
- .google.cm (Cameroon)

- .google.cn (China)
- .google.com.co (Colombia)
- .google.co.cr (Costa Rica)
- .google.com.cu (Cuba)
- .google.cv (Cape Verde)
- .google.com.cy (Cyprus)
- .google.cz (Czech Republic)
- .google.de (Germany)
- .google.dj (Djibouti)
- .google.dk (Denmark)
- .google.dm (Dominica)
- .google.com.do (Dominican Republic)
- .google.dz. (Algeria)
- .google.com.ec (Ecuador)
- .google.ee (Estonia)
- .google.com.eg (Egypt)
- .google.es (Spain)
- .google.com.et (Ethiopia)
- .google.fi (Finland)
- .google.com.fj (Fiji)
- .google.fm (Micronesia)
- .google.fr (France)
- .google.ga (Gabon)
- .google.ge (Georgia)
- .google.gg (Guernsey)
- .google.com.gh (Ghana)
- .google.com.gi (Gibraltar)
- .google.gl (Greenland)
- .google.gm (Gambia)
- .google.gr (Greece)
- .google.com.gt (Guatemala)
- .google.gy (Guyana)
- .google.com.hk (Hong Kong)
- .google.hn (Honduras)
- .google.hr. (Croatia)
- .google.ht. (Haiti)
- .google.hu (Hungary)
- .google.co.id (Indonesia)
- .google.ie (Ireland)
- .google.co.il (Israel)
- .google.im (Isle of Man)
- .google.co.in (India)
- .google.iq (Iraq)
- .google.is (Iceland)
- .google.it (Italy)

- .google.je (Jersey)
- .google.com.jm (Jamaica)
- .google.jo (Jordan)
- .google.co.jp (Japan)
- .google.co.ke (Kenya)
- .google.com.kh (Cambodia)
- .google.ki (Kiribati)
- .google.kg (Kyrgyzstan)
- .google.co.kr (South Korea)
- .google.com.kw (Kuwait)
- .google.kz (Kazakhstan)
- .google.la (Laos)
- .google.com.lb (Lebanon)
- .google.li (Liechtenstein)
- .google.lk (Sri Lanka)
- .google.co.ls (Lesotho)
- .google.lt (Lithuania)
- .google.lu (Luxembourg)
- .google.lv (Latvia)
- .google.com.ly (Lybia)
- .google.co.ma (Morocco)
- .google.md (Moldova)
- .google.me (Montenegro)
- .google.mg (Madegascar)
- .google.mk (Macedonia)
- .google.ml (Mali)
- .google.com.mm (Myanmar)
- .google.mn (Mongolia)
- .google.ms (Montserrat)
- .google.com.mt (Malta)
- .google.mu (Mauritius)
- .google.mv (Maldives)
- .google.mw (Malawi)
- .google.com.mx (Mexico)
- .google.com.my (Malaysia)
- .google.co.mz (Mozambique)
- .google.com.na (Namibia)
- .google.com.ng (Nigeria)
- .google.com.ni (Nicaragua)
- .google.ne (Niger)
- .google.nl (Netherlands)
- .google.no (Norway)
- .google.com.np (Nepal)
- .google.nr (Nauru)
- .google.nu (Niue)

- .google.co.nz (New Zealand)
- .google.com.om (Oman)
- .google.com.pa (Panama)
- .google.com.pe (Peru)
- .google.com.pg (Papa New Guinea)
- .google.com.ph (Philippines)
- .google.com.pk (Pakistan)
- .google.pl (Poland)
- .google.pn (Pitcairn)
- .google.com.pr (Puerto Rico)
- .google.ps (Palestine)
- .google.pt. (Portugal)
- .google.com.py (Paraguay)
- .google.com.qa (Qatar)
- .google.ro (Romania)
- .google.ru (Russia)
- .google.rw (Rwanda)
- .google.com.sa (Saudi Arabia)
- .google.com.sb (Soloman Islands)
- .google.sc (Seychelles)
- .google.se (Sweden)
- .google.com.sg (Singapore)
- .google.sh (Saint Helena)
- .google.si (Slovenia)
- .google.sk (Slovakia)
- .google.com.sl (Sierra Leone)
- .google.sn (Senegal)
- .google.so (Somalia)
- .google.sm (San Marino)
- .google.sr (Suriname)
- .google.st (Sao Tome and Principe)
- .google.com.sv (El Salvador)
- .google.td (Chad)
- .google.tg (Togo)
- .google.co.th (Thailand)
- .google.com.tj (Tajikistan)
- .google.tl (East Timor)
- .google.tm (Turkmenistan)
- .google.tn (Tunisia)
- .google.to (Tonga)
- .google.com.tr (Turkey)
- .google.tt (Trinidad and Tobago)
- .google.com.tw (Taiwan)
- .google.co.tz (Tanzania)
- .google.com.ua (Ukraine)

- .google.co.ug (Uganda)
- .google.co.uk (United Kingdom)
- .google.com.uy (Uruguay)
- .google.co.uz (Uzbekistan)
- .google.com.vc (Saint Vincent and the Grenadines)
- .google.co.ve (Venezuela)
- .google.vg (British Virgin Islands)
- .google.co.vi (US Virgin Islands)
- .google.com.vn (Vietnam)
- .google.vu (Vanuatu)
- .google.ws (Samoa)
- .google.rs (Serbia)
- .google.co.za (South Africa)
- .google.co.zm (Zambia)
- .google.co.zw (Zimbabwe)
- .google.cat (Catalan - language)

8.2.2   List of Bing Domains

Country-specific domains in Bing use the format https://www.bing.com/?cc=XX, where "XX" is the two-character language code. For example, https://www.bing.com/?cc=de will be the German-specific site, https://www.bing.com/?cc=za will be the South African site, and so on. This rule applies for the below list of country codes, according to the list at https://help.bing.microsoft.com/#apex/18/en-US/10004/-1.

- U.A.E (United Arab Emirates): ae
- Albania: al
- Armenia: am
- Argentina: ar
- Austria: at
- Australia: au
- Azerbaijan: az
- Bosnia and Herzegovina: ba
- Belgium: be
- Bulgaria: bg
- Bahrain: bh
- Bolivia: bo
- Brazil: br
- Canada: ca
- Switzerland: ch
- Chile: cl
- China: cn

- Colombia: co
- Costa Rica: cr
- Czech Republic: cz
- Germany: de
- Denmark: dk
- Dominican Republic: do
- Algeria: dz
- Ecuador: ec
- Estonia: ee
- Spain: es
- Egypt: eg
- Finland: fi
- France: fr
- United Kingdom: gb
- Georgia: ge
- Greece: gr
- Guatemala: gt
- Hong Kong S.A.R.: hk
- Honduras: hn
- Croatia: hr
- Hungary: hu
- Indonesia: id
- Ireland: ie
- Israel: il
- India: in
- Iraq: iq
- Iran: ir
- Iceland: is
- Italy: it
- Jordan: jo
- Japan: jp
- Kenya: ke
- Korea: kr
- Kuwait: kw
- Lebanon: lb
- Lithuania: lt
- Latvia: lv
- Luxembourg: lu
- Libya: ly
- Morocco: ma
- Former Yugoslav Republic of Macedonia: mk
- Malta: mt
- Malaysia: my
- Mexico: mx
- Nicaragua: ni

- Netherlands: nl
- New Zealand: nz
- Norway: no
- Oman: om
- Panama: pa
- Peru: pe
- Republic of the Philippines: ph
- Poland: pl
- Islamic Republic of Pakistan: pk
- Puerto Rico: pr
- Portugal: pt
- Paraguay: py
- Qatar: qa
- Romania: ro
- Russia: ru
- Saudi Arabia: sa
- Sweden: se
- Singapore: sg
- Slovakia: sk
- Slovenia: sl
- Serbia: sp
- El Salvador: sv
- Syria: sy
- Taiwan: tw
- Thailand: th
- Tunisia: tn
- Turkey: tr
- Ukraine: ua
- United States: us
- Vietnam: vn
- Yemen: ye
- South Africa: za

8.2.3   List of Yahoo Domains

Each of the websites below also has sub-domains for the other Yahoo search functions. For example, the URL for the image search of the Finnish Yahoo site is https://fi.images.search.yahoo.com; the URL for the image search of the Vietnamese Yahoo site is https://vn.images.search.yahoo.com/, and so on. To see the other sub-domains available for each site, conduct a search using the site: dork with a wildcard. For example, *site:ru.*.yahoo.com* and *site:ru.*.*.yahoo.com* should return the other sub-domains within Yahoo's Russia-based search engine, including images, video, mail, shopping, transit, finance/money, weather, auctions, movies, news, events, or other sites. These will vary by country, as not all services are available for each.

Note: Not all links on the Yahoo site are correct. Those that point only to mail portals were replaced with the search engine link, or removed if only the mail link was available (and the search engine domain was not accessible). The list on the Yahoo site is also missing many links. Some in the list below were obtained by conducting the search *site:*.search.yahoo.com* and consolidating the results.

The below list of country-specific Yahoo domains are from: https://www.yahoo.com/everything/world.

- https://espanol.yahoo.com (Argentina, Chile, Colombia, United States, Mexico, Peru, Venezuela, in Spanish),
- https://au.yahoo.com (Australia in English),
- https://be.yahoo.com/ (Belgium in Dutch),
- https://fr-be.yahoo.com (Belgium in French),
- https://br.yahoo.com or https://br.search.yahoo.com (Brazil in Portuguese),
- https://ca.yahoo.com (Canada in English),
- https://cz.yahoo.com (Czech Republic in Czech),
- https://dk.search.yahoo.com/ (Denmark in Danish),
- https://de.yahoo.com or https://de.search.yahoo.com (Germany in German),
- https://es.yahoo.com (Spain in Spanish),
- https://fr.yahoo.com or https://fr.search.yahoo.com/ (France in French),
- https://in.yahoo.com or https://yahoo.co.in (India in English),
- https://id.yahoo.com or https://yahoo.co.id (Indonesia in Bahasa),
- https://ie.yahoo.com (Ireland in English),
- https://it.yahoo.com or https://it.search.yahoo.com/ (Italy in Italian),
- https://en-maktoob.yahoo.com (MENA region in English),
- https://www.maktoob.yahoo.com (MENA region in Arabic),
- https://malaysia.yahoo.com (Malaysia in English),
- https://nl.search.yahoo.com/ (Netherlands in Dutch),
- https://nz.yahoo.com or https://yahoo.co.nz (New Zealand in English),
- https://at.search.yahoo.com/ (Austria in German),
- https://ph.yahoo.com (Philippines in English),
- https://pl.search.yahoo.com/ (Poland in Polish),
- https://qc.yahoo.com (Quebec in French),
- https://ro.yahoo.com or https://ro.search.yahoo.com (Romania in Romanian),
- https://ch.search.yahoo.com/ (Switzerland in German),
- https://sg.yahoo.com or https://sg.search.yahoo.com (Singapore in English),
- https://za.yahoo.com (South Africa in English),
- https://fi.search.yahoo.com (Finland in Finnish),
- https://se.yahoo.com or https://se.search.yahoo.com (Sweden in Swedish),
- https://tr.search.yahoo.com/ (Turkey in Turkish),
- https://uk.yahoo.com or https://yahoo.co.uk (United Kingdom in English),
- https://www.yahoo.com (United States in English),
- https://vn.yahoo.com or https://vn.search.yahoo.com (Vietnam in Vietnamese),

- https://gr.yahoo.com or https://gr.search.yahoo.com (Greece in Greek),
- https://ru.search.yahoo.com/ (Russia in Russian),
- https://ua.search.yahoo.com/ (Ukraine in Ukrainian),
- https://il.search.yahoo.com/ (Israel in Hebrew),
- https://hk.yahoo.com or https://hk.search.yahoo.com/ (Hong Kong in Traditional Chinese),
- Dictionary Search: https://hk.dictionary.search.yahoo.com/
- https://tw.yahoo.com (Taiwan in Traditional Chinese),
- Dictionary Search: https://tw.dictionary.search.yahoo.com/
- https://th.search.yahoo.com (Thailand in Thai),
- https://pr.search.yahoo.com (Puerto Rico in English),
- https://gl.search.yahoo.com (Greenland in English),
- https://hu.search.yahoo.com (Hungary in English),
- https://ar.search.yahoo.com/ (Argentina in Spanish),
- https://mx.search.yahoo.com (Mexico in Spanish),
- http://jp.search.yahoo.com or https://www.yahoo.co.jp (Japan in Japanese),
- https://mw.search.yahoo.com (Malawi in English),
- https://kz.search.yahoo.com (Kazakhstan in Kazahk),
- https://no.search.yahoo.com/ (Norway in Norwegian),
- https://qc.search.yahoo.com (Quebec, Canada in French),
- https://lu.search.yahoo.com/ (Luxembourg in English).

Note that http://yahoo.co.pt is not the Portuguese Yahoo - it is something else!

8.2.4   List of DuckDuckGo Domains

DuckDuckGo uses the kl = parameter in the URL to designate the country and language combination. The URL of the country/language-agnostic version of the website is https://duckduckco.com. To specify a country and language combination, use the format https://duckduckgo.com/?kl=XX-XX, where XX-XX are the country and language codes. For example, to specify search results geocoded in Japan in the Japanese language, use https://duckduckgo.com/?kl=jp-jp; for search results geocoded in Norwegian using Norwegian, use https://duckduckgo.com/?kl=no-no. DuckDuckGo supports the following combinations using this format:

- xa-ar (Arabia),
- xa-en (Arabia (en)),
- ar-es (Argentina),
- au-en (Australia),
- at-de (Austria)),
- be-fr (Belgium (fr)),
- be-nl for Belgium (nl)),
- br-pt (Brazil),
- bg-bg (Bulgaria),

- ca-en (Canada),
- ca-fr (Canada (fr)),
- ct-ca (Catalan),
- cl-es (Chile),
- cn-zh (China),
- co-es (Colombia),
- hr-hr (Croatia),
- cz-cs (Czech Republic),
- dk-da (Denmark),
- ee-et (Estonia),
- fi-fi (Finland),
- fr-fr (France),
- de-de (Germany),
- gr-el (Greece),
- hk-tzh (Hong Kong),
- hu-hu (Hungary),
- in-en (India),
- id-id (Indonesia),
- id-en (Indonesia (en)),
- ie-en (Ireland),
- il-he (Israel),
- it-it (Italy),
- jp-jp (Japan),
- kr-kr (Korea),
- lv-lv (Latvia),
- lt-lt (Lithuania),
- xl-es (Latin America),
- my-ms (Malaysia),
- my-en (Malaysia (en)),
- mx-es (Mexico),
- nl-nl (Netherlands),
- nz-en (New Zealand),
- no-no (Norway),
- pe-es (Peru),
- ph-en (Philippines),
- ph-tl (Philippines (tl)),
- pl-pl (Poland),
- pt-pt (Portugal),
- ro-ro (Romania),
- ru-ru (Russia),
- sg-en (Singapore),
- sk-sk (Slovak Republic),
- sl-sl (Slovenia),
- za-en (South Africa),
- es-es (Spain),

- se-sv (Sweden),
- ch-de (Switzerland (de)),
- ch-fr (Switzerland (fr)),
- ch-it (Switzerland (it)),
- tw-tzh (Taiwan),
- th-th (Thailand),
- tr-tr (Turkey),
- ua-uk (Ukraine),
- uk-en (United Kingdom),
- us-en (United States),
- ue-es (United States (es)),
- ve-es (Venezuela),
- vn-vi (Vietnam),
- wt-wt (No region).

The above list of country-specific DuckDuckGo domains are generated from: https://duckduckgo.com/params.

8.3   List of Country-Based Search Engines

This book describes many popular regionally focused search engines. There are many others besides those discussed in this book! Consider exploring any of the following regionally focused search engines based on the research problem and desired sources [1]:

- https://gjirafa.com/ (Albania),
- https://find.gbg.bg/ (Bulgaria),
- https://pipilika.com/what (Bangladesh),
- https://www.webwatch.be/ (Belgium),
- http://www.aonde.com/ (Brazil),
- https://busca.uol.com.br/ (Brazil),
- https://www.baidu.com (China),
- https://m.sm.cn (Shenma – Mobile Only) (China),
- https://www.sogou.com (China),
- http://www.zhongsou.com/ (China),
- https://www.sina.com.cn/ (China),
- https://www.sld.cu/ (Cuba),
- https://www.search.seznam.cz (Czech Republic),
- https://atlas.centrum.cz/ or https://volny.centrum.cz/ or https://www.centrum.cz/ (Czech Republic),
- https://www.jubii.dk/ (Denmark – Searches Google.dk),
- https://www.qwant.com/ (France),
- https://www.exalead.com/search/ (France),
- https://www.makupalat.fi/ (Finland),

- https://www.ecosia.org/ (Germany),
- https://metager.org/ (Germany – Metasearch),
- http://www.yellowmap.de/ (Germany),
- https://suche.web.de/web (Germany),
- http://www.bellnet.com/suchen.htm (Germany),
- https://fireball.de/ (Germany),
- https://www.suchmaschine.com/ (Germany),
- https://alpha.infotiger.com/ (Germany),
- http://suchmaschine.com/ (Germany),
- http://kereso.startlap.hu/?sise=s&search=google (Hungary),
- http://www.123khoj.com/ (India),
- https://www.ireland-information.com/engine/ (Ireland) [2]
- www.parsijoo.ir (Iran),
- www.yooz.ir (Iran) [3]
- https://www.virgilio.it/ (VPN may be required) (Italy),
- https://www.goo.ne.jp/ (Japan),
- https://www.infoseek.co.jp/ (Japan),
- http://www.alcarna.net/ (Japan),
- https://search.biglobe.ne.jp/ (Japan),
- https://www.sajasearch.com/ (Malaysia),
- https://www.zoznam.sk/ (Moldova),
- https://gogo.mn/ (Mongolia),
- https://startpage.com/ (Netherlands),
- http://www.botje.nl/ (Netherlands),
- https://www.vinden.nl/ (Netherlands),
- https://www.web.nl/ (Netherlands),
- http://www.searchnz.co.nz/ (New Zealand),
- https://www.kvasir.no/ (Norway),
- https://www.alleba.com/ (Philippines) [4]
- http://www.aeiou.pt/ (Portugal),
- http://www.online.ro/ (Romania),
- https://yandex.ru/ (Russia),
- https://www.rambler.ru/ (Russia),
- https://sakh.com/ (Russia),
- https://www.yamli.com (Saudi Arabia),
- https://www.najdi.si/ (Slovenia),
- http://www.funnel.co.za/ (South Africa),
- https://www.naver.com/ (South Korea),
- https://www.daum.net/ (South Korea),
- https://www.nate.com/ (Searches daum.net) (South Korea),
- https://www.ciao.es/ (Spain),
- https://www.eniro.se/ (Sweden),
- https://www.hitta.se/ (Sweden),
- https://www.picsearch.com/ (Sweden),
- https://swisscows.com/ (Switzerland),

- https://www.search.ch/ (Switzerland),
- https://tiger.ch/ (Switzerland),
- https://www.yam.com/ (Taiwan),
- http://www.chiangmai-online.com/search/ (Thailand),
- https://www.geliyoo.com/ (Turkey),
- https://www.google.com/ (United States),
- https://www.bing.com (United States),
- https://www.yahoo.com/ (United States),
- https://www.aol.com (United States),
- https://www.ask.com/ (United States),
- https://www.gigablast.com/ (United States),
- https://www.lycos.com/ (United States),
- https://www.wolframalpha.com/ (United States),
- https://wbsrch.com/ (United States),
- https://www.zerx.com/ (United States),
- http://www.internetri.net/ (Ukraine),
- https://meta.ua/ (Ukraine),
- https://www.mojeek.com/ or https://www.mojeek.co.uk/ (United Kingdom),
- http://allsearchengines.co.uk/index.php (Meta search) (United Kingdom),
- http://web.curryguide.com/ (Meta search) (United Kingdom),
- https://www.auyantepui.com/ (Venezuela),
- https://coccoc.com/ (Vietnam),
- https://searx.space/ (Metasearch) – special language search capabilities: https://searx.github.io/searx/user/search_syntax.html
- http://arabo.com/ (Various Arab countries),
- http://www.buscapique.com/ (search by country and language),
- https://www.ezilon.com/ (Euro search),
- http://www.buscapique.com/ (Various Countries),
- https://www.zapmeta.com/ (Metasearch, various countries).

Online Database References

1. List created with the help of the following resources: "List of Search Engines by Country," accessed May 21, 2021, https://www.ph4.org/search_searchcountries.php; "Search Engines in all countries in the world," accessed May 21, 2021, https://www.searchenginesindex.com/; "Suchmaschinen-Datenbank [Search Engines Database]," accessed May 25, 2021, https://www.suchmaschinen-datenbank.de; "世界搜索引擎网址 [Word Search Engine URL]," accessed May 23, 2021, http://www.dqxx.com.cn/ForeignTradeWebSite/SearchEngine.
2. This search engine is notorious for producing very limited results, see "Shamrock Search Engine," accessed May 30, 2021, https://en.illogicopedia.org/wiki/Shamrock_Search_Engine.
3. Yooz.ir is only available to users in Iran (i.e. with an Iranian IP address), see Doug Bernard, "Iran's Next Step in Building a 'Halal' Internet," March 9, 2015, https://www.voanews.com/world-news/middle-east-dont-use/irans-next-step-building-halal-internet.
4. This search engine has an associated Web Directory, see "Alleba Filipino Directory - WWW Virtual Library of the Philippines," accessed May 30, 2021, https://www.alleba.com/dir.html.

Index

Printed in the United States
by Baker & Taylor Publisher Services